D0371996

THE
STRATEGY OF
VICTORY

THE
STRATEGY OF
VICTORY

How General George Washington
Won the American Revolution

THOMAS FLEMING

DA CAPO PRESS

Da Capo Press
Hachette Book Group
1290 Avenue of the Americas, New York, NY 10104
dacapopress.com
@DaCapoPress, @DaCapoPR

Printed in the United States of America
First Edition: October 2017

Published by Da Capo Press, an imprint of Perseus Books, LLC, a subsidiary of Hachette Book Group, Inc.

The publisher is not responsible for websites (or their content) that are not owned by the publisher.

Print book interior design by Jeff Williams.

Library of Congress Cataloging-in-Publication Data
Names: Fleming, Thomas J., author.
Title: The strategy of victory: how General George Washington won the American Revolution / Thomas Fleming.
Description: Boston, MA : Da Capo Press, 2017. | Includes bibliographical references and index.
LC record available at https://lccn.loc.gov/2017020803
Identifiers: LCCN 2017020803 (print) | LCCN 2017021930 (ebook) | ISBN
ISBNs: 978-0-306-82496-8 (hardcover), 978-0-306-82497-5 (e-book)
9780306824975 (e-book) | ISBN 9780306824968 (hardcover)
Subjects: LCSH: Washington, George, 1732–1799—Military leadership. | United States. Continental Army—History. | Generals—United States—Biography. | United States—History—Revolution, 1775–1783—Manpower. | United States—History—Revolution, 1775–1783—Campaigns. | BISAC: HISTORY / United States / Revolutionary Period (1775–1800). | BIOGRAPHY & AUTOBIOGRAPHY / Historical.

Classification: LCC E312.25 (ebook) | LCC E312.25 F67 2017 (print) | DDC

973.4/1092 [B]—dc23

LSC-C

10 9 8 7 6 5 4 3 2 1

To Alice

Contents

ACKNOWLEDGMENTS

For a book of this length and complexity, I have many people to thank.

My first thoughts go to Colonel Charles M. Adams, whom I met during my 1960s years at West Point, while I was writing a history of the military academy. It was Adams who helped me grasp the importance of strategy in a professional soldier's thinking. Our discussions were supplemented in much briefer style by my conversations with several generals.

Equally helpful were historians who grasped the idea that George Washington was no mere figurehead. He was a thinker who changed the strategy of the war and a leader who had the equanimity to deal with the barrage of criticism that descended on him from men with little or no military insights, such as John Adams and Dr. Benjamin Rush. A good example of this new view is Edward G. Lengel, former director of the George Washington Papers and author of *General George Washington: A Military Life.*

I have also reached deep into my past and drawn on material on the war in New Jersey by Francis S. Ronalds, former director of Morristown National Historical Park. He generously gave me access to this research, which contained new insights into the British attempt to end the war after the surrender of Charleston in 1780. Equally important were my conversations with the late Don Higginbotham, biographer of Daniel Morgan and author of many other distinguished books, which gave me a new understanding of the importance of the battle of Cowpens. Another friend whose book played a major role in my thinking was Terry Golway, author of *Washington's General*, a superb biography of Nathanael Greene.

I also remain indebted to several librarians. One is Gregory S. Gallagher, until recently the head librarian of the Century Association, whose research talents extended far beyond the relatively small library he managed with such skill and charm. Another is Lewis Daniels, head of the Westbrook, Connecticut, library. Once more he displayed his skill at obtaining rare books from distant libraries, enabling me to devote most of my summers to writing rather than travel. The staff of the venerable New York Society library, of which George Washington and Alexander Hamilton were once members, has also been invariably helpful and encouraging.

My deepest thanks go to my son, Richard Fleming, whose computer and research skills continue to grow and shed new light on topics such as the "Fabian" side of George Washington's generalship. Also helpful was my daughter, Alice, former managing editor of St. Martin's Press, in pursing obscure endnotes and otherwise advising me against repetitions and similar blemishes in the early drafts of the book. My wife, Alice, a gifted writer in her own right, performed a similar task, at times more drastic, in pointing out how much a supposedly "final" draft could be cut, adding new vitality to the narrative.

At least as important were the advice and encouragement of my editor at Da Capo Press, Robert Pigeon. My agent, Deborah Grosvenor, who brought us together, was also a frequently helpful presence. There are many others who have my thanks, confirming one of my favorite adages: No writer works alone. It only looks that way.

Introduction

The year is 1783, the date, March 15—the legendary Ides of March—a day forever filled with foreboding since the assassination of a famous general who sought imperial power, Julius Caesar, more than 2,000 years ago. For the Americans of 1783 the foreboding was especially intense because Caesar's murder led to the destruction of the Roman Republic and to centuries of rule by emperors. Was the fragile new American republic about to experience a similar fate?

We are in the final year of the eight-year struggle that we call the American Revolution. Lieutenant General George Washington is in New Windsor, the American Continental Army's winter camp near Newburgh on the Hudson River in New York. He is about to walk out onto a stage in a building called the Temple of Virtue and confront a galaxy of faces stained with sullen dislike and distrust of his leadership. These ominous visages belong to the officers of the Continental Army. Dangling in precarious balance is the future of the United States of America.

Most twenty-first-century Americans, when and if they learn of this confrontation, can only stare in amazement and disbelief. George Washington, the father of our country, despised and disliked by the men who had spent most of the previous decade risking their lives in obedience to his orders? Why do we celebrate Washington's birthday and consider his home, Mount Vernon, a shrine? Why have we named the capital of the world's most powerful nation in his honor? And erected the world's tallest stone monument to immortalize his name?

The coming pages will provide the answers to these questions. For the moment we can sum them up with the book's title: *The Strategy of Victory*. This confrontation in New Windsor was part of the price Washington was paying for the drastic changes he had made in the way America fought the Revolutionary War. He did not foresee this discord; nor was he sure he and the nation would survive it. More important for today's readers, the crisis forces us to think about the Revolution—and George Washington—in a new way.

My first glimpse of this reality came while I was working on a book about the history of West Point. In the course of my three and a half years at the US Military Academy, I talked to many generals, largely to explore the connection between their educations at the school and their later careers. Beyond this topic our conversations often turned to historical matters, confirming an old aphorism that professional soldiers are all in the history game. They were especially interested when I told them I hoped to write a book about George Washington as a general.

I asked their opinion of him. They all said essentially the same thing: "He was a great general."

"Why do you say that?" I asked. "He lost more battles than he won." At that time, I thought of Washington largely as a figurehead.

"Yes," they replied. "But he changed the strategy of the war. In the middle of the war. That's the hardest thing for a general to do."

I soon grasped that strategy is the essence of a general's job—an idea most civilians may find puzzling or at least surprising. The word derives from the ancient Greek word *strategia*, meaning "the art of troop leader, office of command." It did not become part of Western vernacular languages until the eighteenth century.

One military historian has defined strategy as "a pattern in a stream of decisions." Another scholar describes it as "a system of finding, formulating and developing a doctrine that will ensure long-term success if followed faithfully." A third has summarized it as a human attempt to achieve "desirable ends with available means."[1]

What does all this tell us about Washington's strategy of victory? Perhaps most importantly, it underscores its profoundly human aspect. A winning strategy was not some dry, abstract theory for professors to teach in university classrooms. It could not fit neatly into a single sentence. Essentially it was a cluster of ideas and insights, all linked to a way of winning a specific war.

For George Washington the war was the revolt of the thirteen American colonies against Great Britain, the most powerful nation in the world of 1776. To win was to open a glorious future for America. To lose was to vanish over one of history's precipices, never to be seen and scarcely to be mentioned again. Small wonder that Washington's strategy aroused violent hostility and even more violent affirmations by men who cared passionately about its outcome.

George Washington was one of these caring men. As he would tell the officers he faced in the Temple of Virtue, he had been one of the first to step forward to defend "our common country." Since that time he had "never left your [the army's] side." He was talking about the prime years of his life—from the ages of forty-three to fifty-one. He had devoted most of a decade to creating and maintaining the strategy of victory, sharing it with other soldiers who saw its essential importance, defending it against skeptics and critics, risking it again and again in the most nerve-shredding way imaginable—on battlefields where, veteran soldiers are often inclined to say, if anything can go wrong it will.

This glimpse of the strategy of victory tells us enough about George Washington's ordeal to grasp its central role in America's history. Let us become time travelers and learn how this way of fighting a war emerged from the violence that erupted between the men of Massachusetts and the British army on April 19, 1775. Thereafter we will travel through the years of the war while Washington evolved his new strategy and defended it against ignorant and arrogant critics, until we encounter two battles that demonstrate in breathtaking detail how the strategy of victory succeeded against intimidating odds.

CHAPTER 1

The First Stroke

On April 19, 1775, in the grey interval between dawn and sunrise, some thirty-eight Americans formed two uneven lines on the wet, dandelion-speckled grass of the triangular two-acre common in the center of Lexington, Massachusetts. They had answered the summons of the rolling beat of sixteen-year-old William Diamond's brightly painted drum. Big, burly Captain John Parker, a veteran of the French and Indian War, had given the order to sound this call to arms. Most of the men had spent the night in Buckman's Tavern, a white clapboard building just east of the green; others hurried from twelve houses that faced its three sides. As more men joined the ranks, Parker's numbers grew to seventy-seven, still considerably short of the 130 names on his muster list.

William Diamond's drum had rolled, and the men had formed up in response to a shouted warning from a rider sent out by Captain Parker to scout the road to Boston. A British column, the excited man said, was only fifteen minutes away and marching fast. Parker and his men were on the north end of the common, close to where one branch of the Boston Road led to Bedford. Another branch bent left past the opposite side of the common and continued to Concord. The town's bulky two-and-a-half-story meeting house—where they gathered each Sunday to hear the minister, the Reverend Jonas Clarke, tell them that the British were plotting to deprive Americans of their liberty and that it was every man's sacred duty to resist—blocked their view of the fork, from which the road ran to Boston.

The crisis had been gathering momentum for more than a year—ever since a group of Bostonians disguised as Indians had dumped £9,000 worth of British tea into the harbor to protest the three-cent tax on it. The reaction of Britain's king and parliament had been extreme. They had made the commander of the British army in America, General Thomas Gage, the governor of Massachusetts and passed a series of punitive laws that deprived the people of the state of basic rights, such as the freedom to hold a town meeting without the governor's permission.

Although they had guns in their hands, these men of Lexington were not regular soldiers. They were part-time warriors, known as militia. Under the royal government, every man between sixteen and sixty belonged to the militia. He was supposed to own a gun and a modest supply of ammunition and had to report for military drill at least once a year on training day. Militiamen wore their everyday clothes—loose brown or grey homespun cloth coats and leather knee breeches. They elected their officers once a year and wrote their own rules and regulations.

Since the tea party crisis began, a third of Lexington's men had been meeting every week; supposed to be ready to fight on sixty seconds' notice, they had been designated "minutemen." The same policy prevailed in the province's other towns. Everyone was preparing for a surprise attack by the British army in Boston.[1]

About a quarter of the men were related to Captain Parker by blood or marriage. Most of them came from families that had been living in Lexington for three, four, even six generations, and almost all shared some degree of kinship. The company clerk, Daniel Harrington, whose house stood only a few steps from the common, was a son-in-law of sixty-three-year-old Robert Munroe, one of the company's ensigns—the eighteenth-century term for second lieutenant. Another Harrington—Jonathan—lived in the house next door with his wife and small son. Thirty-eight-year-old William Tidd, the company's lieutenant, was also married to one of Ensign Munroe's daughters. The men included grandfathers like Jonas Parker, the captain's cousin, and Moses Harrington, who were there with their married sons. Six younger men such as John Muzzy were also there with sons in their teens or early twenties.

Incongruous among the two rows of white faces was the glistening black skin of the slave Prince Estabrook. He had become a member of the company by majority vote, in accordance with the regulation that stated, "Any Person Desiring to be Admitted . . . shall have a vote of the Company for the same."

If Captain Parker and his men had any plan, it was to keep as far away as possible from the Concord Road. Thanks to hardworking spies in Boston, they knew Concord was the British column's destination. Earlier in the evening, when riders from Boston had brought the first alarm to Lexington, they told the militia that the British numbered between 1,200 and 1,500 men. Captain Parker and his men had conferred and decided "not to . . . meddle or make with the Regular troops."

The Lexington men soon heard hundreds of feet striking the ground with military precision. The British were very close. Parker and his company waited, their eyes on the Concord Road. But around that side of the meeting house came only a single British officer on a horse, gesturing with a sword. Around the Bedford Road side of the meeting house came six companies of red-coated British light infantry, three abreast, twelve men to a file. Beside them were several officers on horseback and at least six civilians they had captured on the way, hoping to keep their expedition a secret.

There was a split-second pause in the British pace. Then the light infantrymen raced toward the Americans. Shouting furiously, the two lead companies formed a line of battle twelve abreast and three deep. The officer waving the sword was Major John Pitcairn of the Royal Marines. He commanded these light infantrymen, traditionally the toughest, most aggressive soldiers in their regiments. "Lay down your arms," he shouted to Parker's men.

From the other officers on horseback came contradictory commands. "Disperse, ye rebels," one roared. "Surrender," cried another. "Damn them we will have them," bellowed a third.

The appalled Captain Parker turned to his men and told them to disperse without firing. Most of them began to drift away in various directions. Old Jonas Parker and a few others hesitated. Grandfather Parker had vowed never to retreat if the British attacked.

"Surround them," shouted Pitcairn to the furious light infantrymen. But they were not listening to him or to anyone else. Later, Major Pitcairn said he thought he saw a gun held by a man behind a stone wall on the edge of the green "flash in the pan." (The powder in the musket's firing pan flamed but did not ignite the cartridge in the barrel, so the gun failed to go off.) American witnesses—about forty men, women, and children stood around the green or watched from the windows and doorways of the adjacent houses—said one of the British officers on horseback fired a pistol. If either occurred, it only supported the intentions of the light infantrymen from the moment they saw the militia facing them on the common.

The red-coated soldiers in the two lead companies stopped, and the second rank stepped a half pace to the right. The third rank stepped another half pace to the right. The maneuver took the men no more time than it takes to read these words. They had practiced it repeatedly during the preceding winter months. Now every man in the two companies could fire without hitting the soldier in front of him.

Thirty-six muskets crashed on the left, then thirty-six more on the right. A huge billow of white gun smoke swirled in the murky dawn air. Murderous one-and-a-half-ounce bullets tore into Captain Parker's men. Ensign Robert Munroe was dead when he hit the ground. A cousin, John Munroe, gasped as a bullet smashed his arm. Young Isaac Muzzy died at his father's feet. Jonathan Harrington, hit in the chest, crawled painfully to the doorstep of his house and died there, before the eyes of his horrified wife and son.

A wild melee erupted as Parker's men began firing back. A number of men who had lingered in Buckman's Tavern opened fire from the first- and second-floor windows. More guns boomed from the windows of other houses around the common. The rear companies of light infantry stormed into the fight, some returning the shots from the tavern and houses, others charging Parker's men, firing from the hip and lowering their bayonets.[2]

Old Jonas Parker, hit in the first volley, fired his musket from a sitting position and struggled to get a fresh cartridge and flint from his hat, which he had placed on the ground between his feet. A light infantryman stopped him with a bayonet thrust. Asahel Porter of Woburn, one of the men captured on the road, tried to run and was shot dead. He and a Lexington man died north of the common, on the other side of the stone wall. A half dozen more Lexington men were wounded in this vicinity.

"Cease firing. Cease firing," shouted Major Pitcairn. He rode among the milling light infantrymen, striking up their guns with his sword. But they paid no attention to the marine officer—or to any other officer. "The men were so wild they could hear no orders," said Lieutenant John Barker of the King's Own Light Infantry. Squads of furious soldiers rushed toward Buckman's Tavern and the houses, swearing they would kill every man they found in them.

Into this chaos of swirling gun smoke, shrieking women and children, roaring light infantrymen, and cursing officers rode corpulent Lieutenant Colonel Francis Smith. He commanded the seven hundred men who had left Boston at 9:30 P.M. the previous night with orders to destroy the American gunpowder, cannon, and supplies at Concord. Success, they hoped, would cripple resistance to British authority in Massachusetts.

With the help of a lieutenant, Smith found a drummer and ordered him to beat "cease fire." This familiar sound restored some sanity to the berserk light infantrymen. As the companies reformed, some Lexington men on the third floor of Buckman's Tavern fired three shots at Lieutenant Colonel Smith. The soldiers begged for permission to go after them. Smith angrily refused and rebuked them for ignoring the commands of their officers and breaking their ranks.

In perhaps ten minutes, the light infantrymen were in marching formation on the common. Near them, four Lexington men lay dead or dying. Four more were in the same condition just off the green, and another ten were staggering or limping to safety with painful wounds. The British had one soldier wounded in the leg. Major Pitcairn's horse had taken two bullets.[3]

The British officers held a hurried conference. Should they continue their march to Concord now? They knew that every town had companies of militia like the one they had just routed at Lexington. Lieutenant Colonel Smith saw no reason to deviate from his orders. He told the light infantrymen to give three cheers and fire a volley—a British tradition on winning a victory.

By this time the rest of the seven-hundred-man British force had reached the green. They waited on the Concord Road, eleven companies of grenadiers, the biggest soldiers in their regiments, and four additional companies of light infantry, during the performance of the brief victory ceremony. Major Pitcairn's six light infantry companies rejoined the column. In a compact body, their drums beating and fifes skirling, the British marched for Concord, five miles away, oblivious of the fact that they had started a war.[4]

⌒

BEFORE TWILIGHT descended on April 19, one in five of these victorious British soldiers would be dead or wounded. Compounding the irony, they found no gunpowder and very few weapons in Concord, whose residents had, with the help of those numerous American spies, anticipated their haphazard searches and hidden well everything the British hoped to find. While redcoats groped through barns and attics, more than 5,000 infuriated minutemen and militia gathered from dozens of towns in the vicinity and made the soldiers' return to Boston a nightmare. Again and again blasts of bullets hurtled into their ranks from ambushes along the curving road. Only reinforcements from Boston, led by a veteran brigadier, Lord Hugh Percy, rescued them from annihilation. More fierce fighting erupted when the Americans attacked the reinforced column in the final miles to Boston. But they could not pose a serious threat to the British, now over 2,000 men strong.

The British suffered 73 men killed and 174 wounded. Another twenty-six were missing; some had been wounded and left behind along the road; a few had deserted or surrendered. Massachusetts's losses are more difficult to compute. The colony had no organized system for reporting casualties. We are fairly certain that forty-nine died, but the semiofficial estimate of only forty-one wounded is suspicious. The ratio of killed to wounded is usually one to three in land battles. Many of the wounded may have gone home and never reported their injuries.

As the battle fury died away, men on both sides began assessing the experience. Lieutenant Barker wrote in his diary, "Thus ended this expedition, which from beginning to end was as ill-plan'd and ill-executed as it was possible to be."[5] Captain William Glanville Evelyn of the King's Own was convinced that the "Yankey scoundrels" were "the most absolute cowards on the face of the earth." He attributed the valor they had displayed on April 19 to "such a degree of enthusiasm and madness that they are easily persuaded the Lord is to assist them in whatever they undertake, and that they must be invincible."

The chagrined Lieutenant Colonel Smith could only complain, "Notwithstanding the enemy's numbers, they did not make one gallant attempt during so long an action." By gallant attempt he meant a face-to-face confrontation in the traditional battlefield style.

Lord Percy took a more balanced view of Massachusetts's tactics. It was true that the minutemen and militia had attacked in a "very scattered, irregular manner," but Percy noted that they did so with "perseverance & resolution, nor did they ever dare to form into any regular body. Indeed they knew too well what was proper, to do so." Grimly, Percy concluded, "Whoever looks upon them as an irregular mob will find himself much mistaken. They have men amongst them who know very well what they are about." He was now convinced that "the rebels . . . are determined to go thro with it, nor will the insurrection here turn out so despicable as it is perhaps imagined at home."[6]

Percy recognized, with the eye of an intelligent soldier, one of the least understood realities of April 19. The Americans who responded to the British challenge were not a mass of disorganized individuals; they were a well-supplied rudimentary army that had been organizing and training for six months. They were in a state of battle readiness, much better prepared to fight than the British soldiers who marched out of Boston.

A heavy proportion of the American officers were veterans of previous wars who knew how to lead men into battle. Their training and the knowledge that they outnumbered the British five to one added to the confidence with which they responded to the alarm when the fighting began. In short, April 19, 1775, was a victory of preparedness, not a product of spontaneous enthusiasm. The minutemen and militiamen of Massachusetts knew their superior strength and, more importantly, were confident that their months of training would enable them to use that advantage effectively. Unfortunately, this lesson was lost even before it was learned.

CHAPTER 2

Propaganda Meets Reality in 1776

I n reporting their version of Lexington and Concord to the world, Massachusetts's political leaders strove to give the impression that their stance had not been in the least warlike or hostile before General Thomas Gage launched his men on their midnight march. The Yankees were keenly aware that they needed to use the blood spilled on April 19 to win the support of other Americans—especially those living outside New England.

The Massachusetts version of the day denounced "barbarous murders committed on our innocent brethren" and accused the British troops of "driving into the streets women in childbed, killing old men in their houses." The Lexington men comprised "a small party of the inhabitants . . . some with and some without firearms." At other times they were described as "peaceable spectators." In Concord, where attacking Americans inflicted heavy casualties on a British company guarding an important bridge, the armed and angry Americans became "inhabitants . . . collected at the bridge." At no point was there any mention of minutemen or militia. The Americans were simply "provincials, roused with zeal for the liberties of their country," who "assumed their native valor" and fought so well that "the loss on the part of the British troops far exceeded" that of the patriots.

As political propaganda, the report was a masterpiece. It aroused an enormous explosion of sympathy and anger throughout America. Some 20,000 men from western Massachusetts and the other three New England colonies rushed to join the minutemen and militia who had pursued Lord Hugh Percy to Charlestown on April 19. They began building fortifications and organizing themselves into an army that effectively blockaded the British inside Boston. "In the course of two days," wrote one glum British officer, "from a plentiful town we were reduced to the disagreeable necessity of living on salt provisions."

In the southern and central states, long-neglected militia began choosing new officers and drilling regularly. In Virginia, the state's best-known soldier, Colonel George Washington, was among those now ready to fight. "Unhappily, it is to reflect," he wrote, "that a Brother's sword has been sheathed in a Brother's Brest, and that, the once happy and peaceful plains of America are either to be drenched with Blood or Inhabited by Slaves. Sad alternative! But can a virtuous man hesitate in his choice?" A Philadelphia woman, writing to a British officer in Boston, told him, "Nothing is heard now in our streets but the trumpet and the drum; and the universal cry is 'Americans, to arms!'"

This same woman also revealed the cost of this propaganda victory to the Americans. Mockingly, she asked her British correspondent why "the regulars, vastly superior in numbers, were obliged to retreat with [such] rapidity?" By January 1, 1776, the facts about British and American numbers had become so obscured that the editor of the *Pennsylvania Packet* could look back on April 19 and boast, "Two thousand veteran British soldiers were attacked and defeated by 300 peasants, and were saved from total destruction by running 40 miles in a single day." April 19, 1775, had convinced America's political leaders that a rapid gathering of patriot militia could defeat the British army wherever and whenever it dared to invade the continent.[1]

George Washington confronted this strategy when John Adams proposed him as commander in chief of the American army and Congress voted its collective approval. Adams was thinking politically. New England's leaders badly needed a man from the embryo nation's largest state to create at least the illusion of unity. Colonel Washington, as he was generally known, had spent four eventful years commanding Virginia's troops on the western frontier in the French and Indian War.

When Colonel Washington took command of the impromptu army besieging the British inside Boston, he swiftly demonstrated that he could think like a general. He urged Congress to authorize a regular, or "Continental," army of at least 60,000 men and enlist them for the duration of the war. The lawmakers pooh-poohed the figure, cutting it by two-thirds, and all but frothed at the mouth at the idea of enlisting men for more than a year.

Congressman John Adams maintained that only the "meanest, idlest, most intemperate and worthless" men would sign such a contract. Dr. Benjamin Rush of Philadelphia, who exceeded Adams and almost everyone else as a village idiot on military matters, declared, "I should despair of our Cause if our country contained sixty thousand men abandoned enough to enlist for three years or more." Militia would supply Washington with any additional soldiers he needed, the solons grandly declared. It was Congress's first venture—but by no means its last—into eviscerating America's military strength.[2]

Meanwhile the politicians had embarked on a military undertaking that soon prompted them to demand 10,000 of Washington's 20,000 regulars. They invaded Canada on the assumptions that the British had very few troops in this recently acquired "fourteenth colony" and that the descendants of the original French colonizers would be eager to revolt against their new royal masters. British reinforcements and the deep aversion of the French Canadians to the outspoken American Protestants soon turned this experiment into a military fiasco.

General Washington was obliged to accept these decisions. Congress had no intention of letting a general tell it what to do. That idea carried with it the menace of a military dictatorship. In the English Civil War of the previous century, Oliver Cromwell had grown weary of taking orders from Parliament and sent its members home. He had reigned as lord high protector, an experience that convinced most Britons that rule by a king and a parliament was far preferable.

On June 17, 1775, another battle had further convinced Congress that American militia could defeat British regulars with the help of a secret weapon: entrenching tools. On Breed's Hill outside Boston, the amateur Yankee soldiers had inflicted fearful casualties on the king's men as they assaulted the makeshift fort the Americans had constructed in a single night. The battle of Bunker Hill—so called for geographical reasons understood only by Bostonians—taught both the Americans and the British a lesson. The Americans learned the wrong one, the British, the right one.

Bunker Hillism became a key idea in the strategy of the American army, when the New England rebellion became a continental war in 1776. For most of that pivotal year, the Americans expended enormous amounts of time, energy, and money constructing forts on hills and landing sites, hoping to repeat Bunker Hill's bloodletting on a larger scale and to force the British to quit the fight. As Connecticut general Israel Putnam, an architect of the Bunker Hill battle, put it, "Cover [the Americans'] legs and they will fight till doomsday." These seemingly silly words had roots in eighteenth-century fact: soldiers dreaded leg wounds. The primitive medicine of the era knew nothing about infections. The doctor's usual solution was to amputate the damaged limb.

America's politicians—and to some extent their military leaders—were also beguiled by the pronouncements of their chief propagandist, the English radical Thomas Paine, who assured them in his popular pamphlet *Common Sense* that the British army was a collection of hirelings who would not risk wounds and death for their king. The 1754–1761 global war with France (called the Seven Years War in Europe and the French and Indian War in America) had left the British government groaning under a burden of debt so enormous that it could neither finance a large army in America nor pay for its subsistence. This looming debt had equally reduced the Royal Navy. Only 10 percent of the ships on its list could sail more than a mile from a dock. Without debt, sweat, blood, or tears, according to Paine, the Americans could win their independence merely by declaring it.[3]

⌒

FOR HIS first six months as commander of the largely New England army, George Washington concentrated on shaping his men into a coherent fighting force. This was not a simple matter. Washington found the New Englanders almost impossible to discipline; they disliked taking orders from anyone who was not a member of their regiment, often of their company. The idea of obeying someone from Virginia was beyond their contrarian imaginations.

In private, Washington became equally hostile to the Yankees. He was dismayed to learn that the men elected their own officers, many of whom did not qualify in Washington's eyes as gentlemen. He was even more appalled to discover that the officers frequently sat down and ate with their men. One man, who in peacetime worked as a barber, had no compunction about shaving his men and cutting their hair—and charging them for the service.

Washington told his presumed friend Virginia congressman Richard Henry Lee that there was "an unaccountable kind of stupidity in the lower class of these [New England] people which believe me prevails too generally among the officers." Lee showed these letters to John Adams, who did not find them even slightly amusing. Lee had become a friend and admirer of Adams; both were early advocates of independence. Adams was soon sarcastically asking a Massachusetts officer if his "amiable general" thought that "every man from the south of the Hudson River was a hero and every man to the northward a poltroon."[4]

Learning from another friend what Lee was doing, Washington instantly vowed never to say another word about the origins of anyone in his army—a resolution he rarely violated. The experience was Washington's first lesson in understanding the intricacies of Congress, where ideology and friendship played large, invisible roles.

From the start of his career as commander in chief, Washington struggled to create an aura of national unity in his army. He even suggested that regiments should mingle men from different states. Congress—and various state legislatures—vetoed the idea. Washington had to content himself with telling his men that "all distinctions of colonies would be laid aside." Everyone was now a member of "the Army of the United Provinces of North America."[5]

Washington was heartened when six hundred Virginians under backwoodsman Daniel Morgan appeared in camp armed with long-barreled rifles, which were far more accurate than the crude muskets that the rest of the army carried into battle. Morgan's men were forerunners of more non–New England troops to come. Congress had asked Maryland, Virginia, and Pennsylvania to send newly formed regiments.

As commander in chief, Washington had one large advantage: he looked the part. His height, reserved demeanor, and careful attention to his appearance—he always wore polished boots and a crisply pressed blue-and-white uniform, a gleaming smallsword strapped to his waist—impressed everyone. "His personal appearance is truly majestic," wrote James Thacher, a doctor serving with the army. Henry Knox, a Boston bookseller with a passion for the military life, praised his "vast ease and dignity."

$\backsim$

THE GENERAL'S composure had to survive not a few harrowing hours. As 1776 began, his 14,000-man army shrank alarmingly. New Englanders viewed a contract as unbreakable, and the men who had rushed to Boston after Lexington and Concord began departing in droves as the terms of their enlistment expired. Recruiting a new army proved an unnervingly slow process. Not until spring began to green the land did Washington have enough men to think about taking the offensive.

Congress had ordered him to consult his fellow generals, and he soon presented them with a daring plan for an all-out assault on British-held Boston. It called for a frontal attack on the enemy's chief defenses around Boston Neck, while whaleboats landed hundreds of men elsewhere in the city. He hoped to achieve a victory that would force the British to negotiate peace and possibly independence. To Washington's dismay, his subordinate generals voted the plan down. They did not think their largely untrained troops could pull it off—and warned him that a crushing repulse might sink the Glorious Cause.

The admiring Boston bookseller Henry Knox came to the commander in chief's rescue. He led several hundred men on a winter march to Fort Ticonderoga, the British bastion on Lake Champlain in New York State captured a few weeks after the fighting at Lexington and Concord. Using sleds and wagons, Knox and his men dragged several dozen cannons over icy roads and snowy hills to Boston. Washington planted these heavy guns on Dorchester Heights, an elevation south of Boston, where they could fire directly into the city.

Washington hoped for an all-out British attack, which would have enabled him to reenact Bunker Hill on a larger, more decisive scale. Instead the British evacuated Boston, having long since realized that they stood to gain little from occupying the city. Washington wisely decided to let them go without further bloodshed.

Congress and the American people were hugely impressed by the bloodless liberation of Boston. One Virginian declared it would make Washington's name immortal in the annals of America. Congress struck a gold medal in Washington's honor, and Harvard awarded him a Doctor of Laws degree. The easy victory obviously confirmed the widespread opinion of *Common Sense* readers that winning independence would be a simple matter.

General Washington graciously accepted the unrealistic praise showered on him. Privately he admitted his personal disappointment that the British had not attacked the American positions on Dorchester Heights. He was still hoping for the decisive victory that would end the war. At this point he was completely committed to Congress's strategy of victory in one big battle—what military men called "a general action."

〜

ANOTHER CITY had far more strategic value—New York. It was at the center of the thirteen colonies and stood at the mouth of the Hudson River—a waterway that offered a potential avenue for invasion into the American interior. Washington had no doubt that the British intended to transfer their army to New York. "Should they get that town and the command of the North River," he wrote, "they can stop the intercourse between the northern and southern colonies upon which depends the safety of America."[6]

Learning that the British army and navy had retreated to distant Halifax, Washington led his army south to New York in easy marches. He had ordered his second in command, Major General Charles Lee, to proceed to the city several weeks earlier. The defense of New York flummoxed Lee, a veteran professional soldier in the British and other armies. An enemy with a powerful fleet could easily invade the city, surrounded as it was by water, from a dozen different directions. Lee decided the best solution was to erect a series of forts that would exact from the British a serious toll when they attacked. The British-born general had become a convinced Bunker Hillist. Washington still shared this illusion and, on arriving in New York, told Lee he was very pleased with his fortifications.[7]

Washington and his men spent the late spring and summer adding additional redoubts in and around New York. Other bastions rose on Brooklyn Heights across the East River from the city. One New York fort was named Bunker Hill—a graphic illustration of American thinking. Meanwhile Congress was making good on its side of the one-big-battle strategy. It summoned militia from New England, New Jersey, and Pennsylvania, swelling Washington's army to a theoretical 23,000 men. But the commander in chief seldom had an adequate grasp of how many men were available for a battle. Militia came and went as they pleased.

ON JUNE 25, the new British commander in chief, General William Howe, appeared off Sandy Hook, near the entrance to New York Harbor, with 9,000 men and 130 ships. There had been talk of erecting cannons along the Narrows, the appropriately named waterway that led to the inner harbor. But the heavy guns had never materialized. On July 2, Howe and his ships and men dropped anchor off Staten Island. As the army swarmed ashore, the small American garrison fled, and Staten Island's militia switched sides. It was an ominous glimpse of how many New Yorkers were loyalists at heart.

Also on July 2, Congress declared the thirteen colonies independent. Two days later (July 4), the Declaration of Independence was adopted. The momentous news reached New York six days later. The following day, July 9, Washington ordered the Declaration of Independence read aloud to his troops. He thoroughly approved the message it sent to America and the world and felt new confidence when he looked at the numerous forts his troops had built in New York and Brooklyn. The British, he said, would have to "wade through much blood and slaughter" before they could carry even a small part of these defenses. The statement was pure Bunker Hillism.

On July 12, another large British fleet arrived in New York Harbor. Leading it, aboard his huge man-of-war, HMS *Eagle*, was Admiral Lord Richard Howe, older brother of the army's commander. He brought with him another army, swelling the British ranks to 25,000 men. Before the summer ended, additional troops would raise the total to 32,000. It was the biggest army that Britain had ever sent beyond her shores. Among other things, it totally refuted Thomas Paine's claim that the British were too bankrupt to send significant numbers of soldiers overseas. Counting men-of-war and transports, the British fleet in New York Harbor now numbered over four hundred ships—additional proof that former British tax collector Paine did not know what he was talking about.

⌒

FOR THE rest of the summer the Howes played peacemaker with Washington. They had commissions from George III to negotiate a reconciliation. It soon became apparent that they had no power to deal with an independent nation. General Howe, having by this time spent eighteen months in America (including a nightmarish day on Bunker Hill) repeatedly told his brother that he was wasting precious weeks of the summer campaigning season. A serious defeat inflicted on Washington's army would alone quell the rebellion. Only then would the rebels talk peace. The admiral finally agreed and listened to the general's plan for their assault.

On August 22, dozens of small flatboats pulled away from Staten Island and from many of the ships in the harbor. The Howes were utilizing Britain's long experience in amphibious warfare. The flatboats had planked-up sides to protect their passengers from enemy bullets. In the course of the hot, sunny day, 15,000 troops—some of them German mercenaries hired by George III—landed on the shore of Long Island's Gravesend Bay. Washington and his fellow generals were baffled. They had assumed that the British would make New York their first target.

Except for the forts on Brooklyn Heights, built to defend New York City, Long Island's defenses were virtually nonexistent. Washington had stationed only about 4,000 men on its hundred miles of farms and fields. Worse, a brand-new general was in command: Israel Putnam. The hero of Bunker Hill had replaced Washington's first choice, Rhode Islander Nathanael Greene, who had taken ill with one of the numerous fevers then debilitating hundreds of men in Washington's army. Much of this problem came from New York City's polluted water supply.

A healthy General Greene could not likely have made much difference. He knew little about Long Island's geography or people. On August 15, he had complained to Washington that most of his men were in the same state of ignorance. Connecticut-born General Putnam knew even less about the region. The same could be said of his two subordinate generals, John Sullivan of New Hampshire and William Alexander, better known as Lord Stirling, of New Jersey. (The title derived from a claim to a Scottish dukedom.) Even after the British invasion of Long Island, the generals and Washington suspected it was only a feint to lure men from New York's forts before the main attack began there.

When this attack failed to materialize, Washington began to realize the decisive battle would take place on Long Island. On August 22, he journeyed to the forts on Brooklyn Heights and conferred with General Putnam. They invited General John Sullivan to join them and explored the terrain they would have to defend. To the southeast stood a heavily forested ridge known as the Hills of Guan. Washington decided to make this their first line of defense and ordered Putnam to assign his best troops to its summit, with orders to inflict maximum damage if the enemy attempted an assault.

On the night of August 26, heavy skirmishing on the approaches to the Hills of Guan convinced General Putnam that the battle was about to begin. He awoke his two fellow generals, Sullivan and Lord Stirling, and ordered them to prepare their men for a fight to the finish. He also lit signal lights to warn Washington, who had returned to Manhattan.

Except for the skirmishing, the night passed with no sign of a major assault. Much too late the Americans would learn the reason for this puzzling restraint.

⌒

MANY MILES south of the Americans on the Hills of Guan, a 10,000-man British column trudged silently through the darkness. At its head was Captain William Glanville Evelyn, commander of an infantry company in the King's Own Regiment. It was a chilly night, but Evelyn barely gave a thought to his shivering men. The handsome thirty-four-year-old officer was hoping that before the end of the next day, his name would be wreathed in honor. Evelyn also knew that he and his men might head the list of dead and wounded if this march ended in disaster. Fourteen months earlier, Evelyn had led thirty-three men against Americans entrenched on Bunker Hill—and come back with five. A hunger for revenge burned within him and other officers in his regiment.

The eventual targets of this midnight maneuver were the American forts on Brooklyn Heights and the forward regiments on the Hills of Guan. Three passes ran through these hills, and the Americans on the high ground were confident they could inflict prohibitive casualties on any British or German column that attempted to penetrate them. But Americans loyal to George III had told General Howe about a fourth pass on the Jamaica Road, far out on the American left flank. The heights overlooking it were unfortified, and the pass was seldom patrolled. Howe's second in command, General Henry Clinton, saw that a column could use this pass to outflank the entire American position on the Hills of Guan and cut off a retreat to the forts.

As midnight turned into the early hours of August 27, the loyalists guiding Captain Evelyn's men abruptly abandoned the road and led them across farmlands, where they squashed vegetables beneath their boots and cut swaths through fields of corn. They emerged only a half mile from the Jamaica Pass.

A moment later, hoofbeats triggered panic. Had the secret march been discovered? Were Americans in fact crawling all over the area?

Dragoons surged forward and captured five frightened American lieutenants—the only guard posted at the pass. With sabers held high, the cavalrymen demanded to know who else was on the road. No one, the terrified captors answered. Though finding this hard to believe, the British soon confirmed that the winding, steep-sided pass, which a few hundred soldiers with cannons could have defended for hours, was empty. His confidence soaring, General Clinton ordered the men forward, convinced they were closing in on a victory that would end this rebellion and teach Americans a lesson that would sting for a century.

By the time a glaring red sun rose, the British were striding briskly down the road toward the American forts at Brooklyn, well behind the rebel regiments on the Hills of Guan. As they marched, Clinton ordered two cannons fired—a signal to other British and German regiments to launch a frontal assault on the fortified hills.

As the British and Germans forged ahead, Clinton attacked the Americans from behind with 4,000 screaming light infantry. Trapped and panicked, the troops commanded by General John Sullivan surrendered or fled into the woods, where the British and Germans hunted them down like animals. The Germans were especially brutal because their British employers had told them the Americans would give captured mercenaries no quarter. In dozens of nasty encounters, young Americans pleaded with the Germans for mercy, only to be bayoneted with a ferocity that shocked not a few British officers.

Sullivan and his men had taken flight without giving the slightest warning to 2,000 Americans on their right, commanded by Lord Stirling. His men had been more than holding their own. Early in the fighting, they had charged and routed a British regiment on a nearby hill, killing the commander. But panic demoralized the winners of this mini-victory when the Germans who had routed Sullivan's men attacked from the left. At the same time thousands of British infantry from the Jamaica Pass column hit them from behind.

Stirling realized there was only one escape to the American forts—across Gowanus Creek in the rear. But the creek was eighty yards wide and running strong; unless slowed, the British would slaughter his men as they tried to ford it. Stirling turned to the best-trained men in his command, some 250 Marylanders under Major Mordecai Gist. Drawing his sword, the general shouted, "Fix bayonets!" and led a frontal assault on the approximately 10,000 British and Germans attacking them.

Astonished, the king's men recoiled, then began flinging bullets and grapeshot at the advancing rebels from two field pieces. Five times the Americans wavered and broke, but Stirling and Gist rallied them. Washington, watching from one of the Brooklyn Heights forts, gasped, "Good God! What brave fellows I must this day lose."[8]

Marylanders toppled by the dozen in the hail of bullets, and the gallant remnant broke and fled. Stirling, miraculously unwounded, surrendered his sword to Lieutenant General Leopold von Heister, the German commander. At about the same time, another German regiment flushed General Sullivan out of his hiding place in a cornfield. Only nine of the Marylanders and Gist reached the Brooklyn forts. A Connecticut militiaman, Joseph Plumb Martin, later remembered that the terrified survivors who crawled out of Gowanus Creek looked like "water rats. . . . A truly pitiful sight."[9]

Suddenly General Washington recognized a fatal flaw in his forts, the product of a summer of immense labor. Trenches connecting the structures now lay open and undefended. If the British seized them, they could surround and destroy the forts one by one. Washington ordered hundreds of men to pile brush in front of these vital links. On the American left, three New York militia regiments frantically shoveled dirt to erect defenses facing the Jamaica Pass.

General Clinton asked General Howe for permission to order Captain Evelyn and other light infantrymen to assault the New York militia. He was sure he could drive them all the way to the ferry in Brooklyn, cutting off the American retreat across the East River to Manhattan. Other requests to attack poured into General Howe's field headquarters from regimental commanders. One British general wanted to hurl his grenadiers at Fort Putnam, the main bastion on the American left. He was confident he could capture it in minutes.

General Howe said no—again, and again, and again—despite the oaths and pleas of his subordinates. Howe's concern was not British casualties, which had been unbelievably light—only five officers and 56 men killed and thirteen officers and 275 men wounded. Nor was it fear of repeating Bunker Hill's slaughter, though the memory may have quickened his refusal. The general and his brother, Admiral Howe, were pursuing a strategy that sought to preserve rather than destroy Washington's army. The Howes appreciated the Americans' grievances against the British government. Both were political opponents of George III. They feared the growing power of the crown and its hardline supporters in Parliament.

The Howes hoped to force the Americans to ask for peace terms, which the British commanders would make as generous as possible. They worried that the total destruction of Washington's army would give George III free rein to execute the rebel leaders and ruthlessly confiscate lands as previous kings had done in rebellious Ireland and Scotland. When his soldiers brought General Howe the captured American generals, Stirling and Sullivan, General Howe tried to enlist them as peace emissaries to the Continental Congress. Stirling refused; his family had seen the savage way the British had stamped out Scottish revolts. Sullivan, much more naive, agreed to become the Howes' advocate.

ᔐ

THE FIGHTING on the Hills of Guan was over by the afternoon of August 27. For the rest of that day and the next, the Americans in the Brooklyn forts waited for a British attack. Washington brandished two pistols and vowed to shoot the first man who ran. With a characteristic bellow, Putnam repeated his Bunker Hill rallying cry: fire only when you see the whites of their eyes. But the day and night passed quietly.

Still convinced that an all-out attack was inevitable, Washington ordered three more regiments from Manhattan to bolster everyone's courage. The walls of the forts now held the commander in chief, his staff, and almost every available general, plus at least 9,000 men, most of them irreplaceable regulars.

Aboard the frigate HMS *Rainbow* in the harbor, Captain George Collier wrote in his diary, "If we become masters of this body of rebels (which I think is inevitable) the war is at end." Throughout the day, Collier wondered why Admiral Howe had not ordered the *Rainbow* and three other frigates into the East River, where they could cut off a rebel retreat from the Brooklyn Heights forts to Manhattan.

A bone-chilling rain began to fall on the battlefield. Water filled some of the forts' connecting trenches until it reached waist level. At twilight, a brief skirmish broke out as a swarm of British light infantry drove the outlying American pickets inside the forts. At dawn the next day, August 29, the Americans saw what the enemy had gained from this action: a sturdy British redoubt now stood about six hundred yards from the forts; behind it lay a network of trenches. General Howe had taken the first step in the siege technique known as "regular approaches." In a day or two these trenches would be close enough for the British to launch an overwhelming assault.

American morale plummeted. "You must fight or retreat," Quartermaster General Thomas Mifflin told Washington. The American commander resisted the idea. He was still anxious to fulfill Congress's strategy of victory in one general action. A council of war with his other generals revealed that they unanimously favored a retreat. Washington decided they were right. He rushed orders to Manhattan to collect every boat on the East and Hudson Rivers.

At nightfall, amid continuing rain, the retreat began. Fearing a deserter would betray their scheme to the British, Washington told his men that he was repositioning the army. Not until the soldiers marched to the waiting small boats on the East River shore did they realize what was happening.

The best troops, Continentals from Pennsylvania, Maryland, and Delaware, remained in the forts. For two hours, the exodus went smoothly. Then a strong northeast wind began to blow. The small sailboats that made up the bulk of the evacuation fleet struggled against it. Disaster loomed. Brigadier General Alexander McDougall, who commanded the embarkation process, told Washington that there was no hope of getting everyone across to Manhattan before dawn.

At 11:00 P.M. the wind suddenly swung around to the southwest—the best direction to send the boats swiftly across the river. The water became as smooth as the surface of a pond. Boatmen began to pile soldiers and equipment into the vessels until only two or three inches of freeboard remained. A single British cutter with a swivel gun in its bow could have wreaked havoc on these defenseless craft. Plenty of cutters plied the nearby harbor, but none appeared in the East River.

As dawn's first light turned the sky grey, the regulars left behind in the forts grew edgy. An attack was certain the moment the British saw that no one had replaced the men in the connecting trenches. "We became very anxious for our own safety," Major Benjamin Tallmadge of Connecticut said.

Then came another change in the weather that proved even more providential for the Americans. A dense fog engulfed the river and the lines. "I could scarcely discern a man at 6 yards distance," Tallmadge recalled. Even after the sun rose, the fog hung low, enabling every regular to escape undetected. Stepping into one of the last boats was the tall, cloaked figure of General Washington. He had not slept for forty-eight hours.

With the troops now safe in Manhattan, Tallmadge asked Washington if he could return to Brooklyn to rescue his horse. Washington, a fellow horse lover, assented. Tallmadge recrossed the river, and as his oarsmen pulled hard for Manhattan with the steed aboard, they heard angry voices in the fog. British infantry appeared on the East River shore and fired a wild volley that hit no one. They were too late.

⌢

IN MANHATTAN this escape from disaster heartened few civilians. Several thought Washington's men looked "sickly" and "cast down." Over the next few days, a half dozen regiments of militia voted to end the war and go home. Connecticut's part-time soldiers, almost totally demoralized, shrank from 8,000 to 2,000 men within a week.[10]

Meanwhile General Sullivan headed to Philadelphia to fulfill his promise to Lord Howe and delivered to Congress the plea for peace. The politicians delegated Benjamin Franklin, John Adams, and Edward Rutledge to meet with the admiral on Staten Island. Lord Howe earnestly tried to persuade these congressmen to trust in George III's

forgiveness, insisting that Britain did not require unconditional surrender. But the admiral refused to transmit Franklin's proposal to let
the Americans negotiate as spokesmen for an independent nation.
Franklin and the others came away convinced that their best hope was
to fight. We continue to rely "on your wisdom and fortitude, and that
of your forces," Rutledge wrote to Washington in his report of the
meeting.[11]

On September 2, Washington wrote to John Hancock, president of
Congress. He was almost as unhappy with his troops as the troubled
civilian spectators who greeted them on their retreat from Brooklyn
Heights. He judged especially severely the conduct of the militiamen,
who had displayed no enthusiasm whatsoever for fighting the British.
He also admitted that "apprehension and despair" gripped the whole
army.[12]

Washington was by no means alone in this perception. Behind it lay
a much larger question: Should they continue to defend New York?
"Till of late," Washington wrote, he was sure the American army would
make the city the next and possibly decisive battleground. Now he was
no longer confident the army was equal to the task. He asked Congress,
if they evacuated New York, whether they should permit the place "to
stand as winter quarters for the enemy." He was personally inclined to
burn it.

A few days later, Washington received a letter from a revived General Nathanael Greene, who confirmed Washington's growing doubts
about relying on Bunker Hillism in a battle for New York. They should
execute a "speedy retreat" from the island. New York was worthless
compared with "the general interests of America." The country was already "struck with a panick." Another "capital loss" could spell ruin for
their cause.[13] Greene recommended burning New York. Two-thirds of
the city belonged to Tories.

The next day Washington received an answer to his letter to Congress. They sent him a "resolve" ordering him not to burn New York if
he had to abandon it. Washington called another council of war, and a
clear majority of his generals, still devoted to Bunker Hillism, recommended they stand and fight. Most could not bear the thought of

abandoning all those forts that their men had spent the long, hot summer constructing.

Washington was not convinced by this majority opinion. He had begun thinking for himself about fighting and winning this war. The next day he wrote to Congress, revealing a new strategy. He said it was only a question of time before they were forced to abandon New York. He realized that a general and his army might be reproached for retreating. But "the fate of America" was at stake here. With the help of "experienced men," he had decided that his army should "on all occasions avoid a general action, or put anything to the risque, unless compelled by necessity into which we ought never to be drawn." Instead they should "protract the war."[14]

Congress, not grasping the breadth and depth of this change, approved Washington's plan to withdraw from New York if necessary but again forbade him to burn the city. This left Washington to formulate a plan that would not distress the majority of his generals, who still wanted to fight for the city. He calmly began moving most of the army northward, to the high ground known as Harlem Heights, and beyond it to the northern tip of Manhattan, called Kingsbridge. He left only 5,000 men in the forts constructed along the three miles of New York City's shoreline.

To contest a British landing elsewhere, he assigned Connecticut militia and some New York regular troops to defend the coves that indented the East River shore at present-day 15th Street (Stuyvesant Cove), 34th Street (Kips Bay), and 42nd Street (Turtle Bay). These men had neither the time nor the inclination to build serious fortifications. They dug crude trenches and talked loudly to each other about the damage they would inflict on any British soldiers foolish enough to come ashore in their bailiwicks.

For several days, there was no sign of the next British move. Then flatboats began moving up the East River's opposite shore. Landing parties seized two islands in the river. At 7:00 P.M. on September 14, five British frigates dropped anchor in Kips Bay—close enough for the men onboard to exchange insults with the Connecticut militia regiments on the shore. When an American sentry called, "All is well," a sailor on one of the ships shouted, "We will alter your tune before to-morrow night!"

At dawn on September 15, the militiamen awoke to discover that the frigates had moved "within musket shot of us," recalled one of the part-time soldiers. HMS *Phoenix* was close enough for men on shore to read her name. The militiamen shouted insults, waved their guns, and dared the British to try coming ashore. But the sailors were busy loading their cannons. Two hours later, as the sun rose, a hot muggy haze enveloped Manhattan Island. The waiting militiamen began to find the enemy's silence ominous.

Out of Bushwick Creek, on the opposite shore, came dozens of flat-boats. With sailors rowing in steady beats, they began moving across the East River. In the lead boat was General Henry Clinton. Around him were seven battalions of red-coated British light infantry and grenadiers and a brigade of elite British Guards. Nearby were three German battalions of blue-coated grenadiers and green-coated jaegers (huntsmen)—their version of light infantry.

Opposing General Clinton on the Manhattan shore was overage Major General Joseph Spencer of Connecticut—one of too many ranking officers Congress had chosen for purely political reasons. He was little more than a spectator as the British flatboat armada approached. He gave no orders to his scattered regiments. No one tried to concentrate men at Kips Bay. Instead, when the wind and tide bent the line of oncoming British and Germans toward Turtle Bay, militiamen scampered in that direction. Others thought the British would wait for the tide to ebb, carrying them to Stuyvesant Cove, and ran there.

At 11:00 A.M., when the flatboats were about fifty yards from the shore of Kips Bay, the eighty-six cannons aboard the frigates exploded. One militiaman thought his head would fly off with the crash. He dove to the bottom of his trench and lay there, wondering "which part of my carcass was to go first." For fifty-nine minutes the guns pounded the militiaman in their primitive trenches. From the haze of gun smoke emerged the flatboats, in three columns, heading for the shore.[15]

The Connecticut militiaman took one look at these murky, murderous shapes and started running. By the time the first British flatboat grounded several dozen yards from the beach and the men began floundering through the mud to the rocky shore, only the commander of the Kips Bay militia brigade and a handful of men over whom he had immediate control were still in the trenches. Four New York regiments stationed at Stuyvesant Cove and five regiments of Connecticut militia stationed near 23rd Street should have rushed to Kips Bay. But they were paralyzed by the cannonade and the awesome sight of the oncoming British attackers.

As the grenadiers and light infantry reached dry ground, to their disbelief no one fired so much as a shot at them. They had their bayonets leveled and ready. But there was no one to bayonet. The Connecticut militia were legging it north along the Boston Post Road. The British were soon in possession of the gently sloping high ground at present-day 34th Street. The German grenadiers, preceded by a screen of jaegers, approached some nearby woods and fields. From the woods came a blast of musketry. The grenadiers charged with bayonets, and it was Long Island all over again: the mercenaries skewered whimpering, pleading young Americans as they tried to surrender.

By 1:00 P.M. the British had total control of their beachhead and were cautiously expanding it north and south. General Clinton still expected a massive American counterattack. But no such event was forthcoming. George Washington and his staff and other generals, including the hapless Spencer, were frantically trying to rally the fleeing militiamen. They hoped to organize a stand along the Bloomingdale Road around present-day 41st Street, where stone walls divided farms and the corn stood high. The generals brought with them two brigades of Connecticut militia—about 2,500 men. None of them had been anywhere near the Kips Bay beachhead. But when they saw the former defenders of that shoreline running helter-skelter up the road and across the fields, these regiments also collapsed. A glimpse of seven or eight British light infantrymen on the crest of a hill a quarter mile away completed their panic.

In vain General Washington roared, "Take the wall! Take the cornfield!" The men raced past him up the road or scrambled into the fields around him.

Washington saw his military reputation vanishing. He flung his hat to the ground and cried out in anguish, "Are these the men with which I have to defend America?" Cursing stupendously, he lashed runaways within reach of his riding crop. Neither the words nor his blows had the slightest effect. The fleeing troops deserted their commander in chief on the Bloomingdale Road, surrounded by abandoned muskets, knapsacks, canteens, and cartridge boxes.

Washington seldom let his temper get out of control. When he did, the explosion of raw energy drained him to the point of stupor. He slumped in his saddle, staring dazedly around him. A ten-year-old boy with a toy sword could have taken him prisoner. His bewildered aides waited for him to recover. The oncoming British light infantrymen hesitated, suspecting a trap. Finally, one of Washington's aides rode up to the general, took the bridle of his horse, and led him up the road in the wake of his troops. It was the low point of Washington's performance as a commander in chief. It also resolved any lingering doubts he may have had about Congress's strategy of relying on a large turnout of militia.

While this drama unfolded, and the British stood poised to advance across the rest of Manhattan Island, 5,000 men, including most of the army's irreplaceable artillerymen, still manned the supposedly impregnable forts in New York City. Their commander, General Israel Putnam, was looking forward to a replay of Bunker Hill when he received an order from General Washington to retreat immediately. Putnam was inclined to defy the order but a young officer named Aaron Burr convinced him that doing so would lead to disaster. Frantic efforts to load ammunition, guns, and baggage ensued, and a long weary column wended its way up the west side of Manhattan to the safety of Harlem Heights. Its sluggish, almost sullen pace was mute evidence of the regret that tormented almost all these men, who had devoted so many hours to building the forts that they were now abandoning without a fight.

⌒

LATER THAT day, Washington grimly informed Congress of the awful performance of the militia at Kips Bay. Now, he reported, his army was temporarily safe on the "Heights of Harlem," where it could inflict serious damage on the British if they attacked. Such a successful repetition of Bunker Hill required the men to behave with "tolerable resolution." But experience, to his "great affliction," had led him to regard this conduct as "rather to be wished for than expected." He could only hope that some of them were ready "to act like men and show themselves worthy of the blessings of freedom."

As he finished this letter, one of his aides rushed into the room to tell him of an exchange of gunfire on "the plains of Harlem," not far away. At dawn Washington had ordered Lieutenant Colonel Thomas Knowlton of Connecticut, commander of 150 rangers, to prowl closer to the British lines to look for signs of dangerous movement. At about present-day 106th Street, they collided with some four hundred British light infantry camped in a wood. The Americans put up a good fight until Knowlton spotted the 42nd Regiment, the famed Scottish Black Watch, advancing on his left. He ordered his men to begin falling back. The light infantry followed, and the skirmish continued with considerable ferocity all the way to what New Yorkers called "the Hollow Way," a mini-valley at present-day 125th Street.

The light infantry, aware that they were getting dangerously close to the main American army, ceased their pursuit. One of their officers ordered a bugler to sound a call familiar from the fox hunt—a series of whoop-whoops meaning the chase was over, and the fox was dead. It was a peculiarly British touch of arrogance that the Americans understood all too well. Joseph Reed, one of Washington's aides, later told his wife, "I never felt such a sensation before. It seemed to crown our disgrace." He was thinking of the army's awful performance at Kips Bay.

Washington, a veteran fox hunter, shared Reed's feelings. He ordered Knowlton to take his rangers and three rifle companies from a Virginia regiment through the woods on Vanderlyn Heights—present-day Morningside Heights—and get in the rear of the light infantry, cutting off their retreat. (The infantrymen were close to the site of present-day Grant's Tomb.) The light infantry met the challenge with sheets of bullets. Both Knowlton and the major in command of the Virginians went down, mortally wounded. But this only inspired the men in the ranks to press home a ferocious attack. Washington, sensing the chance of a victory that could revive the army's morale, poured in another eight hundred men. Soon the light infantrymen had only one thought in their heads—a retreat to the safety of the British lines. The British ordered the Black Watch into the fight, but even their famed pugnacity could not withstand the pressure from the swarming Americans. Soon the British withdrew into the woods lining the sloping hill along which Broadway now runs.

The sight of the enemy all but on the run galvanized the Americans. Parts of two Maryland regiments charged into the woods, and the red-coated light infantry soon abandoned their shelter. They were temporarily relieved to find reinforcements greeting them, two more battalions of light infantry with two field pieces. This did not in the least discourage the Americans. For another hour, a firefight raged in a buckwheat field between present-day 120th and 119th Streets. The British started running out of ammunition and retreated again. By now everyone in both armies was watching the contest. Even some frigates in Stryker's Bay on the Hudson River tried to help their comrades in arms, blasting numerous cannonades at the Americans. They hit no one. Several regiments of German and British grenadiers now entered the fray, and the Americans, more than satisfied, pulled back to Harlem Heights.

Washington was enormously pleased by the way this minor skirmish lifted the morale of his army. Even some of the runaway militia from Kips Bay stood ready to fight, though no one was inclined to commit them to combat. One man later recalled how they had waited on Harlem Heights for an order to advance, even though some of them were faint with hunger, having had no food for almost forty-eight hours. On the British side, one officer admitted which side had won the fight, telling his diary it was "a most unfortunate affair."

Admiral and General Howe could think of nothing to do next but issue another call for a negotiated peace. From a diplomatic point of view, this decision was a disaster. It confirmed what the three congressmen who talked with the admiral on Staten Island had reported and the newspapers soon printed: the British commanders dealt only in "generalities," which could mean almost anything—or nothing.

Privately the Howes admitted in a letter to their civilian superior in London, the secretary of state for American affairs, that the rebels betrayed not even a hint of an inclination to restore "public tranquility."

Within twenty-four hours, new proof of rebel determination reinforced this pessimism. Shortly after midnight on September 20, the cry "Fire" rang out in New York streets. A stiff wind blew from the south, and the flames, which began near Whitehall ferry slip, swept north with devastating rapidity. Hundreds of seamen from the fleet in the harbor rushed ashore, and two regiments of soldiers joined them. But they could do little. There was a shortage of buckets, and running water was scarce. The British caught a number of men setting fires in advance of the blaze and killed most of these incendiaries without mercy—or questioning.

General Howe feared the fire might signal an all-out attack by the Americans and refused to commit additional soldiers. Only by pulling down dozens of buildings and creating firebreaks did the men fighting the blaze get it under control. By that time it was almost dawn, and at least 600 houses—by some estimates, as many as 1,000—had been destroyed, constituting a third of the city. Washington never admitted a role in this conflagration. But his cryptic comment on it said a great deal. In a letter to his cousin Lund Washington, he admitted that he had asked Congress for permission to destroy the city and been refused. He considered this denial "one of the capital errors of Congress." He was grateful that "Providence—or some good honest fellow—had done more for us than we were disposed to do for ourselves."

∽

Two DAYS after the fire, Washington stole time "from hours allotted to sleep" to write a long letter to Congress. He pleaded with its members to abandon the strategy of depending on short-term militia. He needed the right to enlist enough men for the duration of the war to give him a standing army that he could train and equip to equal that of the British. He knew the term "standing army," with its historical echoes of Oliver Cromwell, made some politicians nervous. But the evils of a standing army were "remote," while not having one as soon as possible would lead to "inevitable ruin."[16]

The general also warned Congress that it was time to show more judgment and care in the selection of officers. The officer corps was "the soul of every army." To find the right men, Washington told Congress, it was time to accept a hard truth—the fervent emotions that persuaded people to support a cause did not last very long. It was foolish to assume that "any other principles but those of Interest" influence most men. To expect otherwise "was to look for what never did, and I fear never will happen." This meant Congress had to pay officers enough to live like gentlemen. At the moment scanty pay was driving a dismaying number of officers to "low and dirty arts." These included looting civilians as well as filching from the public treasury.

This insistence on the significance of "interest" (self-interest) clashed with the largely New England opinion that true patriotism transcended such selfish emotions. No one had paid the militiamen who fought so well on April 19, 1775. (In one or two cases, a town offered to pay its minutemen, only to be told that "volunteers" did not take money.) Serving his country was proof of a man's virtue—the only reward he should seek. No one gave the issue much thought for the moment—but it would engender serious quarrels in the years to come.

⌒

WHILE WASHINGTON was enunciating these basic principles, his army continued to dissolve. Among the Connecticut militia regiments, one had dwindled to fourteen men, another to thirty; several others had fewer than fifty soldiers in their ranks. Some regiments were openly mutinous and threatening to go home. General Howe tried to accelerate this dissolution by putting 5,000 men aboard flatboats in the East River and landing them unopposed on Throgs Neck, a point of land near the junction of the East River and Long Island Sound in the present-day Bronx. The Americans quickly destroyed the only route off Throgs Neck to the mainland—a causeway and bridge. This suggests that Howe's chief purpose was to get the American army off

Manhattan Island. He accelerated this process by moving the 5,000 men north to Pells Point in present-day Pelham, New York, and shipping them reinforcements.

In a council of war, Washington's generals advised him to withdraw from Manhattan as soon as possible. Another nightmarish retreat ensued. There were not enough horses to pull the wagons and guns. Some cannons had to be dragged by hand. The American army was a long, exposed line of 13,000 weary men. But General Howe chose not to attack. He was still pursuing his strategy of knocking Washington's army out of the war without completely destroying it.

The Americans entrenched on the hills around the village of White Plains. Now, at last, Bunker Hill II was sure to happen! The British made a few feints, which local boosters still call the "battle" of White Plains. They captured a hill that outflanked the entire American position. But they again declined to hurl their regiments en masse up the slope at the waiting rebels. Instead General Howe detached a large chunk of his army and sent it back to Manhattan to eliminate the last pocket of enemy resistance there—some 3,000 men entrenched in a large earthwork named Fort Washington. The area around it is now called Washington Heights. Washington had left them there because Congress had urged him to retain control of the Hudson River. Theoretically, the guns of the fort and a fort on the New Jersey shore, named for the army's second in command, Major General Charles Lee, could manage this.

The British attack on Fort Washington was a military masterpiece. From every piece of high ground, artillery rained down shot and shell. A column of Germans struck from the north; the British light infantry assaulted from the south. In two hours, the defenders were driven from their outworks into the central fort, where they milled around, a packed, panicked mob. A German captain stalked in the gate under the protection of a white flag and gave them a half hour to surrender. He made it clear that the Germans intended to honor the military tradition of slaughtering to the last man defenders of a fort who declined to yield. The Americans capitulated.[17]

Major General Nathanael Greene of Rhode Island had played a large part in persuading Washington to leave the men in the fort. Watching from Fort Lee on the New Jersey shore, the two generals saw a fifth of their army vanish. It was the nadir of the American strategy for winning the war in 1776. It was also the last gasp of Bunker Hillism in George Washington's awakening strategic mind.

By this time, Washington had retreated into New Jersey with 3,000 men to rally that state against the oncoming British, who swiftly put 5,000 men across the Hudson River to challenge him. Washington had left General Charles Lee in command of about 7,000 men in Westchester County, with orders to keep the British from invading New England. Instead, the British began reinforcing their New Jersey invaders until they were 10,000 men strong, under the command of one of their most aggressive generals, Charles, Lord Cornwallis. Washington asked Lee to join him for a stand on the Raritan River around New Brunswick. Lee, a headstrong compound of radical political opinions and careening military ambition, ignored Washington's request; he wanted an independent command. In letters to Congress he began referring to Washington's men as "the western army."

Meanwhile, New Jersey's 17,000 militia declined to mobilize. Not a single regiment responded to Governor William Livingston's call. Only about 1,000 individuals showed up at mustering sites, a turnout almost as useless as none at all. The numbers proved the British were waging a very successful war for the loyalties of New Jerseymen. Along their line of march they distributed a proclamation offering pardons and guarantees against "forfeitures, attainders and penalties." Rebels need only appear before a British official within sixty days and sign a statement promising to "remain in peaceable obedience to His Majesty."[18]

On November 29, Washington was in New Brunswick, with an army riven by three months of retreat and defeat. Militiamen broke into stores of rum and got drunk. Others, mostly from Pennsylvania, deserted in droves, despite having been paid to stay until January 1. Men whose contracts expired on December 1 announced they were going home too. Charles Lee continued to ignore Washington's pleas to join him for a united effort in New Jersey. Washington informed Congress that within twenty-four hours, "our force will be reduced to a mere handful." By December 1 he was down to an unstable mix of regular and militia troops that barely totaled 3,000 men. At least 6,000 British were crunching toward the bridges over the Raritan River. Washington told Congress, "We shall [have to] retreat to the west side of the Delaware."

Stunned by its militia's mass defection and Washington's seeming abandonment, New Jersey slid toward collapse. The legislature issued one more appeal to the militia and disbanded. As many as three to four hundred people a day flocked to British army posts at New Brunswick, Elizabethtown, and elsewhere to renew their allegiance. Brigadier General Alexander McDougall was soon writing from Morristown, "This state is totally deranged, without Government or officers, civil or military that will act with any spirit."[19]

Lee finally realized the fate of the infant nation was at stake in New Jersey and crossed the Hudson River into Bergen County. He was not encouraged by what he encountered along his line of march. One sergeant wrote in his diary, "The inhabitants abused us caling us Damd rebels and would not sell Us anything for money." A sergeant sent to buy a hot breakfast for three men stopped at every house for ten or twelve miles before he found one whose occupants sold him some food—at noon. General Lee began saying the mass of New Jerseymen were "strangely contaminated."

Lee's solution was force. An early believer in the dictum that revolutions grew from the point of a gun, he wrote to friends in Congress, urging them to draft militia to fill up the ranks of a new army. He sneered at the idea of volunteers, who drew from "the most idle, vicious and dissolute part of every society." A volunteer standing army would put the "arms of the Republic in the hands of its worst members." On his march through northern New Jersey, Lee gave his mostly New England soldiers carte blanche to rob anyone suspected of loyalism.

Washington took a very different view of New Jersey's collapse. In a letter to General William Heath, who was guarding the Hudson Highlands, the American commander in chief wrote, "The defection of the people . . . has been as much owing to the want of an Army to look the Enemy in the face, as any other cause."[20]

Here, he enunciated another principle of the strategy that would not only win the American Revolution but lay the foundation of the future American regular army. When he wrote that letter, an event had already occurred that enabled him to implement the idea almost immediately. On Friday, December 13, British cavalry captured Major General Charles Lee as he slept at an inn several miles from his troops. Washington promptly took command of Lee's army, which had dwindled to about 4,000 men. He began organizing small armies of militiamen and regulars operating around Morristown and Springfield under the command of Continental officers such as McDougall. He gave the Morristown volunteers three regiments of Lee's troops. He ordered General Heath to invade Bergen County with six hundred Continentals. These mini-armies were soon disturbing the British peace in supposedly pacified New Jersey.

None of this activity impressed the members of Congress in Philadelphia. On December 12 they voted to abandon the city and retreat to Baltimore. They had been debating the structure of a national government for the American nation that they had recently founded. But it was difficult to think clearly with the British only a day's march away. Congressman William Whipple of Connecticut blamed this embarrassing move on Philadelphia. He said the city had been struck "with such a panick in all orders of the people . . . that the contagion seized the nerves of some members of Congress."[21]

General Washington's nerves, on the other hand, remained remarkably steady. On the west bank of the Delaware River, he began planning an attack that would galvanize his army and send a signal to all the people of New Jersey. For his target he chose the British outpost at Trenton, garrisoned by three regiments of German mercenaries. The British had stationed troops there and at Bordentown, Princeton, and other towns across the state to protect the inhabitants who had returned to peaceable obedience to His Majesty. General Howe admitted the posts were a bit exposed. But by now he had decided they could "take liberties" with the hapless Americans.

With a canny combination of espionage, double agentry, and surprise, Washington first befuddled then assaulted the Germans at Trenton in a howling sleet storm on December 26, capturing 868 officers and men and killing or wounding 106. Another four hundred escaped by doing what had heretofore been an American specialty: running for their lives. Returning to Pennsylvania, Washington persuaded his soldiers to stay in the army for another six weeks—virtually the entire force had enlisted only for the year 1776, thanks to Congress's insistence on a twelve-month maximum for all volunteers. With these extremely temporary troops, he recrossed the Delaware, determined to give New Jersey an army to look the enemy in the face. General Lord Cornwallis came after him with every available man and gun.

Washington conducted a fighting retreat but could not hold Trenton. He fell back to the bank of the Delaware River, where, as far as the British could see, Bunker Hillism would soon provide them with the denouement of the Revolution. Washington's position looked hopeless. If he retreated into South Jersey, he was on a peninsula, in another trap. If he tried to flee across the Delaware, at least half his army would be smashed in the process. It never occurred to the British that Washington was planning an attack.

Again he marched by night, leaving campfires burning briskly to simulate the presence of his army. Dawn found him miles in the British rear, mauling three British regiments at Princeton. The astonished Royal Army came puffing and blowing down the road behind him. But Washington had vanished into the country like a will-o'-the-wisp, heading for the main British supply base at New Brunswick. The panicked British marched all night to get there first and took up defensive positions in the hills around the town.

When Washington failed to appear, it dawned on the British—and everyone else—that the king's troops had been outfought, outgeneraled, and, worst of all, made to look ridiculous. Washington settled his weary troops into winter quarters at Morristown, where high ground gave him security and time to begin recruiting a new army. He issued a proclamation to New Jerseyans. Anyone who had succumbed to the British offer of pardon could return to the fold by visiting the nearest military post to swear "allegiance to the United States." The demoralized British contributed to the potency of this tactic by withdrawing from western New Jersey, creating a line of posts around New Brunswick that offered no protection to loyalists in two-thirds of the state. At least as important was the safety of the nation's capital, Philadelphia. An exultant General Henry Knox wrote to his wife, "The enemy were within 19 miles of Philadelphia. They are now sixty miles."[22]

Throughout New Jersey and the rest of America, news of the victories at Trenton and Princeton revived the dying Revolution like a massive jolt of electricity. A loyalist in Virginia reported, "A few days ago they had given up their cause for lost. Now they are all liberty mad again." The British dream of making New Jersey the first state to submit to the king's peace went a-glimmering. Every British officer who rode alone or with a single escort now risked ambush. Foragers looking for food to feed the hungry troops in New Brunswick frequently found themselves fighting mini-battles with militia firing from nearby woods and fields.

General Howe ruefully admitted Washington's successes had "thrown us back further than was at first apprehended from the great encouragement it has given the rebels. I do not now see a prospect of terminating the war, but by a general action"—precisely the climactic battle that George Washington had resolved that General Howe would never get. The strategy of maintaining an army to look the enemy in the face dovetailed with the policy of never risking that army on one roll of the dice of war. The idea was already manifest in Washington's decision not to continue his march to New Brunswick with the half-starved, exhausted troops who had won at Trenton and Princeton. He saw "the danger of loosing the advantage we had gaind by aiming at too much."

For the next five years, Washington fought this protracted war with immense patience and skill. It proved a far more complex task than anyone—including the commander in chief—foresaw, as the war spread north and south, engulfing almost every state. But the victories at Trenton and Princeton had enabled him to obtain from Congress the means of fighting it his way. The shaken lawmakers gave Washington almost dictatorial powers. Henceforth he could enlist men for three years in an army that was truly continental, in name as well as in fact. It would have well-trained artillerymen as well as cavalry, bolstering their ability to confront a British army with similar troops. Also available would be enough money to finance an intelligence operation that enabled Washington to anticipate and move promptly to counter the enemy's plans.

Henceforth victory would be a reasonable possibility—but never a certainty. If there was one indisputable truth about fighting a war, it was its unpredictability. Also problematic were the impatience and personal ambitions of some of the men around Washington, who were hostile to this protracted conflict, and his civilian critics in and out of Congress, who still hungered for a quick victory in one big battle. The next years would continue to provide high drama crowded with opportunities for that other crucial ingredient in wartime: personal courage.

CHAPTER 3

The Year of the Hangman

As 1777 began, British leaders in London took deep breaths and vowed that the war in America would end that year. The Americans had survived thanks to two trifling victories by General George Washington in the final days of 1776. The British remained confident that they could eliminate him in the next twelve months and, to finish the task, were committing not one but two armies to the struggle. General John Burgoyne would descend from Canada at the head of almost 11,000 troops—a figure that included several hundred Indians. General William Howe's 25,000-man army would ascend the Hudson and complete the task of separating New England from the rest of the rebel confederation and smashing the defiant descendants of the Puritans with the thoroughness and savagery the British had displayed in subduing Ireland and Scotland. Then they would join forces and defeat Washington in a general action that would end the war. As the plan became public knowledge, excited loyalists in New York City began calling 1777 the "Year of the Hangman." They saw the three sevens as symbolic gibbets from which guilty rebels would soon dangle.

Almost immediately, this strategy started to go awry. The two generals, rivals for the king's favor and the glory of ending the war, had no enthusiasm for a joint effort. Burgoyne wrote a breezy letter assuring London he did not need Howe's help. Howe never had any desire to offer it. He had another strategy in mind: behead the rebellion by capturing the enemy capital, Philadelphia. Washington would feel obliged to stand and fight or solidify his reputation as the much-derided commander in chief who had been driven from Long Island and New York while half his army ran away. Howe intended to consummate the general action that would end the war long before General Burgoyne got his troops halfway to Albany.

⌒

WASHINGTON HAD spent the winter at Morristown worrying about whether recruiters in the various states would bring him a new army. Congress had authorized sixteen additional battalions of infantry, four regiments of artillery, and 3,000 cavalrymen. As spring advanced, men began to arrive. But Congress—and Washington—soon perceived that these soldiers differed greatly from the enthusiastic volunteers who had enlisted in 1776, when the defiant patriotism generated by Lexington, Concord, and Bunker Hill was paramount in most hearts and minds. Only about 1,000 of the veterans of 1776 had reenlisted. In the spring of 1777, when it became obvious that volunteers were few, Washington had bluntly recommended a draft. "Coercive measures" were necessary, he told Congress. Soon each state had a quota that it could fill by offering bounties or, in a last resort, implementing a draft.

Few of these new recruits resembled the minutemen and fellow militiamen who had fought so well on April 19, 1775. Almost all were young, landless, and poor. They were eager for the bounty that the various states paid to fill their quotas. By May Washington had 9,000 of these mostly new soldiers.[1]

⌒

GENERAL HOWE vowed to make this revival of revolutionary fervor very temporary. On April 13, he attacked the American outpost at Bound Brook, with 4,000 men under the command of Lord Cornwallis. The American garrison of five hundred men made a helter-skelter retreat, losing several cannons and the personal papers of the general in command, Benjamin Lincoln. The British seemed to see it as a muscle-flexing operation. They stayed in Bound Brook only a few hours and fell back to their main base at New Brunswick.

In early June General Howe led 18,000 men into central New Jersey, ostensibly marching toward Philadelphia. He soon discovered that Washington had anticipated him and moved most of his army from Morristown to a protected valley at Middlebrook, about twenty miles south of his winter camp. A brigade under General John Sullivan headed for Princeton, where it could block a sudden push toward Philadelphia. Behind Middlebrook loomed the Watchung Mountains, where any attack on Washington would entail great cost.

Howe marched from New Brunswick toward Somerset Court House. Washington's light infantry skirmished on his flanks, making clear that any attempt to continue to Philadelphia would expose him to a devastating attack. When Howe wheeled to confront Washington, the American commander in chief retreated toward the Watchung Mountains. Meanwhile, Washington's well-funded intelligence operation was sending him interesting news. The British had left all their heavy baggage at New Brunswick. This included boats and bridging equipment, without which any attempt to cross the Delaware River would be ruinous. Washington quickly concluded that General Howe's main interest in New Jersey was enticing him into a general action.

When General Howe retreated toward New Brunswick, Washington followed cautiously. Soldiers from General Nathanael Greene's division skirmished briskly with the British rear guard. General Howe retreated all the way to Amboy, on the shore of Raritan Bay. Washington pursued and ordered his troops to entrench in new positions near Metuchen. On June 26, the British army abruptly surged into New Jersey, again in two columns.

Howe apparently hoped to encircle the camp at Metuchen and force Washington to fight a general action to rescue it. Washington declined to accept a collision on "disadvantageous terms." The British managed to capture three cannons and forced the Metuchen troops to retreat in something close to disorder. But the Americans soon found themselves within the protection of the main army, which Washington led in a fighting retreat to Middlebrook. The British ruefully realized they were back where they had started, with no prospect of that general engagement they wanted so badly.

Fascinating evidence that General Washington knew exactly what he was doing surfaces in a letter that one of his aides, Lieutenant Colonel Alexander Hamilton, wrote to a prominent New York politician, Robert R. Livingston, on June 28, 1777. A recent arrival on the general's staff, Hamilton had attracted Washington's attention with his performance as captain of an artillery company in 1776. Washington soon discovered the energetic twenty-two-year-old had written several impressive pamphlets defending the Revolution before he turned artillerist. Washington was constantly on the lookout for aides with literary talent who could communicate with important civilians in his name, saving him time and trouble.

Hamilton described the Continental Army's maneuvers in New Jersey in lively terms. As the British retired to Amboy for a second time, "We had parties hanging about them." Losses on both sides were "inconsiderable," but Hamilton was confident that British casualties were higher. He told Livingston it was "not unlikely they [the British] will soon be out of the Jersies; where they will go next is mere matter of conjecture, for as you observe their conduct is so eccentric as to leave no certain grounds on which to form a judgment."

Then Hamilton got to the point of his letter. "I know the comments that some people will make on our Fabian conduct. It will be imputed either to cowardice or to weakness: but the more discerning, I trust, will not find it difficult to conceive that it proceeds from the truest policy. . . . The liberties of America are an infinite stake. We should not play a desperate game for it or put it upon the issue of a single cast of the die. The loss of one general engagement may effectually ruin us, and it would certainly be folly to hazard it, unless our resources for keeping up an army were at an end, and some decisive blow was absolutely necessary, or our strength was so great as to give certainty of success. Neither is the case."[2]

⤳

THE MOST important word in this letter is "Fabian." Hamilton was looking back more than 2,000 years to the struggle of ancient Rome with its chief Mediterranean rival, the North African city of Carthage.

In 215 BC, the gifted young Carthaginian general Hannibal invaded Italy by marching over the Pyrenees and the Alps with a 60,000-man army. He quickly won three stunning victories. The third triumph annihilated Rome's two best legions. The shocked Romans turned to an aristocrat named Quintus Fabius Maximus.

Rome's allies in other parts of Italy were wavering toward submission to Carthage. Needing to raise and train a new army, Fabius decided Rome's best hope was to avoid an all-out battle until Hannibal's men grew weary of endless skirmishing and marching. Fabius also attacked their foraging parties and scorched the earth in their path to make it difficult for them to find sustenance. This cautious strategy was not popular with most people in Rome. They began to call Fabius "Cunctator," meaning "the Delayer" or, worse, "the Dawdler." Eventually Fabius was forced to resign his command.

A new general took over the Roman army and challenged Hannibal near the town of Cannae in southeastern Italy. At first the battle looked like a total victory for the Romans. Hannibal's center gave way, and he began a seemingly panicky retreat. Both wings of the Roman army joined the pursuit. Hannibal counterattacked with forces concealed on both flanks, and suddenly the Romans were encircled and trapped. Hannibal had achieved a double envelopment, one of the most difficult feats of generalship. Almost the entire Roman army of 88,000 men was slaughtered.

The frantic Romans turned again to Fabius for their salvation. He kept his legendary composure and patched together another army strong enough to resume his tactics of delay and attrition. Eventually a discouraged Hannibal abandoned Italy and retreated to Carthage, where he suffered defeat in a climactic battle with a younger Roman general, Scipio Africanus. Looking back, the Romans realized that Fabius had saved their city.[3]

⌒

COLONEL HAMILTON assured Robert R. Livingston that if General Washington continued to fight the war Fabian style, victory was more than possible—it was even probable. Only intelligence that the British were about to receive large reinforcements, necessitating an attack before they became too strong to resist, would justify a change in policy. But the news from abroad "contradicts this," Hamilton assured him.

Most European powers hoped for a British defeat in America. They disliked Britain's arrogant displays of power on sea and land around the world. There were rumors of certain countries giving America "more effectual aid." Without naming a specific nation, Hamilton mentioned that the Americans had just received a shipment of the latest artillery, which had slipped through the British blockade and was being rushed to the army.

By the end of the summer, Hamilton predicted, the British would begin to "dwindle away," and Washington could attack with considerable hope of success. In the meantime, Hamilton urged Livingston to circulate the thinking behind the Fabian policy to "take off disagreeable impressions our caution may make."[4]

This letter would prove much too optimistic. Two ships, carrying cannons, thousands of muskets, and tons of gunpowder had reached New England—products of a clandestine operation put together by the French, with ample room for the government to deny any and all responsibility. But the Americans heard nothing more from Paris for the next twelve months—while military developments teetered toward disaster. Recruiting for the new army became more and more difficult. Voluntarism dwindled away almost completely. General Nathanael Greene wrote to his wife, Caty, in Rhode Island, "We have got together a small force . . . by no means equal to our expectations."[5]

༄

MEANWHILE BAD news arrived like random thunderclaps from the northern front. The first shock threw everyone into dismay. Fort Ticonderoga, looming between Lake Champlain and Lake George in northern New York, was considered "the Gibraltar of America." Others called it "the key to the continent." Many Americans had been confident that it would keep General Burgoyne from reaching Albany. Now they learned that the troops garrisoned there had abandoned the great bastion with scarcely a shot fired in its defense.

Militia from New York and New England, intimidated by the news, were not turning out to oppose the oncoming British. It was a replay of Washington's 1776 retreat through New Jersey, where there had been no army to look the enemy in the face. General Burgoyne exultantly issued proclamations calling on soldiers and civilians in his path to surrender without a fight.

General Washington remained in close contact with the war north of Albany. He did not rely on stories drifting into his headquarters. He had already dispatched two major generals to help deal with the deteriorating situation: Benedict Arnold of Connecticut and Benjamin Lincoln of Massachusetts. The fat, affable Lincoln was adept at persuading reluctant militia to join the fighting. The fiery Arnold had proven himself a first-class battlefield leader during the 1775 invasion of Canada. Washington hoped his tactical prowess would supplement the northern commander, General Philip Schuyler, who excelled more at organizing and supplying an army than leading it on the battlefield.

On August 16, 1777, Washington wrote a revealing letter to New York governor George Clinton, commander of the state's militia. Washington told him he had seen a letter from General Lincoln to General Schuyler telling him that they planned to "unite all the militia and Continental troops in one body." The commander in chief made it clear that this was no longer an acceptable policy. He called it "a very ineligible plan."[6]

The militia should perform another important task: it should make "Mr. Bourgoigne anxious for his rear," forcing him to advance "circumspectly and to leave such strong posts behind that must make his main body very weak, and extremely capable of being repulsed by the force we shall have in front."

This letter marked another step in Washington's evolving use of militias. He had said harsh things about the amateur soldiers in 1776. But the limited availability of recruits for his regular or Continental Army was forcing him to realize that he still needed the militias as partners in fighting the war, even if he could not expect them to face British regulars face-to-face in a battle line. With Burgoyne, their task was to constantly render the British general concerned for his "convoys" of supplies from his rear.

At the same time, concerned that the Northern Army have as many Continentals as possible, Washington told Clinton that he had ordered two regiments guarding the Hudson Highlands to join up with it as soon as possible. Also on his way from Washington's army was Colonel Daniel Morgan of Virginia, with his corps of six hundred frontier riflemen. At this point in his career, Morgan was known largely for his reckless courage—a trait he had exhibited repeatedly during Congress's ill-judged 1775 invasion of Canada. His bravery had not saved him from being trapped in the winding streets of Quebec City and forced to surrender. Like many other officers in the Continental Army, he was still learning the art of revolutionary leadership. After six months in a Quebec prison, he was paroled and, in the fall of 1776, exchanged for a British prisoner of equal rank.

∽

ON JUNE 17, 1777, the adjutant general of the Northern Army of the United States had presented Major General Arthur St. Clair with a "return" of the ten Continental regiments under his command. It made dolorous reading. Only twenty-three men in Colonel Seth Warner's regiment had bayonets. Colonel Nathan Hale's New Hampshire regiment was minus 264 powder horns and 334 priming wires. All the regiments were pathetically understrength. Warner had only 173 men instead of 640; another regiment had dwindled to 85. Companies comprised as few as 41 men. Overall, the regiments were short 3,506 rank and file and proportionate numbers of officers.

With barely 1,576 Continentals and two regiments of militia—about 900 men—St. Clair, newly arrived for three months' duty, was supposed to defend not only Fort Ticonderoga but an even more extensive, unfinished work, Fort Independence, on a height across the narrow neck of water connecting the two parts of Lake Champlain. If he put every man in his army on the lines, he would have only one soldier per yard of front—and not a musket in reserve. Worse, he would have to abandon a number of outlying redoubts covering Ticonderoga's exposed northwest flank.

The Scottish-born forty-year-old St. Clair (pronounced Sinclair), a former British lieutenant who had distinguished himself in the French and Indian War, had arrived at the fort on June 12. He replaced Major General Horatio Gates, who had retreated to Philadelphia to persuade his numerous New England friends in Congress to dismiss General Schuyler and give him command of the northern department.

St. Clair was aware that he was dealing with soldiers burdened by defeat. The British had driven the Northern Army from Canada in 1776 with humiliating ease. St. Clair had participated as a colonel in the ignominious rout at Trois-Rivières, in which a 2,000-man American force had disintegrated into fleeing fragments, making headlong retreat from the fourteenth colony inevitable. Only desperate defensive fighting on Lake Champlain by an impromptu fleet commanded by General Benedict Arnold—and the onset of winter—had prevented the British from taking Ticonderoga in late 1776.

Descending onto Lake Champlain as St. Clair nervously read his returns was a British army of 7,586 fighting men, backed by a fleet of gunboats and pinnaces manned by 700 Royal Navy sailors. In command was Major General Burgoyne, a soldier who had made his reputation as a daring cavalryman in Europe. His men called him "Gentleman Johnny," a term of respect and affection because he treated them well. In canoes beside the 260 batteaux carrying the royal rank and file paddled several hundred war-painted Indians eager to collect a bonanza in American scalps.[7]

Incredibly, no one in the American army—or Congress, for that matter—knew that Burgoyne had orders to invade America with this imposing force. The screen of Indians spread by the British along the border had frustrated American attempts to scout into Canada. The Americans remained convinced that the main British army of 25,000 men under Sir William Howe would soon sally from New York to attack Philadelphia and that Burgoyne, who they knew was in Canada, would assemble every man the defense of that colony could spare and sail south to join him.

Even when Burgoyne's fleet and army appeared in full view from Ticonderoga's ramparts on June 30, 1777, St. Clair refused to take them seriously, believing the display of armed might a feint. Not until his pickets clashed with a British patrol and captured a drunken Irish soldier, who told them in convincing detail about the size of the British host, did the Americans realize they were in imminent danger of annihilation.

St. Clair spent the next three days in an agony of indecision. In memoirs written decades later, Assistant Adjutant General James Wilkinson said he "lacked the resolution to give up the place, or in other words to sacrifice his character for the public good." The remark pithily, if heartlessly, summed up St. Clair's dilemma. Acutely aware that his reputation would probably never recover if he retreated, he also understood that the Continentals under his command were precious, irreplaceable assets.

As the British began surrounding him, St. Clair convinced himself that they planned an immediate assault. He toyed with the possibility of replicating Bunker Hill here in the northern woods. But he also remembered the disastrous fate of the 3,000 Continentals who tried to restage Bunker Hill at Fort Washington on Manhattan in the fall of 1776.

General Burgoyne, an appalled spectator of the mistakes made at the original battle of Bunker Hill, had no intention of repeating them. On July 4, his engineering officer, a lieutenant named Twiss, slogged to the top of an outlying hill called Sugar Loaf. Several American engineers had urged previous commanders of Ticonderoga to fortify it, because from its 750-foot-high crest cannons could fire into both forts. But shortages of men and equipment—and the complacent assumption that no one could manhandle a cannon up its steep, forested slope—had left it exposed to an enterprising enemy.

By July 5, Twiss had two twelve-pounders on top of Sugar Loaf, firing at vessels in the narrows between the two forts. St. Clair took one look and said, in the stilted style of Wilkinson's memoirs, "We must away from this because our situation has become desperate." We can be fairly sure this professional soldier's real words were a lot more graphic. In a hastily convened council of war, his brigadier generals agreed unanimously that retreat was the only option.

The painful decision revealed that all had learned a fundamental lesson that Washington had gleaned from the disasters of 1776. They were no longer fighting a "war of posts." They should sacrifice forts, even cities, to the all-important task of preserving an army to look the enemy in the face.

⌐

PILING AMMUNITION and stores, along with numerous sick, into a fleet of two hundred batteaux and sloops, six hundred Continentals sailed that night for Skenesborough, now Whitehall, at the narrow southern end of Lake Champlain. The militia and the rest of the Continentals retreated with St. Clair down a rough road cut through the forest toward the same destination. In the confusion, they almost left behind 1,000 men in Fort Independence, largely because their brigadier, a French volunteer named Roche de Formoy, got drunk and forgot to pass along the evacuation order.

The Continental rank and file, most of them New Englanders, remained confirmed Bunker Hillists. They wanted to fight it out on Fort Ti's ramparts. "Such a retreat was never heard of since the creation of the world," wrote one fuming New Hampshire soldier. "I could scarcely believe my informant was in earnest," recalled Dr. James Thacher of Massachusetts, who was awakened at midnight with the news that it was time to flee.[8]

In Ticonderoga St. Clair left four artillerymen manning a battery of guns loaded with grapeshot, trained on the bridge between the two forts. These ambushers had orders to fire the guns and run when a sufficient number of British went to work on repairing the bridge, into which the Americans had hastily chopped some large holes. The British methodically replanked the bridge without a shot fired. Mounting Ticonderoga's ramparts, they found the four heroic gunners dead drunk beside a case of madeira.

No wonder British confidence soared. Burgoyne immediately ordered the 850-man British light infantry battalion, commanded by another enterprising soldier, forty-eight-year-old Brigadier Simon Fraser, to pursue the retreating Americans. In hot humid weather, they marched at a killing pace from 4:00 A.M. until 4:00 P.M. on July 6. Not far behind them slogged 1,280 German troops under portly, aggressive Major General Baron Friedrich Adolf von Riedesel. The British scooped up another twenty drunkards and numerous other stragglers along the rutted road. From them they got a good idea of the size of the American rear guard, which consisted of Colonel Ebenezer Francis's 11th Massachusetts Regiment, reinforced by selected companies from the rest of St. Clair's army.

The Americans retreated at a frantic pace. One man said they "hurled thro' the woods at 35 miles a day . . . oblidged to kill oxen belonging to the inhabitants wherever we got them; before they were half-skinned every soldier was oblidged to take a bit and roast it over the fire, then before half done oblidged to march." In Hubbardton, a "town" consisting of exactly two houses, St. Clair paused to let Francis catch up with him. When the colonel did not materialize, he left Colonel Seth Warner and his regiment with orders to reinforce Francis and join the main army at Castleton, six miles down the road. When Francis finally showed up, he had with him over five hundred stragglers, guarded by Colonel Nathan Hale's New Hampshire regiment. Recently recovered from the measles, the sick men were utterly spent by the pace of the retreat. As the senior officer, Warner decided to spend the night in Hubbardton.

Although they knew the British were pursuing them, Hale's men, who camped closest to the enemy, posted only one sentry. Arising at 3:00 A.M. on July 7, Fraser's light infantry reached the American camp at dawn and routed Hale's regiment and the invalids as they were cooking breakfast. But Warner's and Francis's Continentals gave them a very different reception. A big, brawny New Hampshireman, Warner had commanded the rear guard on the retreat from Canada in 1776 and knew his business. Posting most of his men behind log barricades on high ground, he cut down twenty-one attackers as they came up the steep slope, including a British major who made the mistake of climbing up on a fallen tree to reconnoiter the position.

A ferocious firefight erupted along a half-mile front. Fraser expertly shifted men to the right to envelope the American left flank. Francis promptly demonstrated that the Continentals had learned some tactics in two years of warfare by attacking the British left. For a little while the battle seesawed, with muskets crashing, gun smoke billowing through the woods, and men falling fast on both sides.

In Castleton, the gunfire made St. Clair wonder if he should march to Warner's rescue. He found no enthusiasm for the idea among his brigadiers. He contented himself with dispatching two aides to order his two militia regiments, camped several miles closer to Hubbardton, to support the embattled rear guard. The aides met the militiamen on the road and barely avoided being trampled in the amateurs' mad rush to put as much distance as possible between them and the shooting.

On the battlefield, the British were growing panicky in the face of the ferocious American resistance. Suddenly through the booming musketry came the astonishing sound of a military band. Baron von Riedesel had arrived with a 180-man advance guard; he struck up the band to make the Americans think he was leading a brigade. Some one hundred of his men were jaegers armed with short, accurate rifles and the training to counter the Americans' woodland tactics.

The Germans swiftly enveloped Francis's flank and, when the Yankee colonel tried to rally his men, cut him down with a bullet to the heart. His shaken soldiers scattered into the woods, and a chagrinned Warner ordered his New Hampshiremen to do likewise as their left flank became more and more indefensible. Colonel Hale, still trying to protect his invalids, surrendered with 270 of them soon after the firing ceased.

The two-hour brawl temporarily ended British thoughts of hot pursuit by land. Fraser had lost 50 killed and 134 wounded, roughly 21 percent of his light infantry. The small German detachment, in action only a few minutes, had lost 13 percent. American casualties were 41 dead and 91 wounded, plus 324 captured, most of them invalids. Lieutenant Thomas Hadden of the Royal Artillery confided to his journal that the light infantry had discovered that "neither were they invincible nor the rebels all poltroons. On the contrary, many of them acknowledged that the enemy had behaved well and looked upon General Riedesel's fortunate arrival as a matter of absolute necessity." It deserves noting that Hubbardton was fought entirely by Continentals.

The pursuers soon learned their army had achieved a sensational success on the water the previous day. The American fleet had cruised down Lake Champlain, enjoying band music and a bit of tippling, secure in the illusion that a massive chain across the narrows blocked the entrance to the lower part of the lake. British sailors broke the chain with a few well-placed cannon balls. They descended on the dismayed Americans at Skenesborough, capturing most of their fleet and forcing them to abandon all their cannons and staggering amounts of flour and salted meats.

With the road through Skenesborough blocked, the mortified St. Clair had to lead his men on a seven-day detour into the wilderness east of Lake George to reach Fort Edward on the Hudson River. Along the way he discharged his two militia regiments for fear that their panic and insubordination would contaminate his Continentals. At Fort Edward, he found a distraught General Philip Schuyler with a paltry 700 Continentals and 1,400 jittery militia—the sum total of the Northern Army's reserve.

⌒

THE FALL of Ticonderoga, the apparent rout at Hubbardton, and the debacle at Skenesborough sent shockwaves of panic and consternation throughout northern New York and New England—and the rest of America. "No event could be more unexpected nor more severely felt throughout our army and our country," Dr. Thacher morosely admitted in his journal. George Washington got the news from Schuyler, along with a chilling portrait of the Northern Army's prospects. The enemy, Schuyler wrote, was "flushed with victory, plentifully provided with provisions, cannon and every warlike store," while the Americans were "dispirited, naked . . . without camp equipage, with little ammunition and not a single cannon."

At dilapidated Fort Edward, the disgruntled Ticonderoga fugitives had no sooner arrived than they began accusing Generals Schuyler and

St. Clair of treason. They filled the mails with letters home, claiming the British had fired "silver balls" from their cannon into Ticonderoga to bribe them. "The Indignation and distrust [of Schuyler] that prevails here are extream," James Warren wrote from Boston to John Adams in Philadelphia. "The want of confidence in your commanders [is] such, that if it be not removed by Lincolns being sent there to command, the militia will very much impede our reinforcements."[9]

Simultaneously, General Horatio Gates trumpeted his detestation of Schuyler to New England delegates in Congress. Schuyler owned huge swaths of land along the Hudson and Mohawk Rivers and found it hard to practice the rude and often crude democracy favored by the New Englanders. In military matters Schuyler tended to be a martinet, often showing up at outposts in the dawn to make sure sentries were on the job—another trait that failed to endear him to the men in the ranks. But few men made a larger contribution to the American cause. His skillful diplomacy kept most of the Iroquois neutral for the first years of the war. Without his talents for organization and supply, the Northern Army would have collapsed long before.

⌐⌐

SCHUYLER SOON reported more bad news to Washington. "A very great proportion of the [local] inhabitants are taking protection from General Burgoyne." Copying a leaf from Howe's book, Burgoyne had issued an orotund proclamation, warning the Americans in his path that if their "Phrenzy of hostility should remain," he would execute "the Vengeance of the State against the wilful outcast."[10] Worse, another British army was headed for Albany. Some 1,800 regulars, Indians, and Tories under the leadership of Lieutenant Colonel Barry St. Leger had sailed across Lake Ontario and debouched toward Fort Stanwix, the bastion that guarded the Mohawk River valley. The mere threat made it impossible to raise any militia from this populous region to defend the Hudson River valley from Burgoyne. The news could have been much worse. Thanks to Schuyler's foresight, Stanwix had been rebuilt earlier in the year and garrisoned with 650 Continentals, who defiantly declined St. Leger's invitation to surrender.

In New Jersey, General Washington continued to worry about General Howe's army. Scouts brought him news that they were boarding ships off Amboy. Was Howe about to ascend the Hudson River and join Burgoyne in an all-out assault on New England? In that case the main Continental Army would be expected to join the battle. Washington ordered General Sullivan to march his men to a place called The Clove in the Ramapo Mountains, overlooking the Hudson River. It was close enough to make General Howe nervous about attempting an ascent of the Hudson.

On July 23 Washington heard truly startling news: the British fleet of more than 270 ships was heading out to sea—and turning south. Washington decided that Howe was planning to attack Philadelphia by landing at some convenient place on the Delaware River. In the heat of summer he ordered his men on a forced march to the nation's capital. When they reached the Delaware, he gave his weary troops two days to recuperate on its banks. Washington himself rode ahead to confer with congressmen and Pennsylvania state officials about the best way to defend Philadelphia.

Washington had barely arrived when he heard even more startling news. The British fleet had paused at the mouth of the Delaware River—then headed out to sea again and disappeared. What had happened? An unexpected intrusion of good luck had rescued the Americans from a possibly ruinous situation. The British captain of the frigate HMS *Roebuck* informed General Howe that the Delaware was so heavily fortified with cannon on its banks that attempting to penetrate it would be almost suicidal.

This report exaggerated more than a little. Only two forts blocked the ascent of the Delaware. They may have fired briskly on the *Roebuck*, but Admiral Howe's battle fleet backed by General Howe's 18,000-man army could have eliminated both forts rather quickly. Instead General Howe decided on an alternate plan that had its own advantages—to sail south and ascend Chesapeake Bay. From its northern banks he would be within an easy march of Philadelphia, with no costly obstacles like the Delaware River forts to clear.

Washington still wondered if the whole maneuver might be a ruse to wear out his army with marching and countermarching. After more days of uncertainty, he finally led the Continental Army to a camp on Neshaminy Creek, twenty miles north of Philadelphia. Meanwhile the British army was undergoing an ordeal at sea. It sat becalmed on the sweltering Atlantic. Horses died, and men sickened from spoiled food. Not until August 24, after drifting helplessly for most of thirty-two days, did Howe's men stumble ashore on the northern banks of Chesapeake Bay. American resistance was negligible. A few dozen militiamen fired a cannon and their muskets at the 18,000 redcoats and their German confederates, then hastily dispersed.

Confident in his safety from attack, General Howe allowed his men to rest and recuperate from their enervating voyage. He still hoped that Washington would fight to defend Philadelphia and give him the all-out battle he needed to end the war. The American commander in chief said he had every intention of fighting to defend his nation's capital. He knew he had to make the attempt if he hoped to retain the support of Congress.

Washington chose to make a stand at Brandywine Creek, a winding stream twenty-six miles from Philadelphia. He positioned his 12,000-man army—3,000 of them militia—along the Brandywine's banks. The waterway was traversable only at several fords. In an ironic echo of the battle of Long Island, a loyalist told General Howe of two unguarded fords far out on the American left flank. Aware of these, Washington had asked General Sullivan, who was in command on this flank, to watch for a British attempt to use them. Neither Sullivan nor the cavalry colonel to whom he delegated this responsibility performed well.

Meanwhile about a third of the British army, mostly the German troops, began a demonstration at Chadds Ford. They blasted cannons and muskets at the Americans and gave every evidence of launching an all-out attack. Not deceived, Washington planned a counterstroke that would smash up this pseudo-assault. Before he could issue the order, a messenger from General Sullivan informed him that the British were advancing on the left flank in ominous numbers. General

Howe and half his army had crossed the unguarded fords without a shot fired at them.

Accompanied by the Marquis de Lafayette, Washington galloped toward the sound of the guns. They met Sullivan's men falling back in disarray. Lafayette sprang off his horse and tried to rally them. He took a bullet in the leg and accomplished little except to display his reckless courage. Back at Chadds Ford, the Germans attacked across the Brandywine. Washington decided it was time to retreat.

Unlike the battle of Long Island, it was not a panicky rout. Washington's rear guard fell back from one patch of woods to the next, fighting hard until the oncoming British drove them out. Howe's men soon showed signs of weariness; already weakened by their ordeal aboard ship, they had marched more than seventeen miles before going into action. Without cavalry because so many of his horses had died on the voyage to the Chesapeake, Howe abandoned the pursuit as darkness fell.

* * *

FOR THE next month Washington and Howe maneuvered through the web of rivers and creeks around Philadelphia. The British commander repeatedly tried to trap the American army or some part of it. He succeeded only once, on September 21, when he caught an American division commanded by Major General Anthony Wayne camped near Paoli. Washington had detached Wayne and two other division commanders with orders to attack Howe's flanks and rear. Wayne moved too close to Howe's camp, under the illusion that the British were not aware of his presence. In a night attack, bayonet-wielding British light infantry killed or wounded more than three hundred men.[11] Most of the time Washington, marching and countermarching his ragged soldiers more than one hundred miles, skillfully zigzagged west. This not only gave him ample room to keep retreating but kept his army between the British and Reading, a main American supply depot.

Finally, in the last week of September, Howe abandoned hope of an all-out battle and marched into undefended Philadelphia. Congress fled to York, Pennsylvania. An angry John Adams, more and more disillusioned with his army's commander in chief, raved about the need for a general of "active masterly capacity" who would "save this country." He clearly had no clue about Washington's Fabian strategy.

Washington kept his army within an easy march of the capital. He had no intention of letting the campaign end on such a sour note. Spies soon informed the commander in chief of an opportunity for a "stroke." General Howe had camped 8,000 men in the village of Germantown outside Philadelphia. Washington concocted one of his most daring battle plans. He divided his army into four columns and hurled them at the British in a dawn attack on October 4, 1777.

The Americans came whooping out of a dense fog and routed British outposts. The Continentals in the two center columns drove 1,000 yards and seemed on their way to tearing the British apart. But the fog that had concealed their advance became a fatal disadvantage. American units began to fire on each other, and many regiments lost contact with their commanding officers. Six British companies under a fighting colonel named Musgrave turned a large stone house owned by loyalist Benjamin Chew into a fortress that distracted and disrupted the American rear. Several regiments stopped to assail it instead of maintaining the momentum of the general attack.

General Sullivan's division ran out of ammunition. Soon confusion turned to panic in many regiments. Howe in the meantime had summoned 3,000 reinforcements from Philadelphia. Washington again decided to retreat. The battered British, with more than five hundred men dead or wounded, made no attempt to pursue.

The battle of Germantown, though a military failure, put an end to British hope of fulfilling the vengeful prophecy of the Year of the Hangman. In northern New York, the American army confronting General Burgoyne, strengthened by Washington's reinforcements, was ready to write an even more final coda to the fading British expectation of a swift victory.

⌣

AT THIS point in the drama, Congress intervened by firing Generals Schuyler and St. Clair and appointing Horatio Gates commander of everything north of Albany. Gates was one of the few generals on the American side who understood the tangled British psychology that had so much to do with unraveling the Year of the Hangman. Nothing else explains the eagerness with which he sought the seemingly thankless job of commanding the Northern Army despite its history of headlong retreat.

Grey-haired and ruddy-faced, with thick spectacles that often slid down his long, pointed nose to give him an old-womanish look, the fifty-year-old Gates was an ambitious man, even if he did not look like one. The son of a duke's housekeeper, he had risen to the rank of major in the British army thanks to his talents as a staff officer. As the American army's first adjutant general, he had proven himself a valuable organizer and administrator in 1775.

Gates's combat experience was almost zero—he fought for about fifteen minutes in the 1755 debacle known as Braddock's Defeat, before being struck down by an Indian bullet. In the attack on Trenton on Christmas night of 1776, Washington had offered him command of the right wing. He had excused himself for reasons of "health" and rushed to Baltimore to lobby Congress for command of the Northern Army.

Gates's New England admirers ignored his shortcomings and attributed to him near miraculous powers. One declared that his mere arrival in Albany lifted them from "this miserable state of despondency and terror." Unquestionably, just getting rid of Schuyler and St. Clair eliminated the rampant paranoia in the New England Continental regiments. Gates also benefited from Burgoyne's decision to rebuild a twenty-three-mile road through the forest from Skenesborough to Fort Edward on the east bank of the Hudson, a task that consumed three weeks and gave the rattled Americans time to regroup.

Schuyler had skillfully impeded Burgoyne's progress with tactics that the original Fabius Maximus would have warmly approved. A thousand axmen felled huge pines and hemlocks in the British path. They also destroyed some forty bridges over the numerous creeks and ravines. Burgoyne dispatched neither his Indians nor his light infantry to deal with this scorched-earth policy. Relaxing in the fine stone house of William Skene, the principle citizen of Skenesborough, Gentleman

Johnny enjoyed a new mistress, the wife of his commissary, and remained euphoric over the easy capture of Ticonderoga.

Gates also benefited from the first good news the Northern Army had received in a long time. On the left flank, eight hundred Mohawk Valley militia marching to bolster Fort Stanwix had fought a bloody drawn battle with St. Leger's army at Oriskany, inflicting heavy casualties on his Indian allies. On the right flank, New Hampshire militia under Colonel John Stark and Continentals led by Seth Warner had attacked and virtually destroyed a 1,500-man force of Germans that Burgoyne had dispatched to Bennington to seize stores and horses.

By the time Gates took command of the Northern Army, Schuyler had retreated to Van Schaick's Island, at the mouth of the Mohawk River, nine miles north of Albany. There he was able to block the main road and stay in touch with operations in the vital Mohawk Valley. New England officers told Gates that Schuyler's constant retreating had disgusted the men. Gates decided that a march north "to meet the enemy" would be good for morale. Some say Major General Benedict Arnold had not a little to do with urging this move on Gates.

Starting on September 8, the army marched thirteen miles north to Bemis Heights, rugged country overlooking the Hudson and named for a tavern on the riverbank. There, Polish engineering officer Thaddeus Kosciuszko constructed an elaborate array of field fortifications on the one-hundred-foot-high bluffs and the five-hundred-foot-wide strip of level ground along the Hudson. To the west, should the British try to outflank rather than storm the position, the ground was thickly forested, broken by occasional clearings, and cut by deep east–west ravines—ideal terrain for American light infantry maneuvers.

If Arnold was responsible for this move, it was the last advice Gates took from his fellow major general. An intriguer himself, Gates saw conspiracies everywhere. He had rudely excluded Schuyler from his early war councils in Albany. When it came to touchiness, Arnold was in a class by himself. As Gates began excluding him from staff meetings, the stocky ex-apothecary grew surly and obnoxious in return.

General Burgoyne had no idea where the Americans were. Crossing the Hudson on September 13 on a bridge of boats near Saratoga (present-day Schuylerville), the British commander groped southward in slow, cautious marches. Not until September 18, when an American patrol fired on a group of his soldiers digging up potatoes on an abandoned farm, killing and wounding twenty of them, did he realize the rebels were close. Although he still had only the dimmest idea of the American position on Bemis Heights, Burgoyne decided to attack it the next day.

In the ensuing battles of Saratoga, the officers that General Washington had sent to the northern front played crucial roles. General Arnold commanded a wing of the American army and demonstrated brilliant tactical ability. Rather than staying on the defensive, as was General Gates's preference, Arnold led his men in fierce attacks on the oncoming British. Samuel Downing, a soldier who followed him across the bullet-thick battlefields, said, "There wasn't any waste timber in him, and a bloody fellow he was. He didn't care for nothing; he'd ride right in. It was 'Come on boys'——'t wasn't 'go boys'. He was as brave a man as ever lived."

At the climax of the second battle Arnold led a charge that seized a key redoubt overlooking the British camp. As he joined his men in swarming over the walls, a bullet smashed the leg already shattered once in the assault on Québec in 1775. It ended his career as an active soldier.

At West Point, in the Old Cadet Chapel, there are memorials to America's revolutionary leaders. Benedict Arnold's plaque has no name. It simply reads, "Major General, born 1740." On the Saratoga battlefield, another memorial is a stone carving of a man's booted leg. Both pay silent tribute to the sacrifice Arnold made to win this crucial victory.

Almost as important was General Benjamin Lincoln's role. He more than fulfilled the words George Washington wrote to the anxious New York Council of Safety on the loss of Fort Ticonderoga. He told them he was sending "very valuable officers": Lincoln and Arnold—"particularly the former, than whom, there is, perhaps, no man from the state of Massachusetts, who enjoys more universal esteem and popularity." Lincoln played a crucial role in raising and organizing a body of militia that operated on Burgoyne's left flank and in his rear. He wrote letters to officials in Massachusetts, telling them to forward newly requisitioned militia, with an emphasis on men who had performed "partisan duty" led by officers "able, active and experienced." Setting up headquarters in Manchester, Vermont, Lincoln soon had 2,500 men under his command.

In the middle of September, as Burgoyne clashed with the main army, Lincoln sent his men out in groups of five hundred. One group, led by Colonel John Brown, assaulted the British post on Lake George, captured four hundred British soldiers, released one hundred American prisoners, and seized "a vast quantity of plunder." Another group tested the defenses of Fort Ticonderoga. These moves by mostly militia bands unnerved Burgoyne and his top commanders. They saw their supply line to Canada severed—and cut a half pound of bread and a half pound of meat from their soldiers' daily rations.[12]

Meanwhile, Daniel Morgan and his five hundred riflemen were joining Benedict Arnold in challenging the British on the main battlefield. Again and again their deadly guns turned British advances into panicky retreats. At the climax of the second battle of Saratoga, when a desperate Burgoyne had committed every soldier in his battered army to an all-or-nothing gamble of another frontal assault, his light infantry commander, Simon Fraser, did a superb job of rallying the redcoated foot soldiers. General Arnold rode up to Morgan and pointed to Fraser. "That man on the grey horse is a host unto himself and must be disposed of," he shouted. Morgan passed the order to a half dozen of his best sharpshooters, who soon put a bullet through Fraser's belly. The brigadier's fall consumed what little heart was left in the British attack, and the survivors ran for the protection of their fortified camp.

Burgoyne's situation rapidly grew hopeless. While rations dwindled and horses starved to death, the surrounding Americans sniped by day and bombarded by night. By this time, Lincoln had joined the main army with his militia. Gates's army swelled to 14,000 men, 8,000 of them militia. The British could not tell the difference between a militiaman and a Continental. Each had a gun in his hand. Desertions multiplied among Burgoyne's dispirited men. Finally Gentleman Johnny asked Gates for surrender terms.

On October 17, Burgoyne's men marched out and stacked their arms in a meadow north of Fishkill Creek. The gleeful Gates wrote to his wife, "Burgoyne and his great army have laid down their arms to me and my Yankees." With New England's politicians behind him in Congress, Gates thought he was now in a position to supplant George Washington as the American commander in chief.

It has become traditional to point to Saratoga as a historic turning point that transformed the war by persuading France to become America's public ally. The victory unquestionably contributed to the French decision. But Louis XVI and his ministers were equally impressed by Washington's skill at keeping the main American army intact outside Philadelphia, aggressively staring the enemy in the face. His ferocious attack on Howe's army at Germantown on October 4, only three weeks after the defeat at Brandywine, provided explosive proof that Britain's 1777 campaign had failed on all fronts.

Meanwhile, the militia marched home to spread fabulous tales of how they had bagged Johnny Burgoyne—a tradition that still lingers in not a few history books, which portray Saratoga as a triumph of American farmers à la Lexington and Concord over another British professional army. The Continentals, if they heard such hot air, dismissed it. They knew who had beaten Burgoyne. Some of them also knew that they now had a strategy for victory—if they had the perseverance and courage to make it work.

CHAPTER 4

The Perils of Fabius

I n Pennsylvania, General George Washington began encountering many of the criticisms that had dogged the original Fabius. The fugitive members of the Continental Congress, one hundred miles west of Philadelphia in the provincial town of York (population 1,700), were profoundly unhappy with their lot. Most of York spoke only German. The food varied from bad to awful. These hardships led to something close to a legislative exodus. When congressional president John Hancock arrived, he was dismayed to find only nine delegates on hand to deliberate the policies of the nation. Over the next few weeks, the number rose to eighteen—still far from the fifty-six who had issued a resolute Declaration of Independence little more than fourteen months ago.

In and around Philadelphia the local population began switching sides. The city had long been the engine of a regional economy that included the farmers of western New Jersey, southeastern Pennsylvania, Delaware, and northern Maryland. In an average year, the city exported as much as 57,000 tons of wheat, plus thousands more tons of salted meat and bar iron from nearby forges. This gross domestic product frequently totaled $40 million—roughly $600 million today. The locals knew only that Washington had fought two battles and lost both and that the enemy occupied their capital. Even more importantly, the British had "hard" money, whereas the Americans could only offer the paper dollars being churned out by the printing presses of Congress. The British accelerated their declining value by counter-feiting them by the millions.

Worsening matters was the American attempt to block the Delaware with the two forts built below Philadelphia. The British lost almost 1,000 men, and two warships ran aground and were destroyed in ferocious fighting. But the enemy eventually prevailed, and Admiral Lord Richard Howe's fleet had acquired access to the city, another defeat on General Washington's escutcheon.

Inside the Continental Army, not a few generals—as disillusioned and discouraged as the civilians—were ready to listen to the general who had won the most recent victory: Horatio Gates. Wealthy Philadelphian Thomas Mifflin was one of the first to express his disillusion with General Washington. On October 8, 1777, he resigned as major general and quartermaster general and did not hesitate to tell members of Congress why. On November 23, Richard Henry Lee of Virginia informed Samuel Adams that Mifflin had been in York and reiterated that "the military knowledge and the authority of Gates" were needed "to procure indispensable changes in our army"[1]

On November 17, Mifflin had written to Gates in even more extravagant terms. "You have saved our northern hemisphere, and in spite of our consummate & repeated blundering you have changd the Constitution of the southern campaign on the part of the enemy from offensive to defensive." Mifflin went on to explain why the "southern campaign"— a nice way of minimizing Washington's role—might have succeeded if Gates had remained with Washington's army. He would have counteracted "the deep rooted system of favoritism which began to shoot forth at New York & which has now arrived to its full growth and maturity. Repeated slights and unjustifiable arrogance combined with other causes to drive from the army those who would not worship the image and pay an undeserved tribute of praise and flattery to the great and powerful. The list of our disgusted patriots is long and formidable—their resentments keen against the reigning cabal and their powers of opposition not despicable." An explorer of this thicket of words will soon see that the men being trashed were General Washington and his two closest advisors, Generals Nathanael Greene and Henry Knox.[2]

⌒

GENERAL MIFFLIN was striking notes that were already reverberating through Congress. On October 26, 1777, John Adams told his wife, Abigail, that he was glad Gates had won and almost as glad that Washington and his "southern troops" had failed. Adams feared "idolatry and adulation would have been unbounded, so excessive as to endanger our liberties for what I know. Now we can allow a certain citizen to be wise virtuous and good without thinking him a deity or a Savior."[3]

Another anti-Washington voice that became noticeably louder in Congress belonged to James Lovell, a devoted follower of Samuel Adams. They shared the widespread New England dislike of a regular army and a persistent preference for militia, which supposedly would not endanger American liberties. On November 27, 1777, Lovell wrote to General Gates, "Good God! What a situation are we in! How different from what might have been justly expected! You will be astonished when you come to know accurately what numbers have at one time and another been collected near Philadelphia to wear out stockings, shoes and breeches? Depend upon it for every 10 soldiers placed under the command of our Fabius, 5 recruits will be wanted annually during the war."[4]

Lovell begged Gates to take charge of the Board of War, a hitherto inert congressional creation theoretically empowered to issue orders to everyone, including General Washington. Were it not for Gates, Lovell was convinced, our affairs would be "fabiused into a very disagreeable posture."[5]

⌒

GEORGE WASHINGTON never mentioned his supposed historic model, Quintus Fabius Maximus, in the eight long years of the Revolution. His version of protracted war differed significantly from the Roman general's. The original "Cunctator" would have deemed much too risky the "strokes"—fierce attacks such as Trenton, Princeton, and Germantown—that Washington constantly looked for an opportunity to make. Virtually from the start of his generalship, Washington saw he had to keep up the morale of American civilians as well as soldiers. He understood that he was fighting a war in which public opinion was crucial. His use of the militia as auxiliaries to the Continental Army's regulars was even more inventive. One scholar who compared Washington's generalship to Fabius's concluded that Washington was not an imitator; he was a new and original Fabius in his own right.[6]

This did not prevent other members of Congress from condemning him. New Jerseyan Jonathan Sergeant wrote to Lovell, "We want a general. Thousands of lives and millions of property are yearly sacrificed to the insufficiency of a commander-in-chief. Two battles he has lost for us by two such blunders as would have disgraced a soldier of three months standing." Sergeant said he agreed with fellow New Jerseyan Congressman Abraham Clark, who declared, "We may talk of the enemy's cruelty as we will. But we have no greater cruelty to complain of than the management of our army."[7]

In his letter to Gates, General Mifflin saw the situation in equally dark terms. "We have had a noble army melted down by ill judged marches—marches that disgrace their authors & directors and which have occasioned the severest and most just sarcasm and contempt of our enemies. How much are you to be envied my dear general? How different your conduct and your fortune!" Mifflin mentioned a half dozen high-ranking officers who were contemplating resignation. "In short this army will be totally lost unless you come down and collect the virtuous band who wish to fight under your banner and with their aid save the southern hemisphere. Prepare yourself for a jaunt to this place. Congress must send for you. I have 10,000 things to tell."[8]

The insight that Washington adapted, rather than copied, Fabius's strategy gathers weight when we watch him deal with Horatio Gates. The commander in chief well knew that Gates participated willingly in the intrigue to replace him as commander in chief. Instead of reporting General John Burgoyne's surrender to Washington, as would be expected in any well-organized army, Gates sent his report to Congress via his talkative aide, James Wilkinson. Almost a full month passed before Gates mentioned the great event in a letter to Washington, adding that he supposed the commander in chief had already heard the news.

In response to this performance, Washington dispatched his aide, Alexander Hamilton, to Albany to request—if necessary, to insist—that Gates send most of his army to Pennsylvania without delay. The choice of Hamilton is interesting. Washington had several older, more mature aides, such as Tench Tilghman of Maryland. But they lacked Hamilton's brashness. Gates, perhaps sensing he had gone too far in ignoring Washington, had already dispatched Daniel Morgan and his men, plus a brigade of Continentals, to the main army when Hamilton arrived on his doorstep in early November 1777, after riding three hundred miles in five days. Hamilton pronounced himself dissatisfied with General Gates's detachments in the bluntest imaginable terms. Gates, in a letter he decided not to send, protested his peremptory style. Some historians have censured Hamilton for a lack of deference and pointed out that Washington's orders to him made no such extreme demands. But it seems equally likely to this writer that the orders were an artful cover. At the very least, Hamilton reflected what Washington and his headquarters staff thought of Gates's insulting behavior. Hamilton's report of his combative visit oozed sarcasm. "I found insuperable inconveniences in acting diametrically opposite to the opinion of a gentleman whose successes have raised him to the highest importance."[9]

∽

WASHINGTON MARCHED his reinforced army to Whitemarsh, twelve miles northwest of Philadelphia. There he was protected by two commanding hills. The army's generals debated a surprise attack on the British in Philadelphia, which Howe had ringed with redoubts to prevent another Germantown. A majority voted against it. Nathanael Greene, rapidly emerging as Washington's favorite general, wrote, "The probability of a disappointment is infinitely greater than that of success. We must not be governed in our measures by our wishes."[10]

On December 3, a committee from Congress arrived to report an almost unanimous vote in favor of an immediate assault. Washington showed them the opinions of the generals, and they reluctantly changed their minds. The Pennsylvania state government, also fugitives from British-occupied Philadelphia, met in Lancaster and informed

Washington that they too wanted action. All these politicians, oblivious of Washington's strategy, were also unaware of the deterioration of the army's equipment. Almost half the Continentals lacked blankets. The constant marching had worn out shoes and uniforms.

A few days later, on December 5, two-thirds of the British army marched out of Philadelphia and paraded before Whitemarsh, virtually daring the Americans to attack. After the frustrations and disappointments of the last months, not a few officers and men in Washington's ranks hungered to make an all-out charge. But Washington refused to issue the order. He knew that some politicians would soon denounce his decision in York and Lancaster. Letters about it would fly to Horatio Gates in Albany. But he calmly, steadfastly declined to attack. After looking at the men and guns on those two commanding hills for most of the week, General Howe marched glumly back to Philadelphia.[11]

THE GENERALS now began debating where the Continental Army should spend the winter. Some favored places far from Philadelphia— Reading or more distant cities, where the troops could rest and receive new equipment and clothing. But Washington decided this would enable the British to export their influence throughout the entire region around Philadelphia. To retain the loyalty of the citizens in this populous and wealthy quarter, the Continental Army must seem determined to continue the war. It would have to camp close enough to Philadelphia to be poised to deliver a blow.

On December 19, 1777, beneath lowering grey skies, with snow swirling in a savage winter wind, the 11,000-man Continental Army trudged to a mix of wooded tableland and forbidding hills called "the Valley Forge." There the men began building a veritable village of log cabins, while the commissary department frantically sought food to feed them. Philadelphia was only twenty miles away, enabling Washington to patrol the roads around the city with fifty-man detachments of picked troops and arrest farmers caught selling the British food for their army. He also set up an espionage system that enabled him to learn well in advance of British plans for an attack. Valley Forge was on high ground, easily fortified, and Washington made sure the redoubts and trenches were strong enough to discourage General Howe from an assault.

Washington now had time to deal with the generals who were backing Gates as his replacement. Along with General Mifflin, a French volunteer, General Thomas Conway, was especially outspoken. He had written Gates a fawning letter, which Gates's aide, Lieutenant Colonel Wilkinson, described during a late-night drinking session with William Alexander, the New Jersey major general also known as Lord Stirling. Infuriated by Conway's treachery, Stirling reported the letter to Washington, writing down the contents as he remembered them. The commander in chief sent a copy of this message to Conway, asking for an explanation.

Conway replied sneeringly and warned Gates that someone was stealing his private correspondence. Undone, the Saratoga victor lashed out in several directions. He wrote to Washington wondering if Alexander Hamilton were the thief and wondered how the commander in chief could tolerate such conduct. Washington coolly replied that the man who had revealed the contents of Conway's letter was Gates's talkative aide, Lieutenant Colonel Wilkinson.

In Congress General Washington's critics remained determined to embarrass him into resignation. They revived the Board of War, empowering it to launch campaigns and review the army's policies without consulting the commander in chief. They appointed Gates the board's chairman, named General Mifflin as his right-hand man, and made Lieutenant Colonel Wilkinson the board's secretary.

With considerable power at their fingertips, the conspirators decided to launch a military campaign without so much as consulting General Washington. After considerable discussion they decided on their target: Canada. Who would conduct this winter campaign? They chose a general for whom they were sure it would have great personal appeal—the Marquis de Lafayette. He would be instantly popular with Canada's French majority. Already active in the Continental Army was a regiment of Anglo-Canadians who had joined the Revolution. They would supplement's Lafayette's popularity with his fellow Frenchmen. Best of all, practically no British soldiers remained in Canada. Little more than 2,500 to 3,000 well-equipped troops could conquer the vast territory.

At first thrilled by the proposal, the young marquis was far less enthused when he discovered that General Conway was to be his second in command. Lafayette flatly declined to serve with the man who was blatantly disloyal to General Washington. Next, the plotters learned that Lafayette would not report to them about the exploits of the expedition. All his letters would go to General Washington, with copies to the Board of War. The squirming Gates and Mifflin could only agree to these conditions, barely concealing their discomfiture.

Lafayette headed for Albany, where he was supposed to find men, guns, and supplies. He was soon a very distressed general. Instead of 2,500 enthusiastic Continentals, he found 1,200 troops shivering in summer uniforms, many as shoeless as their fellow soldiers at Valley Forge. New Hampshire's John Stark, supposed to be eager to summon hundreds of his aggressive militiamen, had nothing but questions about how to feed these men and supply them with ammunition and winter uniforms. Soon an enraged Lafayette was writing wild letters to the new president of the Continental Congress, Henry Laurens, denouncing Gates and Mifflin. Laurens swiftly forwarded them to George Washington. General Gates's reputation as a brilliant planner was soon in tatters. Even more decrepit were his hopes of becoming commander in chief.

On February 19, 1778, Gates capitulated to Washington. In a labored letter he disowned General Conway and the congressional critics. He vowed that he had never promoted dissension in Congress or anywhere else. He closed this catalog of lies with a whopper: "I heartily dislike controversy even on my own account." Gates added the hope that Washington would not allow "his own suspicions or the prejudices of others" to prolong the quarrel.[12]

With his congressional critics reeling, Washington greeted a five-man committee from Congress sent to Valley Forge. Their mission, in James Lovell's nasty words, was "to rap a demigod over the knuckles." Washington presented them with a 16,000-word report, ghostwritten by Alexander Hamilton, analyzing the army's problems in the quartermaster and commissary departments, both of which Congress had badly mishandled. The head of the committee, Francis Dana, had been Lovell's Harvard roommate. After Dana had time to read the report, which recommended, among other things, that officers be promised half pay for life, Washington invited him to dinner. After the meal, Dana joined him for a stroll outside his headquarters. Abruptly, Washington said, "Mr. Dana—Congress does not trust me. I cannot continue thus."[13] The staggered Dana replied that a majority of Congress had not lost faith in him. Soon the congressman was a Washington ally. Back in York, to the consternation of Lovell and the other critics, he supported all Washington's reforms. Before long a man Washington trusted, General Nathanael Greene, was head of the quartermaster department, guaranteeing new energy in finding food for the army. Other men chosen by the commander in chief took over the commissary department.

Even more important than these breakthroughs was another change Washington persuaded the members of the camp committee to support: pensions for his officers. During the Valley Forge ordeal, over three hundred officers had resigned. Washington had decided that only a solution the British army had long since adopted would keep qualified men in leadership positions: half pay for life. He was aware that this change directly challenged the New Englanders' insistence that patriotic virtue alone should motivate men to bear arms in the revolutionary cause. Necessity had forced them to yield this illusion when it came to recruiting men in the ranks. But for officers to require the incentive of so much cold cash was certain to infuriate the opinionated Yankees and their allies in other colonies. The proposal stirred a violent debate in Congress. After weeks of impassioned oratory, the pro-Washington wing of Congress suggested a compromise: half pay for seven years. It passed, six states to five, with two state delegations deadlocked. Did

Washington realize this topic would haunt the rest of his military and political career? If so, he was prepared to face it.

~

THE ARMY'S military training was by no means neglected at Valley Forge. In charge of it was another foreign volunteer, former lieutenant general Baron Friedrich Wilhelm von Steuben. The title was imaginary. In fact the baron had never been more than a captain in the German army, although he had a wealth of knowledge derived from experience as a general staff member of the Prussian army. It was the greatest deception for a good cause in history. Endorsed by the French minister of war and promoted by Benjamin Franklin, he was introduced to Washington as a lieutenant general, which greatly enhanced his actual credentials. The baron proceeded to create a new training system for the American army. For the first two years of the war, the Americans had followed the British system, in which sergeants drilled the men, and officers had very little to do with them. Under the baron's tutelage, the officers drilled the men and devoted not a little time to winning their affection as well as their obedience. Steuben's approach was revolutionary and would make a huge difference not only in future battles in this war but in the future of the US Army.[14]

With General Greene as quartermaster and commissaries who reported to General Washington rather than Congress, the last few months of the Valley Forge encampment were almost pleasant for both officers and men. New recruits poured in as the various states improved their drafting systems; Washington's manpower soon reached 15,061. On April 30, astounding news arrived via a courier from Bethlehem, Pennsylvania. The letter writer told the American commander that he was en route from Paris to York to deliver to Congress copies of a treaty signed with France, creating an alliance in which King Louis XVI guaranteed the independence of the United States. Washington rushed the letter to the president of the Continental Congress, saying, "No event was ever received with more heart-felt joy."[15]

A week of celebrations followed. Washington began telling correspondents there was a good possibility that the war would end soon.

"The game, whether ill or well played hitherto," he wrote, "seems now to be verging toward a favorable issue."[16] He would soon discover that the game was far from over. Within two months the Continental Army that Baron von Steuben had trained to near perfection would be fighting for its life, and the commander in chief would face another challenge to his leadership—one that did not merely criticize his Fabian tactics but dismissed the whole idea of a trained regular army.

CHAPTER 5

General Double Trouble

I n May 1778, a new and potentially troublesome character appeared in Valley Forge. As readers will recall, General Charles Lee, second in command of the American army, had been captured in New Jersey in late 1776 when he carelessly spent the night several miles from his troops. By that time he had exasperated General George Washington by ignoring repeated requests to join the commander in chief's dwindling army for an attack on the British. Now, eighteen months later, the British had agreed to exchange Lee for a captured British general of equal rank and permitted him to return to the American army on parole.

Washington set aside the unpleasant memories of Lee's uncooperative 1776 performance and gave a dinner for him at his Valley Forge headquarters. Superficially cordial, Lee had little to say about serious matters. Instead he headed for York, where he claimed he wanted to lay a "hobby horse" before Congress—a plan for remodeling the American army. As was typical of his arrogant style, Lee offered the commander in chief no further explanation. He was soon in York, dining with New England delegates, most of whom worshipped him as much as they adored Horatio Gates. As John Adams had revealed in saying he was pleased that Washington had lost the battle of Brandywine, the Yankees instinctively favored other generals, fearing Washington might become too powerful and threaten American liberties.

Lee explained his "hobby horse" to these gentlemen, probably knowing in advance they would like it. He called for "the formation of the American Army in the least expensive manner possible." They should forget all the complex maneuvers Baron von Steuben had been teaching Washington's men. Lee's maneuvers were so simple that the soldiers could learn them in a few weeks.

General Lee derided Washington's and von Steuben's efforts to create a well-trained professional army. Lee said Americans would never master this "European plan." The British would laugh at them, and the Americans would lose every battle that depended on formal maneuvers. It was "nonsense" to expect Americans to outdo British regulars in this department. Instead Lee called for a vast increase in the number of militia, with a special emphasis on cavalry. The Continental Army might as well disband and join in harassing the British army militia style.[1]

We again glimpse Lee's arrogance in a letter to congressional president Henry Laurens. He urged Laurens to reinstate him as soon as possible; Washington needed him. In fact, "considering how he is surrounded . . . he cannot do without me." Here Lee was referring to Nathanael Greene and Henry Knox, who many New England congressmen believed were responsible for the bad advice that had lost the battles of Brooklyn, Brandywine, and Germantown. Lee cast numerous aspersions on Washington's ability as a general, further delighting his Yankee admirers.

After obtaining what he thought was the approval of Congress—President Laurens diplomatically avoided disagreeing with him—Lee finally got around to sending General Washington a copy of his plan. Meanwhile he dashed off a letter to Laurens suggesting his own promotion from major general to lieutenant general—giving him equal rank with General Washington. Laurens submitted this proposal to Congress, which voted it down six states to three. Francis Dana and the other members of the committee that had gone to Valley Forge and become converts to Washington's policies pointed out that if anything happened to him, Lee would then be the army's de facto commander in chief. Having listened to his scheme for reorganizing the army, they had no intention of allowing this ascension to take place.

‿

BACK IN Valley Forge, Washington continued to treat Lee with the greatest cordiality. He was aware that he was dealing with another congressional favorite, in some ways more potent than Gates. The standing-army-hating congressmen around Samuel Adams were eager to renew their secret war with the commander in chief. Having defeated Gates, Washington was determined to show no hostility to General Lee unless the latter provoked it.

Lee persisted in criticizing the current organization of the Continental Army to anyone who would listen. He conjured a deep concern about the lack of intimate connection between a major general and the men he commanded. He felt a general should lead in battle only the men he had personally trained. He seemed oblivious of the role of the brigadier generals, who had such a connection and were more than able to fill this spurious gap. Obviously Lee was attempting to acquire a piece of the Continental Army and make it his personal possession.

General Double Trouble also urged Washington to station part of the American army on the lower Susquehanna River because he was sure the British were planning a foray in that direction. Next came a warning that Lee was now convinced the British were going to seize control of the Chesapeake Bay region rather than retreat to New York. The Continental Army should do something to counter the threat. The "something" almost certainly involved giving a chunk of the army and an independent command to Major General Lee.

Washington finally wrote to Lee, saying he was always ready to discuss the major general's ideas but hoped he would stop talking about them to anyone with ears. The commander in chief preferred proposals to "come directly to myself." It did not do the army any good to have generals discussing problems that might simply be "unavoidable."

Annoyed by his failure to overawe Washington, Lee told a favorite correspondent that, looking back, he saw the whole war as a series of blunders committed first by the Americans and then topped by the British. Now the Yankees had been rescued by the French alliance, without which "we were inevitably lost"—not exactly a compliment to the commander in chief.

THE KNOWLEDGE that Lee was hurling these smears in all directions did nothing to improve Washington's temper—as Horatio Gates found out when he ignored an order to send all the muskets in the northern department to Valley Forge as soon as possible. On discovering that someone on his staff had obeyed this command, Gates countermanded it instantly. By that time a substantial number of guns had reached Easton, Pennsylvania. A deputy quartermaster general in Easton told Washington about this inexplicable recall.

The commander in chief drafted a ferocious rebuke. "What could induce you to give these orders or how you can justify this countermand I cannot conceive." He crossed out this blast and in a revision told Gates he had "2500 men in camp without guns." He ordered Gates to send every available gun in his possession to Valley Forge "without the least delay." Gates's countermand had "greatly disappointed and exceedingly distressed me." In another revision, Washington crossed out "me" and wrote "injured the service." The letter closed with another ferocious sentence, which he did not cross out: "You will consider the above as an order not to be dispensed with in the present situation of affairs." If Gates held any illusion that he had persuaded Washington to forget his intrigues, this letter annihilated them.[2]

At Valley Forge, Washington did not need spies to tell him that the British were planning to evacuate Philadelphia. Fleeing loyalists and deserters were streaming into the countryside, talking of the British plans. General William Howe had resigned. His replacement was second in command General Henry Clinton. London had warned Clinton that a French fleet was on its way to America. He had no time to spare if he wanted to get his army to New York, where the British fleet could support it. Admiral Lord Richard Howe had made clear he had no intention of allowing his ships to be trapped in the Delaware River.

◡

ON JUNE 17, Washington and his generals discussed their options. The British fleet—cabins crowded with loyalist refugees and decks and holds loaded with baggage—had already sailed for New York. Much of the British army had crossed the Delaware River, obviously planning to march across New Jersey to the same destination, accompanied by a twelve-mile-long wagon train loaded with food, ammunition, and weapons of war.

What to do? Launch an all-out attack and bring on a general action? Let the troops go unchallenged and parade the Continentals through Philadelphia like a vanquishing army? Attack the British rear guard and content themselves with a minor victory? Washington, with more trained men in his ranks than he had commanded since the war began, was strongly inclined to a general action. He was definitely no slavish imitator of Fabius Maximus.

General Charles Lee seized the floor and held forth on the folly of fighting even a minor battle with the British. He reiterated his conviction that Americans could not defeat British regulars. Risking a general action would be "criminal," he declared. Only General Anthony Wayne favored an all-out attack. Washington said nothing but clearly wanted to wipe from the public record the taunts and sneers directed at his Fabian leadership that had emanated from York and Lancaster during the winter months. He was eager to give his revived army a chance to prove itself in battle.

By now, however, Washington had learned not to make emotional decisions. He ordered a Continental division under General Lee across the Delaware River north of Trenton, where it could strike the British if they traversed New Jersey by a central route. He attached a string of orders to Lee's assignment. He should march his troops only from 4:00 A.M. until noon because of the summer heat. He was to follow a route laid out for him by Quartermaster General Nathanael Greene so that the division could take advantage of magazines stocked with food, water, and ammunition. He was reminding Lee that Lieutenant General George Washington was in command of the Continental Army.

Washington led the rest of the army across the Delaware River not far from where the British had crossed, opposite Philadelphia. He then issued a stream of orders aimed at slowing Clinton's progress toward New York. New Jersey's Continental brigade and over 1,000 Garden State militiamen harassed the flanks of the British column. To these Washington added Colonel Daniel Morgan and his riflemen, their numbers bolstered by volunteer sharpshooters from other regiments. Jeger captain Johann Ewald, assigned to protect the British flanks and rear with his marksmen, wrote in his diary, "Each step cost human blood."[3]

Washington's men burned bridges on the retreating army's route, chopped down trees to block roads, and removed buckets and ropes from wells to sharpen British thirst. The enemy soon slowed to a crawl. In the first seven days Clinton's men covered barely forty miles. To shorten his march, the British general decided to alter his route. He turned southeast and headed through Monmouth County toward Sandy Hook, where the British fleet could meet him and transport his men to New York.

The summer heat, already ferocious, became almost unbearable in Monmouth's virtually waterless terrain. Almost 1,000 British troops deserted. The American army, on the other hand, remained in good spirits, thanks to the efficiency of Nathanael Greene's quartermaster department. Well-stocked magazines guaranteed ample food and water. Each night, on arriving at a campsite, the army found latrines dug, plenty of straw for bedding, and barrels of vinegar to ward off intestinal diseases.

On June 24 Washington called another council of war. This time he bluntly asked his generals whether they should "hazard a general action." Or should they attempt only a partial attack on the rear guard and let General Clinton decide whether he wanted a winner-takes-all battle? That way the Americans could fight on the defensive and extricate themselves if the battle started to go against them. Once more General Charles Lee wildly opposed an offensive, saying that if he had the power, he would "build a bridge of gold" to assist the British to New York as swiftly as possible. Again Lee declared the Americans could not possibly defeat British regulars in a standup, open-field encounter. He intimidated enough generals to convince a majority that only an attack on the rear guard could be justified.[4]

That night Quartermaster General Greene wrote to Washington, lamenting that as a staff officer he could no longer speak out in councils of war. He told the commander in chief that he thought an attack should be in far greater force and the main army should be "in supporting distance" to confront the British if they chose to fight an all-out battle. He reminded Washington of the criticism that had emerged in Congress and from the Pennsylvania state government for their failure to strike another blow after the battle of Germantown.[5]

Washington was thinking along similar lines. He expanded the force that was to attack the rear guard until it totaled 4,500 men—almost half his infantry. In command he put Major General Marquis de Lafayette, with Brigadier General Wayne as his chief deputy—the two generals most in favor of a major attack.

A few hours after the troops marched, General Lee appeared at Washington's tent to say he had changed his mind. Letting the far younger Lafayette command the attack would impugn his honor. Washington was obviously unhappy. Lafayette, hearing that Lee wanted to replace him, willingly surrendered the top command, solving that problem. The marquis became the advance guard's second in command.

On June 27, Henry Clinton rested his men at Monmouth Court House (now Freehold). The weather remained unbelievably hot. The British army was now only a day's march from Middletown, New Jersey—high ground where it would be safe from assault. From there it could easily reach the Atlantic coast at Sandy Hook.

General Washington ordered General Lee to attack the British rear guard as soon as possible. Lee replied that he was sure Clinton would counterattack with most of his army. Unimpressed, Washington informed Lee that he expected him to proceed with the assault. He wanted Lee to hold the rear guard in place until Washington arrived with the rest of the army. If the British reinforced the rear guard, so be it. Washington had confidence in his Continentals.

For the next twenty-four hours General Lee did nothing. He made no attempt to weaken or distract the enemy. He did not detach five hundred men to assault its wagon train and throw it into confusion at the right moment. He did not select a jump-off site for his attack. When he summoned Lafayette, Anthony Wayne, Charles Scott, and the other generals under his command to discuss the assault, Lee did not give them a plan. Nor did he ask them what they had seen from their forward positions. He simply told them to be ready to advance in the morning at 5:00 A.M.

∽

AT DAWN the next day, Washington received a message from the commander of the New Jersey militia telling him that the British army had begun its march toward Middletown. Washington ordered the main army to begin its advance and sent one of his aides galloping to Lee, telling him to launch an attack as soon as possible. With the temperature in the nineties, Washington's 7,800 men trudged down a sandy road toward Monmouth Court House. The commander in chief scribbled a hasty note to Congress president Henry Laurens warning that a battle was imminent—if the British did not elude General Lee.

Washington had scarcely finished this dispatch when a messenger arrived from Lee's headquarters reporting that the major general had found a little-used road that would enable him to cut off the 2,000-man British rear guard. An exultant Washington sent an aide galloping to tell Lee he was on his way with the rest of the army. By noon Washington was close enough to strain his ears for the sounds of battle. There were none—except for a few tantalizing cannon shots. He sent another aide forward to find out what was happening.

As the perspiring Continentals advanced down the main road, Washington, on horseback at the head of the column, met a man who told him Lee's men were retreating. A thunderstruck Washington asked where he had gotten this information. The civilian pointed to a young fifer who confirmed the bad news. The commander in chief had barely ridden another fifty yards when he met three men, one of them wearing the remnants of a soldier's uniform. They told him Lee's whole force was falling back. Washington still refused to believe it. After those agonizing winter months at Valley Forge and the weeks of relentless training under Baron von Steuben, could Lee retreat without a fight?

The agitated commander in chief rode to the crest of a ridge and saw two regiments retreating down the road in serious disorder, all but staggering with heat exhaustion. One of their colonels told the stunned Washington that the whole advanced corps was abandoning the battle—information confirmed within minutes. Columns of men trudged down the road, many looking frightened or bewildered or both. Washington asked Colonel Israel Shreve, commander of the 2nd New Jersey Regiment, why he was retreating. With a strange half smile, the portly Shreve said he did not know. He had been ordered to retreat, and that was what he was doing. Washington saw no wounds or gunpowder-blackened hands or faces. Shreve's men had obviously done no fighting.

Finally there appeared the one man who could answer Washington's questions: General Charles Lee, followed by several aides and hundreds more retreating men. An infuriated Washington rode up to him and shouted, "What is the meaning of this?"

Lee could only goggle in amazement at the enraged commander in chief. "Sir? Sir?" he stuttered.

"What is all this confusion? This retreat?" Washington roared in his face.

When Lee responded that Americans could not and would not stand before British bayonets, Washington responded, "You damned poltroon! You never tried them!"

At this point, according to some eye (or ear) witnesses, Washington's temper flew completely out of control. Brigadier General Charles Scott said the commander in chief cursed Lee "until the leaves shook on the trees. Never have I enjoyed such swearing before or since." Lafayette later confirmed the outburst.[6] Whether there was some exaggeration after the fact remains debatable. This much is certain: Washington ferociously demanded an explanation for Lee's decision to retreat without bothering to inform him.

Lee responded with incoherent babble. There was no confusion in his ranks, but there had been "disobedience of orders, contradictory intelligence and the self-importance and presumption of individuals." In other words there was plenty of confusion, but it was not Lee's fault. He tried to blame it all on Brigadier Generals Scott and Wayne for disobeying his orders. Washington made no effort to conceal his contempt. Lee was confessing his ineptitude as a general. He had lost control of his troops. Most of them did not know where they were going or why.

On Lee babbled. He claimed that when he advanced, he found himself "in the most extensive plain in America." If he had not retreated, British cavalry would have annihilated his regiments. He had not bothered to discover this supposedly dangerous terrain on June 27, when he did nothing all day but putter about his headquarters. In a desperate attempt at a summary, Lee declared that "he did not choose to beard the British Army in such a situation." Finally he uttered a sentence that approximated the truth: "Besides, the thing was against my opinion."

"All this may be true, sir," Washington snarled, "but you ought not to have undertaken it unless you intended to go through with it!"

∽

A MOMENT later, Washington's aide Robert Hanson Harrison rode up to report that masses of British troops were advancing in battle formation and were less than fifteen minutes away. As if Clinton were adding exclamation points, cannonballs began plowing the sandy earth in the Americans' vicinity. The general had heavily reinforced his rear guard. It now comprised 6,000 men—almost half his army.

With two-fifths of the Continental Army—Lee's men—groggy with fatigue and falling back with no orders to take a position and Washington's main army coming up the road behind him, also without a plan, the stage was set for a rout that might destroy the Continental Army and would certainly ruin the commander in chief's reputation forever. Did General Lee have precisely this in mind when he embarked on this withdrawal without giving Washington the slightest notice?

Washington had assumed the British, satisfied with Lee's retreat, would resume their march to Sandy Hook. Instead General Clinton obviously hoped for an all-out battle. For a long, agonizing moment, Washington sat in the saddle, dazed. He knew nothing about the forested landscape that surrounded him, having planned to fight the battle on the "plain" beyond Monmouth Court House that General Lee had found so forbidding.

One of Washington's senior aides, Tench Tilghman, sensed his commander in chief's thoughts. He told Washington that a lieutenant colonel in a New Jersey regiment knew the local terrain intimately. His family owned a great deal of it. Washington ordered Tilghman to find this man without a moment's delay. In a few minutes, the officer was at Washington's side, explaining the local geography in urgent detail.

As he listened, Washington experienced what might be called a military epiphany. In a letter to his younger brother Jack, he later wrote that the certainty suddenly gripped him that the "bountiful Providence which has never failed us in the hour of distress" had arranged for him to encounter General Lee at this place. It was all but perfect for defense. A nearby hedgerow could serve as a rampart, and a wooded hill overlooking the road on the left could become a fortress bristling with cannons that commanded the long slope up which the British army would have to charge. In their rear was a swampy ravine, traversed by a narrow passage, that the Americans could easily defend if they had to fall back.[7]

Washington issued a stream of orders. He sent a New York regiment behind the hedgerow and added other regiments as quickly as they materialized. He ordered two regiments to occupy a fringe of hilly woods on the left and told them to attack with the bayonet to check the enemy's advance even if it cost them every man in their ranks. When Anthony Wayne appeared with the rest of his men, marching in perfect formation, Washington put him in command of the front line. An admiring Marquis de Lafayette said Washington's presence "stopped the retreat." Alexander Hamilton later wrote that he "never saw the General to such advantage. His coolness and firmness were admirable."[8]

⁓

FIFTEEN MINUTES later, the British army attacked. First came the cavalry. Wayne's men were ready for them. Cannons and musketry demolished dragoons and horses. They were soon fleeing for their lives. Then came the infantry. The best troops led the assault. Tall grenadiers, their high, brass-fronted busbies adding to their fearful appearance, occupied the front ranks. After them came the elite Foot Guards, also huge, a walking (or, more precisely, charging) aristocracy. Here, if ever, was a test of General Lee's thesis that the Americans could not meet Britain's best regulars in face-to-face battle.

In the fiery heat, Americans belied any and all myths. Steuben had worked a miracle. They had become not only a band of brothers, officers and men, but also that mysterious spiritual organism known as an army. At a drumbeat or a barked order, they pivoted left or right, defending flanks and even the rear with selfless ferocity. Their musketry exploded in coordinated blasts that tore unspeakable gaps in the redcoated ranks. Commanding the center, Washington watched as amazement transformed face after aristocratic enemy face. A new American army was being born here!

As the sun slid toward twilight, the British survivors staggered back to that controversial plain beyond Monmouth Court House, where heavy cannons stood poised to protect them from more damage. For the moment they were in no danger from the victorious Americans. The day's diabolical heat had drained them of all but the most minimal respiration. When Washington considered an attack using the men of Lee's advance guard, whom Baron von Steuben had reorganized, he realized that, although willing to make the attempt, they simply lacked the physical strength. He ordered his men to rest for the night in their forward positions and resume the battle in the morning.

On the other side of the battle line, General Clinton had wisely decided to put as much distance as possible between his battered battalions and the Americans. After giving the men a half dozen hours to rest, he ordered them to resume their march to Sandy Hook at midnight. An American patrol that probed the edge of the plain at dawn found it vacant. Washington ordered Daniel Morgan and his riflemen to pursue the British with harassing tactics. But as the June sun resumed its ferocious glare, he saw no hope of spurring his still-weary men to overtake them.

⌒

DURING THE night, Washington had slept in his cloak beside Lafayette. They had discussed Charles Lee's conduct. Lafayette believed him a coward and possibly a traitor. Henry Laurens, the president of Congress, agreed. For the next two days, Washington chose silence as the best means deal with the antagonism that had exploded on the Monmouth battlefield. Lee, however, was incapable of this wise tactic. He wrote letters to members of Congress, claiming that if he had not ordered his men to retreat, "this army, and perhaps America, would have been ruined." What had he received for his generalship? "Thanks from his Excellency . . . of a singular nature." Lee soon made his discontent known to newspapermen and to his fellow soldiers.

On June 30, Washington congratulated numerous officers and the army in general for their performance in the battle. He conspicuously omitted Charles Lee. General Double Trouble responded with an angry, insulting letter to the commander in chief. He told Washington that neither he nor the "dirty earwigs" who filled his head with flattery were in any position to judge why and when he had retreated. Once more Lee claimed the success of the day was "entirely owing" to his actions and decisions. Lee demanded a court-martial, confident that he could justify his actions "to the Army, to the Congress, to America, and to the world."[9]

Washington responded in turn with a curt letter informing Lee that his accusations and insulting tone were "highly improper." If he wanted a court-martial, Washington was more than ready to prove that Lee was guilty of "a breach of orders and misbehavior before the enemy . . . in not attacking them as you had been directed, and in making an unnecessary disorderly and shameful retreat." When a political friend urged Lee to stay silent, he sneeringly declared he was not in the least worried about "His Deityship."

Lee got his court-martial. Hamilton and other aides testified to his insulting language. Generals Wayne and Scott portrayed him as a man who did not know what he was doing on the battlefield. To save their men they had made their own decision to retreat. General Lee's aides struggled to defend him. They got some help from anti-Washington officers such as Aaron Burr. The court-martial board deliberated for three days and found Lee guilty of failing to attack the enemy as directed. They also found him guilty of disrespecting the commander in chief in his angry letters. But they found Washington's overheated description of Lee's retreat somewhat excessive. They eliminated the word shameful and described the retreat as "unnecessary . . . and in a few instances disorderly." They sentenced Lee to suspension from the army for a year.

᠊ᢏ

OUTRAGED AND as vocal as ever, Lee took his case to Congress, where he found that many of the same politicians who feared and disliked a regular army were ready to dismiss the court-martial's decision. Congressional outliers, such as ideologue Benjamin Rush, joined the call to dismiss the charges. By the time the verbiage subsided, it was December 5, 1778, and the country regarded Monmouth as an American victory for which Washington was responsible. A solid congressional majority voted to uphold the verdict.

It was the beginning of the end for General Double Trouble. When Lee began flinging at the politicians the same vituperation that he had hurled at Washington, they dismissed him from the military. The year ended with America's Fabius in complete command of the Continental Army without a challenger in sight.

CHAPTER 6

A Surplus of Disappointments

After the battle of Monmouth, George Washington and his men began to think of themselves as soldiers of destiny. The alliance with France transformed everyone's perspective. There was excited talk about an early end to the war. Final victory—the destruction of the British army and fleet—seemed just over the horizon.[1]

This optimism multiplied exponentially when a massive French fleet appeared off the American coast. In command was a distant cousin of the Marquis de Lafayette, Charles Hector Theodat, Comte d'Estaing. He heightened American expectations with a florid letter to Washington, praising his "talents and great actions . . . [which] have insured him in the eyes of all Europe the title, truly sublime, of deliverer of America."[2]

The Americans expected the French admiral to fight his way into New York Harbor and destroy Admiral Lord Richard Howe's fleet, which d'Estaing outgunned 850 cannons to 534. Aboard the French ships were 4,000 marines. With their addition to his battlefield strength, Washington was certain he could overcome General Henry Clinton's army, regain New York, and end the war.

The Marquis de Lafayette boarded d'Estaing's flagship to function as his interpreter, as the admiral spoke no English. Lafayette returned with unpleasant news. Lord Howe had positioned his ships just inside the narrow entrance to the harbor. Each French man-of-war would have to survive a series of broadsides. Admiral d'Estaing's enthusiasm for a decisive victory rapidly dwindled. His orders did not obligate him to fight a costly struggle in American waters. His ultimate destination was the West Indies, where the French government was eager to seize St. Lucia, Grenada, Jamaica, and other immensely valuable British "sugar islands." In the eighteenth century sugar was the equivalent of oil—a magic commodity that produced wealth. D'Estaing told Lafayette his ships drew too much water to penetrate the inner harbor—not a very convincing excuse.[3]

THE CONQUEST of New York vanished into a suddenly dubious future. But Admiral d'Estaing claimed he was still eager to strike a blow before he departed for the West Indies. A disappointed Washington suggested another target. For more than a year, the British had maintained a 6,000-man garrison in Newport, Rhode Island, to guarantee the Royal Navy's possession of a deep-water harbor that would not freeze over. The New England states regarded the men stationed there as potential invaders and would willingly call out their militias to help destroy the garrison. The amateurs volunteered by the thousands when they learned that Washington had given Major General John Sullivan 4,000 Steuben-trained Continentals, to which d'Estaing would add his 4,000 marines.

For a while it seemed that the British Newport army would have no choice but abject surrender. But the blunt, swarthy Sullivan did not get along with the elegant, aristocratic admiral. The French officers mocked the irregular mixture of uniforms in the American army, especially among the officers. D'Estaing scoffed at the militias and was appalled that Washington had not sent more troops. Lafayette, as the man in the middle, was soon half frantic, trying to settle various disputes. Nevertheless Washington remained hopeful. Capture of the Newport garrison a year after General John Burgoyne's surrender might be "the finishing blow to British pretensions in America."[4]

Then came unsettling news from New York. Admiral Lord Howe had gone to sea with his New York squadron. The British high command spread the word that additional warships were on their way from Britain to reinforce him. Were they planning a rendezvous at sea, followed by an assault on d'Estaing? On August 9, 1778, Admiral d'Estaing discovered that Howe's ships had arrived off Newport but not attempted to attack him.

D'Estaing decided to accept the challenge. He canceled plans to land his marines and headed out to sea, promising General Sullivan he would return when he had disposed of the British threat. He had what sailors called "the weather gauge"—the wind was blowing from behind him—giving him the power to maneuver. But Lord Howe declined to fight with the wind against him. Instead, he headed south, content to draw the French ships and their marines away from Newport. For most of the day and into the night, the flight and pursuit continued, with the French always six or eight miles behind.

At midday on August 11, the sky began to darken, and the sea became more and more turbulent. In the first hours of the night a ferocious gale struck both fleets, scattering them in all directions. For the next two days, the storm raged, inflicting fearful damage on many men-of-war. D'Estaing's immense flagship, the *Languedoc*, lost its bowsprit and all three masts. Next its rudder snapped, making it impossible to steer. Other French ships lost two out of three masts. For a while, on the day after the storm, it looked as if the *Languedoc* would be easily captured. But other less damaged French men-of-war came to her assistance.

After two or three indecisive clashes between single ships, Admiral d'Estaing managed to reassemble his fleet off Sandy Hook, where he replaced missing masts and conferred with his captains about what to do next. They voted against returning to Newport. The fleet was too badly damaged. Only a major port such as Boston could repair their ships. D'Estaing dropped anchor off Newport and sent a messenger to General Sullivan to inform him of their decision to withdraw from the battle.

An infuriated Sullivan sent the Marquis de Lafayette and two other generals to persuade D'Estaing to stay and help them win a victory that the Americans badly wanted and needed. If he would delay his departure for only forty-eight hours, the emissaries told him, they could smash the British Newport garrison. D'Estaing replied that he did not think they could overcome the heavily fortified British in so short a time. "Six thousand well entrenched men . . . could [not] be carried in twenty four hours or in two days." On August 21, without further discussion, the French sailed for Boston.

〜

GENERAL SULLIVAN's anger exploded. He wrote—and persuaded his subordinate generals to sign—"A Protest of the General Officers on Rhode Island," a ferocious blast that listed nine reasons why the French should have stayed in the battle and ended with the nasty assertion that d'Estaing's withdrawal damaged "the honor of the French nation." In his orders to his troops, Sullivan added another verbal slash: "The General cannot help lamenting the unexpected departure of the French fleet" and urged his men to win the victory that "their allies refuse to assist" them in obtaining.

The French admiral thus abandoned the American Continentals and their militia supporters on Newport Island, face-to-face with a well-armed enemy, with a mile of deep water between the Americans and the mainland. General Sullivan continued to fling so many insults at the French that Lafayette almost challenged him to a duel. The New England militia began going home "in shoals," one officer reported, further imperiling the survival of Sullivan and his 4,000 regulars.

When Sullivan tried to withdraw to the mainland, the British and their German mercenaries attacked, hoping to drive the Americans into the sea. Like the British at Monmouth, the king's men were shocked by the ferocity and skill of the Continentals. Among the best fighters were the men of the 1st Rhode Island Regiment, which included 125 African Americans. The stunned attackers fell back, and Sullivan managed to get his troops off Newport Island just in time. The next day, Sir Henry Clinton arrived from New York with 5,000 reinforcements, who would have almost certainly overwhelmed the isolated Americans.

〜

Washington urged Lafayette to extend a "healing hand" to repair the bad feelings between the French and Americans. The marquis did his best but could not change the minds of the disillusioned Bostonians, who insulted French officers on the streets. An officer who attempted to stop rioters pillaging a bakery was shot and killed. A furious d'Estaing decided to sail for the West Indies without bothering to tell anyone when or if he would return. Thus the soaring hopes created by the French alliance dwindled to disillusion, and the summer that began with high hopes after the battle of Monmouth ended in frustration and disappointment.[5]

Desperate to create even an aura of French triumph, Lafayette journeyed to Philadelphia and, without Washington's permission, attempted to persuade Congress to back an invasion of Canada. On hearing about this, Washington had to summon all his self-control to stay calm. He had no intention of wasting Continentals on another northern adventure. He was finally in charge of the war and determined to fight it his way. Lafayette's collapse with a debilitating fever averted a confrontation. When the marquis recovered, Washington suggested that he return to France and persuade his countrymen to send the Americans more substantial aid than d'Estaing's sail-by fleet.

∽

WASHINGTON AND his army finally had to face the disagreeable fact that the war was not over. Even more unpleasant was the realization that the entry of the French into the conflict had given the British a new reason to fight on. London's one hundred years of intermittent struggle with Paris for world power stirred deep feelings of patriotism among all ranks of British society. Moreover, England, with its sophisticated tax system, had the resources to stay in the struggle. Americans, on the other hand, found themselves confronting an invisible enemy that eroded their confidence and sapped their war effort: the depreciation of their paper money.

By the end of 1777, Congress and the states, most of which also printed their own currency, had issued $72 million in Continental dollars. But they levied no taxes to support this paper avalanche. Under the

Articles of Confederation, the primitive constitution Congress had created, the legislature had no power to tax. Washington's strategy of protracted war had saddled the lawmakers with decisions that they lacked the power—or the courage—to make. They had bet on a short war. A win in one big battle had been central to their strategy. They found admitting their error extremely difficult.

Money lay at the heart of a quarrel that began at Valley Forge and revealed alarming fissures in congressional unity: Washington's insistence on pensions for the Continental Army officers. He thought they had settled the issue with the congressional compromise in the spring of 1778—half pay for seven years after the end of the war. But many New Englanders still insisted the policy would "debase human kind" and vowed to resist the supposed greed of "the gentlemen of the blade."

The issue came back to life when inflation began eroding the value of the officers' salaries. In October 1778, a worried Washington wrote Congressman Gouverneur Morris, wondering, "What officer can bear the weight of prices, that every necessary article is now got to. A rat, in the shape of a horse, is not to be bought at this time for less than 200 pounds; a saddle under 30 or 40; boots, 20, and shoes and other articles in like proportion. How is it possible for officers to stand this without an increase in pay?"[6]

The depreciation of the American dollar also posed an immediate problem for Washington: it brought recruitment to a virtual halt. Payments of bounties in paper money lost their appeal. Worse, there was no way that Congress or the states could bear the expense of a large army. The cost of feeding the current one was almost prohibitive. Washington divided his forces, keeping most of the troops in New Jersey and sending detachments of cavalry and light infantry to Westchester County, where they could find food in the nearby countryside—and prevent the British from foraging for this vital necessity.

⌒

IN NEW YORK, General Sir Henry Clinton was planning an operation that would, he hoped, show the Americans that the British could invade their countryside to forage on a grand scale whenever they chose.

On the way back from his failed foray to Newport, Clinton had detached General Charles Grey and several hundred light infantrymen to raid east of that city. They sailed into Buzzards Bay and up the Acushnet River to ravage Fair Haven and Bedford, Massachusetts. They burned ships, barracks, and a fort with eleven pieces of artillery. Resistance by local militia was sporadic and ineffective.

Encouraged, Grey sailed out of Buzzards Bay to the island of Martha's Vineyard. There the inhabitants had apparently heard about the damage done to Bedford and Fair Haven and surrendered without firing a shot. They agreed to hand over the guns of their militia, plus three hundred oxen and 10,000 sheep. Grey rushed the news to the British in Newport, who sent him transports that removed most of these succulent animals. Grey's ships took the rest of them, stirring pleasant thoughts in Sir Henry Clinton's otherwise unhappy mind. He had orders to ship 8,000 men to fight the widened war in Florida and the West Indies, which meant he would have little choice but to stay on the defensive in New York.

Before he could detach these men, they would need tons of food for their journey. Clinton decided to convert this necessity into a very large operation that might encourage more Americans to imitate their war-weary brethren on Martha's Vineyard. Perhaps trying to raise his own spirits, he told a fellow general back in London that he thought a few such invasions would "convince these poor deluded people" to give up a war they could not win—especially if his gambit included a great deal more "devastation."[7]

On September 22, 1778, Sir Henry invaded Bergen County, New Jersey, with 5,000 men. Bergen was then twice or perhaps three times the size of the current county. It stretched from Hackensack down through what is now Hudson County to the river that divided so much of northern America. The county was an almost ideal target from the British point of view. Bergen was heavily loyalist. In 1776, when the Americans tried to raise militia there to help defend New York City, they had managed to recruit two companies, each with twenty enlisted men.

While this 5,000-man army forced an American cavalry regiment to retreat, another equally impressive army, complete with cavalry, artillery, and light troops, invaded Westchester County. By September 24, Clinton had put 10,000 men into the territory Washington was supposedly guarding and started stripping farms of forage and animals. In Bergen County, the British built two forts and several smaller redoubts to improve their chances of resisting an American attack.

The locals in Bergen County generally provided the opposite of resistance. The loyalists were more than ready to sell their produce and animals for hard money, which the British paid promptly. Soon flatboats were moving up and down the Hackensack River, carrying tons of food for horses and men to New York City.

Washington made no attempt to interrupt these hardworking harvesters. He was unaware of Sir Henry Clinton's orders to ship 10,000 men southward. But he probably noticed a rather large concentration of flatboats in the Hudson River opposite the mouth of the Hackensack River. They were mute witnesses of Sir Henry's hope that Washington would attempt an assault on one of the two halves of the army now in Bergen and Westchester. The flatboats would enable him to unite the army and give him a chance to meet Washington in a general action.

But America's Fabius remained Fabian in the face of this provocation. Washington saw no immediate risk in letting the British forage until their warehouses and transports were overflowing. The war's outcome did not depend on how well fed the enemy was. The only test that mattered would take place on the battlefield, and Washington still had no intention of risking a major clash without a virtual guarantee of success. For a full month, the British continued to forage. Occasionally their light troops and cavalry tried to surprise a nearby American outpost. They succeeded only twice. In Bergen County they caught a cavalry regiment appallingly unprepared for a surprise attack and virtually wiped it out.

In Westchester, the Americans took consolation for a few days from an ambush they staged. Infantry under fiery Colonel Richard Butler of Pennsylvania caught two patrols of German troops by surprise and inflicted heavy casualties on them. A few weeks later, the enemy repeated the Bergen performance with another cavalry regiment. They surprised an outpost of some thirty sleeping dragoons and killed or captured all of them.[8] An angry Washington urged General Charles Scott to conduct a thorough investigation of the regiment to see if some officer had been guilty of negligence. No charges resulted from this probably half-hearted examination.[9]

⁓

IN SEPARATE detachments, General Sir Henry Clinton sent 5,000 men to the West Indies, with orders to attack the French island of St. Lucia. Another 3,200 men headed for Florida, where General Augustine Prevost was assembling an army to attack Georgia. Sir Henry remained on an unhappy defensive in New York City. Elsewhere in America, the British were less quiescent. In northern New York and western Pennsylvania, loyalist raiders and their Indian allies struck savagely at exposed settlements, especially in the Mohawk Valley. Soon hundreds of farms in this fertile region had been abandoned, depriving the American army of a prime source of flour. The British also used their sea power to ravage the coastlines of New Jersey, Connecticut, and Chesapeake Bay. Clinton had already enunciated the goal after General Grey's raid on Martha's Vineyard—to discourage the rebel Americans and make them yearn for peace.

The close of 1778 brought with it new worries. The southern department had been largely quiescent since 1776. In 1777, Congress chose Major General Robert Howe as its commander. In Charleston, he discovered officials from South Carolina and Georgia were hostile to his appointment. Not a little of their enmity sprang from his North Carolina origins. Howe returned their dislike with stiff criticism of South Carolina's failure to recruit—and pay for—more Continentals.

In the spring of 1778, General Howe undertook an invasion of East Florida, hoping to defeat the army that the British were raising there under General Prevost. The Americans had only five hundred Continentals. The rest of their army consisted of militia. The expedition ended in fiasco, when the mostly South Carolina militia colonels refused to take orders from Howe.

News of this disunity reached London and inspired orders sent to General Clinton in New York to support General Prevost in an attack on Savannah. There were good grounds for supposing that a successful assault might induce the surrender of the rest of Georgia. The sparsely populated colony was virtually undefended.

The attack on Savannah was amazingly successful. General Howe and the city's 1,200-man garrison retreated after little more than token resistance. The British fanned out through the Peachtree State with virtually no opposition. Loyalists by the hundreds eagerly welcomed them. Soon Georgia was so thoroughly pacified there was talk of inviting the exiled royal governor to return and set up a civil government.[10]

⌁

IN THE north, Washington had little opportunity to use his dwindling regular army. But he never ceased looking for an opportunity to launch one of his "strokes" where the British least expected it. In June he began eyeing a British fort overlooking the Hudson River just below Peekskill, on a promontory known as Stony Point. On three sides it rose 150 feet above the river and jutted a half mile into the stream. On the fourth side was a swamp bridged by a causeway to the mainland. A similar fort stood on the river's opposite bank, on Verplanck's Point.

To increase the power of a stroke, Washington had organized a 2,600-man light infantry corps and made Major General Anthony Wayne its commander. The leadership and courage he had displayed at the battle of Monmouth had attracted Washington's attention—and more than removed the stain of the battle of Paoli.

Together, the commander in chief and Wayne studied the two forts for the better part of a week. Wayne concluded that both were too strong to take in a frontal assault. But a surprise attack on Stony Point in the dark of the night might succeed. Washington approved the proposal and told Wayne to draw up a plan. This turned out to be a six-page memorandum full of details that made clear how much thought Wayne had given this daring gamble. He also paid not a little attention to his men's uniforms and appearance. On that morning's parade, he insisted that everyone be "fresh shaved and well powdered." Wayne deemed a good appearance essential to a regiment's or corps' confidence and pride.

He also announced that he would reward bravery. The first five men to enter Stony Point's main works would receive bonuses that ranged from $500 for the first down to $100 for the fifth.

By this time some readers may be wondering how Wayne got the nickname still associated with him: "Mad Anthony." A talkative soldier in Wayne's ranks, who was less than enthusiastic about his battlefield style, had pinned it on him. It did not mean he was insane or mentally erratic. Once the battle began, he was impetuous, roaring curses at the enemy (he was perhaps the boldest swearer among the Continental Army's generals), shouting encouragement to his men, acting the leader in every sense of the word. Off the battlefield he was an assiduous student of the art of war as articulated by European thinkers such as France's Marshal Maurice de Saxe. Wayne liked to quote one of Saxe's favorite lines: "War is a trade for the ignorant and a science for the expert."[11]

When the officers and men of the light infantry corps had absorbed the intricate plan of attack, Wayne marched them twenty miles down the river from West Point, detaining all civilians they encountered along the way. Secrecy was essential. If the five hundred British regulars in the fort knew what was coming, the attack would degenerate into a slaughter.

Precisely at midnight on July 16, a party assigned to the causeway connecting the fort to the mainland began firing blasts of musketry, designed to throw the defenders into confusion and panic. Meanwhile the bayonet wielders stormed the fortifications, led by small groups, grimly called "forlorn hopes," with orders to clear away any obstructions. They attacked in two columns, on the left and right flanks. General Wayne led the left flank column, and Pennsylvanian colonel Richard Butler led the one on the right.

At first British resistance was fierce. Seventeen of twenty men in one of these forlorn hope groups were killed. Wayne went down with what at first seemed a mortal wound—a bullet in the head. But it was only a graze, and he was soon on his feet, roaring encouragement to his men. The British commander totally misjudged Wayne's plan. He rushed toward the musketry with six companies, assuming this was the main assault. Into the fort's interior surged both columns to attack the rest of the garrison with bayonets. For fifteen minutes a wild melee ensued. Then the outnumbered British surrendered, and the companies attacking the detachment of musketeers had no choice but to do likewise.[12]

The victory was immensely gratifying for the Americans. They had not only outfought but outthought the British. A vastly pleased Washington told Congress, "The event will have a good effect upon the minds of the people, give our troops greater confidence . . . and depress the spirits of the enemy accordingly." Congress was equally pleased. They voted to award General Wayne a medal and directed that the value of the guns, ammunition, and provisions captured at Stony Point be distributed to Wayne's light infantry: more than $158,000 in paper dollars—inflated but still welcome to men not being paid regularly.[13]

⌇

WHEN CONGRESS looked south, its members were far less pleased. They decided to replace General Robert Howe as the man in charge. Without consulting Washington, they chose General Benjamin Lincoln, the New Englander who had distinguished himself as the leader of the militia that had so effectively wrecked General Burgoyne's supply lines. The genial Lincoln had managed to remain friendly with both Washington and Horatio Gates.

Washington could only hope for the best. Appointing a New Englander to a southern command was a risky move. But Congress insisted on retaining the authority to name the commanders of the military departments. In his camp outside New York, Washington must have been hoping for the return of the French fleet. His army lacked the strength to assault the city without substantial aid in men and guns. Admiral d'Estaing had won important victories in the Caribbean, capturing the sugar islands of Granada and Dominica. With the hurricane season looming, it seemed logical for him to sail north and join the Americans in an all-out attack on New York. To tempt him, Washington called out 12,000 militia from five nearby states.[14]

Instead, Admiral d'Estaing decided he would be satisfied with a quick victory over the British garrison in Savannah. He appeared off the city on September 4, 1779, and called for its surrender "to the arms of the King of France." The phrase offered another glimpse of his refusal to accept Americans as equals in their alliance.[15] In Savannah, General Prevost stalled for twenty-four hours and used the time to draw his scattered forces together until he had a respectable defending army of 3,200 men.

The Americans under General Lincoln managed to muster only 600 Continentals, 750 militiamen, and 250 cavalry to support the admiral. By this time, Lincoln was as unhappy with South Carolina's approach to the war as General Robert Howe had been. Its leaders still refused to recruit additional Continentals. At one point after the surrender of Savannah, General Prevost had advanced into South Carolina, and the state's government panicked. They offered to drop out of the war and become neutrals if the British promised not to burn Charleston.

Nevertheless, on paper, d'Estaing had reason for confidence. He again had over 4,000 troops aboard his ships. With considerable reluctance the admiral agreed to take Lincoln's advice and begin a siege. The Americans expended huge effort to build roads and transport cannons from the warships to positions for an effective bombardment. For five days the big guns pounded the city. But the barrage did not produce an offer of surrender. Admiral d'Estaing grew impatient. His captains worried about the possibility of a wandering hurricane. Scurvy was rampaging through his fleet, killing thirty-five men a day.

The admiral overruled General Lincoln and ordered an assault at dawn on October 9, 1779. General Prevost had built rugged defenses in and around Savannah. He also had plenty of cannons. When the allies attacked, they encountered storms of grapeshot and musketry that killed several ranking officers. The British counterattacked and drove many French and Americans into nearby swamps. In one hour, the allies lost more than 1,000 troops. Admiral d'Estaing was wounded twice trying to rally his shaken men. Thoroughly disgusted, he retreated to his ships and sailed back to France. General Lincoln and his battered army retreated to Charleston, where anxiety became the emotion of the hour.[16]

⌢

IN NEW York the news of the failure of d'Estaing's siege of Savannah had an electrifying effect on General Clinton. He was particularly impressed when he learned how well numerous loyalists in General Prevost's army had fought. Clinton decided to commit a major part of his army to winning the war in the south. He described the victorious defense of Savannah as "the greatest event that has happened in the whole war. I need not say what will be our operations in consequence."[17]

The crudity of the French abandonment of General Lincoln and Admiral d'Estaing's departure for Europe sent the sinking Continental dollar into the abyss. In two months the cost of basic commodities such as wheat and beef doubled. The appalled Congress, face-to-face with bankruptcy, stopped printing money. By this time perhaps 200 million dubious paper dollars were in circulation. Washington was soon telling Congress and anyone else who would listen that it now took "a wagon load of money to buy a wagon load of provisions." His army began to run short of food.

Congress's solution to the crisis shrieked desperation. It ordered the states to stop printing money and start supplying the army "in kind." This meant that each state must ship tons of food over the awful roads of the day with neither money to pay wagon men nor forage for their horses. Washington warned, "Unless the states will . . . endow Congress with absolute powers in all matters relating to the great purposes of the war and of general concern . . . we are attempting an impossibility and very soon we shall become (if it is not already the case) a many headed monster."

⌢

HIS CONFIDENCE soaring, General Clinton withdrew the garrison from Newport and left New York on December 26, 1779, with 8,700 of his best troops. His destination was Charleston, South Carolina. Behind him in New York he left about 10,000 men under General

Wilhelm von Knyphausen, commander of the German troops in America. That was more than enough men to cope with Washington's army, which had shrunk to 9,000 men.[18]

On February 10, 1780, General Clinton's armada of ninety transports and ten warships appeared off Charleston. The South Carolina legislature immediately adjourned and gave Governor John Rutledge dictatorial powers to deal with the crisis. Rutledge loftily informed General Lincoln that he assumed nothing but "an invincible and extreme necessity" would induce the departmental commander to withdraw his Continental troops from the defense of the city, and "such a necessity will never exist."

Lincoln knew well that this thinking clashed with Washington's strategy of retaining at all costs a trained army to keep the Revolution alive and attract militia. In his New England heart, Lincoln disliked and even feared the criticism that this strategy had evoked. His fellow general, Arthur St. Clair, had been reviled and condemned for eighteen months after abandoning Fort Ticonderoga. Washington himself had endured similar obloquy in his dispute with Congress and with hostile generals such as Thomas Mifflin after the British captured Philadelphia.

Washington declined to give Lincoln any direct advice, even when his subordinate wrote plaintive letters, trying to decide what to do. The commander in chief remained determined to avoid further quarrels with Congress, who had appointed Lincoln without consulting him. Washington did his best to help by sending Lincoln additional regulars. Soon almost the entire Virginia Continental line was inside Charleston, joined by six hundred North Carolina Continentals. Washington hoped that with enough trained soldiers Lincoln might be more inclined to escape the city. Alas, instead Lincoln's determination to fight it out behind his fortifications only intensified, as the British army slowly surrounded Charleston.

Early in the siege General Lincoln made one attempt to adopt Washington's strategy. He sent General William Moultrie with a mixed force of Continental infantry and cavalry to Bacon's Bridge twenty miles west of Charleston to encourage militia to turn out and "hang on the enemy's flanks." But no militia materialized, and the venture was

soon abandoned. The reason for the failure is plain: even with the recent reinforcements, Clinton's host still drastically outnumbered Lincoln's army. Clinton also had a secret weapon: a cavalryman named
Banastre Tarleton who commanded a six-hundred-man legion that
stood ready to disperse any attempt to rally militia to help defend
Charleston.

This thick-shouldered, compact man of middle height with bright
red hair and a hard mouth would soon become the most feared and
hated British soldier in the south. In 1776 he had come to America, a
twenty-one-year-old cornet—the British equivalent of a second lieutenant. He was now a lieutenant colonel, a promotion so rapid for the
British army of the time that it left older officers frigid with jealousy.
Tarleton had achieved this spectacular rise almost entirely on raw courage and fierce energy. His father had been a wealthy merchant and lord
mayor of Liverpool. He died while Tarleton was at Oxford, leaving him
£5,000, which the young man promptly gambled and drank away while
ostensibly studying the law in London. He joined the army and discovered he was a born soldier.

In America, he was a star performer from the start. In 1778 he was
appointed brigade major of the British cavalry. After retreating from
Philadelphia, the new British commander, Sir Henry Clinton, gave Tarleton another promotion. Loyalists had begun volunteering in large
numbers, many forming troops of dragoons. Clinton decided to com-
bine these units into a 550-man force that he christened the British
Legion. He made Tarleton their commander. Half cavalry, half infantry,
a legion was designed to operate on the fringe of a main army as a
quick-strike force. Clinton issued them the green coats and tan breeches
worn by most loyalist regiments.

The situation spiraled downhill for Lincoln. The British siege lines
moved closer and closer to the American fortifications. Meanwhile
promised southern militiamen failed to show up. South Carolina
raised 2,000 part-timers, but they refused to enter the besieged city.
North Carolina promised 3,000, but only 1,000 appeared, and true to
militia form, in March, at the end of their term of enlistment, they
went home.

By April, Lincoln had 3,500 Continentals and about the same number of undependable militia and volunteers. Meanwhile, the British had received reinforcements from New York, raising their numbers to 10,000 men. The end became apparent when Banastre Tarleton surprised and smashed American cavalry guarding the last escape route from the city. The ring of guns and bayonets was now complete.[19]

Food supplies dwindled ominously. Clinton's artillery began bombarding civilian houses as well as the city's fortifications. One British officer noted in his diary the loud wail from women and children with every salvo. Soon a civilian committee was urging Lincoln to negotiate surrender terms. General Clinton had foreseen this moment. He remarked that he did not worry very much about more Continentals reinforcing Lincoln. He looked forward to capturing all of them. To prove his point, he subjected Charleston to a savage two-day bombardment. On May 12, 1780, Lincoln surrendered.

When the pathetically small American army marched out to lay down its guns, a British officer asked, "I take this, sir, to be your first division?" Lincoln replied, "This body, sir, contains my first and last division. They are all the troops I have." The following day, a search of the city turned up hundreds of militiamen who had been hiding out in barns and basements, avoiding the battle. A bitter General William Moultrie said, "It was three times the number of men we ever had on duty."[20]

Clinton's victory, the British and the loyalists quickly pointed out, more than equaled the surrender of Burgoyne's army. Sir Henry had captured not only more men but the fourth-largest city in the nation, the capital city of the south. Suddenly the momentum of the war had changed. As the news traveled north, loyalists and British and Hessian regulars rejoiced. They began talking about the American lands that a grateful king would bestow on them.

No one listened to these cheerful predictions more closely than the 10,000 men in the New York garrison. For the previous months, loyalists had been telling General Wilhelm von Knyphausen that when Charleston fell, he could and should attack Washington's shrunken American army and end the war. The stage was set for the ultimate test of Washington's strategy of victory.

CHAPTER 7

Lexington Repeated—with an Army to Look the Enemy in the Face

A cool night wind stirred the shallow waters of Newark Bay. It was close to midnight on June 8, 1780. Clouds cut off even the feeble light provided by the stars, making the darkness almost impenetrable. For the light infantrymen of the 37th and 38th British Regiments, sitting stiffly upright on the thwart seats of their attack flatboats, the total darkness was doubly unnerving. The high planked-up sides of the boats made them disconcerting craft. Even in daylight soldiers liked to see where they were going. Now, under the double weight of darkness and danger, they felt like living men in floating coffins.[1]

In the lead boats, guides with distinctively American accents gave muted directions to the sweating oarsmen. A few minutes later, to the light infantrymen's intense relief, they heard the hissing sound of marsh grass against the sides and bottoms of the boats. Oars were shipped and poles produced to shove the boats a final few dozen yards into the salt meadows that fringed the shore of Elizabethtown, New Jersey. Finally the grunting pole wielders swore they could not move the boats another foot. The planked-up sides were lowered and the men sprang out—to find themselves up to their knees in muck. Cursing eloquently—they had been issued generous rations of rum—and holding their bayonet-tipped muskets at shoulder height to keep them dry, they followed the American guides. After some fifty floundering yards, they at last found firm earth beneath their feet.

Now Brigadier Thomas Stirling, commander of the expedition, took charge. A tough, cool professional who had spent fifteen of the twenty previous years soldiering in America, he had been the first man out of the lead flatboat. Swiftly he sent one company of light infantrymen to probe a nearby orchard. Another company moved cautiously down a long, narrow pasture to the nearest road. If challenged, they had orders to use only their bayonets.[2]

Brigadier Stirling did not expect to encounter anyone. British raiding parties from Staten Island had so demoralized the Americans that they had practically abandoned posting sentries along the shore. Stirling waited until runners returned with reports that there was no sign of rebel Americans anywhere in their vicinity. He sent an aide mucking back across the salt marsh to summon the rest of the 37th and 38th Regiments, waiting offshore in forty flatboats. With them came Stirling's batman, leading his horse.

As soon as the flatboats had landed their human cargo, they pulled away for the Staten Island shore again. A half hour later they were back with the rest of Brigadier Stirling's division—two regiments of green-coated soldiers from the Duchy of Hesse-Cassel, led by Colonel Ludwig Johann Adolph von Wurmb, one of the toughest, cleverest young officers in the war.[3]

Faced with the American fondness for Indian-style skirmishing, von Wurmb had organized the light infantry companies of the German regiments into a separate corps and trained them to fight the Americans in their own manner. Two companies of these sharpshooters were with von Wurmb as he came ashore. By now Stirling had over 1,300 men in Elizabethtown, more than a match for anything the Americans had in the area.

Colonel von Wurmb was in high spirits; he looked forward to daybreak, when the full four-hundred-man Jaeger Corps would join him to fight for the first time in America under a German commander in chief. Lieutenant General Wilhelm von Knyphausen had issued the orders that sent Stirling and von Wurmb to this midnight rendezvous in Elizabethtown's marshes. Before the night was over, General von Knyphausen was to join them with another 4,500 troops. Their destination was Morristown, where, spies told them, the American army under George Washington had dwindled to a mere 3,500 sullen, mutinous men.

Destruction of Washington's army would provide an almost perfect complement to the news of Charleston's surrender. The rebellion would evaporate in New Jersey and in nearby states, just as it was withering in the south. Waiting in New York was the most famous loyalist in America, William Franklin, son of Benjamin Franklin, eager to resume his duties as royal governor of the Garden State. With the king's authority restored in this cockpit colony at the center of the rebellious thirteen, the rest of the revolution would soon fragment into diehard pockets that the British could mop up at leisure. General von Knyphausen would sail home as the conqueror of America.[4]

Brigadier Stirling did not share Colonel von Wurmb's enthusiasm for this scenario. He had no desire to make a hero out of "Old Knyp," as the British (and Americans) called the trim, erect Hessian martinet. Stirling considered the expedition a dangerous, pointless adventure. As the commandant of Staten Island, he knew more about the dwindling rebellion than any other officer in the British army. Loyalists on his intelligence payroll rowed back and forth across the narrow waters of Arthur Kill constantly, bringing him the latest news. Their reports convinced Stirling the rebellion would collapse from bankruptcy and internal discord in a few months.[5] Why waste men, money, and horses to destroy an army that was about to fall apart?

In fact, Stirling feared that attacking Washington's regulars might revive their fighting spirit. The same principle applied to the amateur soldiers of New Jersey—the militia—which, on paper, amounted to 16,000 part-time troops. But Stirling had swallowed his doubts and opinions and was obeying Knyphausen's orders. By sunrise he was supposed to be seven miles northwest of Elizabethtown in firm possession of both the town of Springfield and Hobart Gap, a crucial pass that ran through the heart of the Watchung Mountains—better known even then as the Short Hills. Hobart Gap was the doorway to

Morristown, eleven miles away across flat terrain, made to order for the steamroller tactics that the British army executed so well.

∽

THE REPORTS of imminent American disintegration brought by loyalists to Stirling and Knyphausen were not exaggerated. Thirteen days before Stirling and von Wurmb landed on the Elizabethtown shore, the entire Connecticut Continental brigade had mutinied at Morristown and attempted to march home to the Nutmeg State. Only the leveled muskets of regiments from other states had stopped them.[6]

For months George Washington had been warning his supporters in the Continental Congress that his army was on the point of dissolution. He told one congressman that his men were eating "every kind of horse food but hay." For days at a time the men lived on a sickening compound of buckwheat, rye, and Indian corn, which they pounded into "firecakes" and heated on their crude stoves. Clothing was in equally short supply. One captain wrote a friend, "Many a good lad has nothing to cover him from his hips to his toes save his blanket."[7]

Shortages of food and clothing were not new in the Continental Army. The country's apparent indifference to their plight, however, enraged the soldiers and depressed Washington and his officers. Quartermaster General Nathanael Greene looked out his window at the snowbound army on January 4, 1780, and exclaimed, "Poor fellows . . . more than half naked and two thirds starved. A country overflowing with plenty are now suffering an army employed for the defence of everything that is dear and valuable to perish for want of food."[8]

To compound Washington's woes, the 1779–1780 winter was the coldest in living memory. The Hudson River froze so solidly that cannons weighing a ton or more were towed across it. For a full week the temperature hovered at or below zero. Frostbite disabled dozens of men on sentry duty. Many of the soldiers began trying to desert the starving army legally. They swore they had enlisted for three years and their time was up. A number of men in New Jersey's regiments demanded hearings with the chief justice of the state. He passed the buck to the New Jersey legislature. An alarmed Washington warned New Jersey's governor,

William Livingston, that if they went ahead with the proposed hearings, the military system "would be nearly unhinged."

Still, Washington refused to abandon the tough discipline of a regular army. On the day after the near mutiny of the Connecticut brigade, fifty men from each regiment mustered at the grand parade ground in Morristown. Soon eleven condemned deserters appeared, with drummers and fifers playing the dead march before them. After letting them shiver in expectation of doom for a few minutes, Washington pardoned all but one, convicted of forging discharges that enabled at least one hundred men to desert without fear of retaliation when they reached home.[9]

The next day, Colonel Elias Dayton, commander of the 3rd New Jersey Regiment, stationed in Elizabethtown, sent Washington a copy of James Rivington's *Royal Gazette*, which featured the news of Charleston's surrender. Dayton added a note hoping the story was a fake. A glum Washington replied that it bore "too many marks of authenticity" and urged Dayton to be on his guard. There was a good chance that the British, looking to build on the momentum of this victory, would "make an attempt on you."[10]

Dayton could do little to act on Washington's warning. American security in Elizabethtown had all but collapsed. Every second man seemed to have drifted toward some sort of accommodation with the British. Dayton had withdrawn his regiment to the town of Springfield, twenty miles inland. James Caldwell, the outspoken pastor of the Presbyterian Church in Elizabethtown, had retreated with his family to the nearby village of Connecticut Farms. But Dayton himself, with a handful of soldiers to give him a semblance of protection, continued to spend most of his days and nights in Elizabethtown.

On the night of June 6, Dayton was in his house when a furtive figure came to his front door and handed him a note. The message, from an American spy on Staten Island, warned that the British had massed 5,000 troops near the New Jersey shore. Dayton summoned nineteen-year-old Moses Ogden, an ensign (second lieutenant) in the 4th New Jersey Regiment, and ordered him to take twelve men to the crossroads where two main roads from the shore met. If he saw any British, he was to give them one "fire" and retreat.

Dayton and the men of his 3rd New Jersey Regiment would wait for Ogden in the center of Elizabethtown, where he hoped to make a stand on some high ground known as Jelf's Hill. Ogden marched his men on the double to the crossroads and deployed them in a pasture on the left side of the road. For an hour they heard nothing but wind sighing through the marsh grass.

Suddenly everyone recognized the tramp of marching feet. A large black blur that could only be a man on a horse emerged from the darkness. Beside him walked guides carrying dark lanterns that shed no light ahead—only behind. Their glow illuminated gleaming belt buckles, white crossbands, and shiny muskets by the dozen. Ensign Ogden told his men to aim at the man on horseback. "Fire," he growled.

Twelve muskets erupted simultaneously with a blast of flame and a great gush of white smoke. Ogden and his men whirled and ran. Behind them they could hear excited shouts and cries and a barked order followed by repeated volleys of musketry. Not a ball came close to them. In ten minutes they came panting into the center of Elizabethtown to be challenged by Colonel Dayton's sentries. Ogden told Dayton he had just seen the 5,000-man army reported in the spy's letter.[11]

Colonel Dayton ordered his son, Captain Jonathan Dayton, to rush a note to General Washington in Morristown. Minutes later the horseman was on the road. The message read,

> *Sir:*
> *I am directed by Colo. Dayton to inform your excellency that the enemy landed this night at 12 o'clock, from the best intellegence four or five thousand men and twelve field pieces, & it is his conjecture they intend to penetrate into the country.*[12]

⌒

BACK AT the crossroads, the front ranks of the British column milled around Brigadier General Thomas Stirling in wild confusion. A musket ball had smashed the general's thigh. He lay on his back in the road, almost delirious with pain, while the surgeons of the 37th and 38th

Regiments worked on him. A tourniquet stopped the bleeding, but the general was clearly out of action, probably for the rest of the war.

Colonel von Wurmb, marching with the German troops, joined the disorganized crowd at the crossroads to murmur his sympathy. Through teeth clenched with pain, Stirling handed the command over to him. The brigadier was lifted onto an improvised litter and carried down the road to Elizabethtown Point, where the rest of the army was supposed to land.

Stirling's fate shook von Wurmb. He decided not to move another step into Elizabethtown until daylight gave him something to shoot at. He knew how easily soldiers could panic when attacked in the darkness. Up in the acrid gun smoke from Moses Ogden's muskets went the plan to seize Hobart Gap before dawn.

On Jelf's Hill in Elizabethtown, Colonel Dayton prepared for a desperate defense. He knew it was madness to make a stand in the center of the town. Not only would he and his handful of men probably be wiped out, but much of Elizabethtown might be destroyed. Yet he was ready to make the sacrifice to give Washington time to move the main army from Morristown to the Short Hills.

A huge horseman came pounding down the road from Newark to solve Dayton's problem. Major Aaron Ogden, uncle of Ensign Moses Ogden, was aide de camp to General William Maxwell, commander of the New Jersey brigade. He had been asleep beside Maxwell in brigade headquarters in Bound Brook when he heard the gunfire of his nephew's patrol. Major Ogden had been on his horse within minutes, riding toward the sound of the guns.[13]

"Scotch Willie" Maxwell had probably called a warning after him. The last time this big, reckless son of Elizabethtown had ridden toward a British raid, he had cantered alone down a road into the marshes and found himself surrounded by an enemy patrol. Ignoring their demand to surrender, he had wheeled his horse and dashed for freedom. He made it—but not before a British bayonet sank deep into his chest.

Everyone assumed the wound was mortal. But the twenty-four-year-old giant had been tenderly nursed by the women of Elizabethtown—so tenderly by one of them, pretty Elizabeth Chetwood, that they had fallen in love and were now engaged.

The commander of the 4th New Jersey Regiment, Colonel Oliver Spencer, some of whose men had rallied with Dayton's soldiers on Jelf's Hill, joined Ogden and Dayton for a tense conference. Could the rest of the brigade join them here? Not without an exhausting march, Ogden pointed out. Moreover, even if they arrived in time, they would still be little more than 600 men, counting sergeants, corporals, and commissioned officers; 205 of the brigade's 741 men were sick or on detached duty. Better to fall back and obey two prime military maxims: concentrate your force and seize the high ground.

The nearest high ground was in the village of Connecticut Farms, where a branch of the Elizabeth River had dug a long, narrow ravine. The two regiments with General Maxwell in Bound Brook could easily join them there.[14] Colonel Dayton was not convinced. He hated to abandon Elizabethtown, where he had a handsome house to lose to British torches. But he decided to get his men off Jelf's Hill and fall back to the edge of town, near Governor William Livingston's mansion, Liberty Hall.

There, about an hour later, Scotch Willie himself joined him. The brigadier had already made up his mind. Defending Elizabethtown made no sense militarily. The men of the 1st and 2nd New Jersey Regiments were on the march to Connecticut Farms. He told Dayton and Spencer to join them there.

It was not an easy decision for Maxwell to make. He was abandoning Liberty Hall, the house of his good friend, Governor William Livingston, to the enemy. As Dayton's men filed down the road toward Connecticut Farms, the crusty Scot rode into the yard of Liberty Hall and awoke the Livingston family. As usual, the governor was not at home. He had not slept in this house for several years. Maxwell suggested that Mrs. Livingston and her two daughters, Susan and Kitty, depart for the interior of the state. But they decided to stay, hoping to preserve the house from random burning and looting. Only the governor's son, William, knowing the British fondness for carting male rebels off to New York prisons, decided he would be safer with Maxwell.[15]

As the young man and the old soldier rode into the night, Scotch Willie's usually dour face was extraordinarily grim. How could 600 men make a stand against 5,000? The American army had only one hope for survival: the New Jersey militia.

Maxwell barked an order, and a horseman raced for Hobart Mountain in Springfield. On this highest hump of the Short Hills stood a wooden pyramid, some eighteen feet square at the bottom and twenty feet high, the center filled with dry brush. Beside it stood a squat mortar, affectionately known as "the Old Sow."[16]

The men guarding this equipment were awakened in their nearby houses and told what to do. As soon as they saw the British and Germans emerge from the northwestern outskirts of Elizabethtown—it would be easy enough to spot the red and blue column winding through the green fields—they were to ignite the fire signal and put the Old Sow to work. But they were not to alarm the countryside until they had unmistakable proof that the British were moving inland.

General Maxwell knew his militiamen. It was a mistake to summon them unnecessarily. The next time, when the emergency was real, they would not come. Scotch Willie no doubt wondered how the militia would react to this call after a winter of having their farms stripped by Continental Army commissary officers who gave them nothing more valuable than a certificate, payable at some future date, for their cattle, grain, and forage. Even more important was the question of whether the militia would stand and fight a full-scale invasion. Would they—could they—face 5,000 trained regulars?

Under laws passed by the thirteen state governments, militia companies were supposed to meet regularly and learn the essentials of soldiering. Above all, they were supposed to practice the difficult art of loading and firing a musket swiftly. But it was hard to get politicians to pass laws that guaranteed regular performance of this training duty. Washington and his generals repeatedly begged for a New Jersey law with teeth, but Governor Livingston could never persuade the legislature to pass one.

The legislators' timidity disgusted the acerbic Livingston. Earlier in the war, he had told his son-in-law, John Jay, that the New Jersey Assembly, "after having spent as much time in framing a militia bill as Alexander would have required to subdue Persia, will at last make such a ridiculous business of it, as not to oblige a single man to turn out who can only bring him[self] to consume three gallons of . . . Toddy per annum less than he does at present." The governor was referring to the small fine the legislature imposed on the militiamen who refused to report for duty.[17] Even these fines were seldom collected. The failure to pass a tough militia law was one more illustration of the precarious condition of the Revolution in New Jersey.

Largely thanks to Livingston the New Jersey militia had, on paper at least, an effective organization. When the legislature failed to pass a decent law, Livingston and his thirteen-man executive council took charge of the situation. The council met at least once a month, and in times of emergency much more often. During the first six months of 1780, it had met forty-seven times.[18]

In May 1780, it issued a two-page document, "Alarm Posts and Places of Rendezvous of the Militia of New Jersey," which carefully spelled out where the regiments were to gather when an alarm sounded. The colonels north of the Raritan River were to assemble at the Short Hills. If the enemy advanced into the country, they were to "endeavour to keep on one or both flanks and as near their front as possible and to keep up a constant Fire with small Parties in different places." If the enemy pushed toward the mountains and seemed inclined to penetrate them, the colonel in command was to possess himself of the gap they moved toward and give them all the annoyance and obstruction in his power.

Note the realistic nature of these instructions. There is no exhortation to fight the British army to a standstill or drive them into Raritan Bay. They were obviously written after consultation with that veteran student of how to use militia in concert with a regular army, the governor's good friend General Washington.

When the British retreated from Philadelphia in 1778, Washington had put Maxwell in charge of the New Jersey militia. They had done a good job of harrying the enemy's line of march until the pursuing

Continentals caught up with them at Monmouth Court House. There, on June 28, 1778, the Continentals proved they could equal and even best the British in a toe-to-toe slugfest. But Washington's army had numbered 13,503 officers and men at Monmouth. Now, two long, discouraging years later, it numbered 3,760.[19] As Elias Dayton and Scotch Willie Maxwell fell back toward Connecticut Farms, both knew that the militia and Washington's thin line of Continentals were about to face a supreme test.

DOWN AT Elizabethtown Point, the rest of Lieutenant General Knyphausen's army was coming ashore in five "divisions," each about 1,300 men. Colonel von Wurmb's four regiments, still hesitating at the crossroads, made up the 1st Division. Major General Edward Mathew, who had led a devastatingly successful raid against Portsmouth, Virginia, in the late spring of 1779, commanded the 2nd Division. In his charge were two more veteran British regiments, the 22nd and the 57th. With them came two regiments whose troops did not wear red coats and white cross belts; their coats were green, and they fought under an American commander, William Franklin's close friend Brigadier Cortlandt Skinner, former attorney general of New Jersey. They were the 1st and 4th New Jersey Volunteers—"Skinner's Greens"[20]—every man a loyalist fighting to regain property he had forfeited in the cockpit state because of his devotion to the king.

Other regiments coming ashore with Knyphausen included the 43rd, which had fought at Quebec under James Wolfe and at Bunker Hill under General William Howe, as well as a battalion each of the Scots Guards and the Coldstream Guards. These were elite troops.

General von Knyphausen arrived with the 3rd Division. He grew alarmed as the night slipped away and fully half his army was still on Staten Island. As the tide ran out, the men found themselves sinking up to their thighs in marsh mud. The engineers had to build two bridges down to the water's edge. It soon became obvious that the 4th and 5th Divisions, mostly German troops and a regiment of British cavalry, the 17th Light Dragoons, would not get over before daybreak.[21]

The trim, stiffly erect German general had another worry on his mind. He had been reluctant to launch this expedition without orders from the British commander in chief, Sir Henry Clinton. Only strenuous persuasion from New York's loyalists, who fanned his envy of Clinton, had persuaded him to take the gamble. At 3:00 P.M. the previous day, Clinton's shadow had suddenly intruded on the operation—in the person of his aide-de-camp, Major William Crosbie.[22]

With shaky fingers, Major William Beckwith, Knyphausen's aide, who had been instrumental in talking him into the expedition, ripped open Sir Henry's dispatches. As he read them, he relaxed. They contained no orders. Beckwith swiftly summarized them for Knyphausen, who neither read nor spoke a word of English. Sir Henry was telling them what they already knew: he had captured Charleston at very small cost.

Among the generals, irritation replaced alarm. As usual, Clinton was telling them nothing of his plans. Everyone turned on Crosbie, testily asking about Sir Henry's intentions. Was he returning to New York with the Carolina army? Was he planning a strike into the Chesapeake? What sort of summer campaign did he have in mind?

Major Crosbie was nonplused. He was on the stickiest wicket that any aide-de-camp ever encountered in the history of warfare. Sir Henry had indeed told him his plans—but enjoined him to strictest secrecy. Crosbie would give Knyphausen only "hints."[23]

In fact, Sir Henry had a very good plan for ending the war within a few days after his return from Charleston. Clinton was a gifted military planner and thinker. If the British had taken his advice at Bunker Hill, the Revolution might have ended on June 17, 1775. He had suggested to Sir William Howe the flanking movement that enabled the British to thrash Washington at the battle of Brooklyn on August 27, 1776. In 1777, Sir Henry had urged Howe not to abandon General John Burgoyne and his army in northern New York, advice that, if followed, would have averted disaster and might have turned those three sevens into gibbets as loyalist believers in the Year of the Hangman hoped.

In his memoirs of the war, Clinton revealed the plan the agonized Crosbie had in his head. The moment the fleet from Charleston arrived at Sandy Hook—it was already en route—Clinton intended to land the 4,000 men he had with him at Perth Amboy. Knyphausen was to land at Elizabethtown Point with 6,000 men. "The two corps," Clinton wrote, "marching immediately in concert . . . might have a fair chance of reducing the enemy's general to the hazardous dilemma of either moving out against one or the other, or exposing himself to the united attacks of both by staying in his camp."

The Americans would have faced two armies, each stronger than their half-starved, desertion-riddled brigades. Moreover, the geography of New Jersey improved Clinton's plan's likelihood of success. From Amboy the road to Morristown ran through Mordecai's Gap, an opening in the mountains at least as large and inviting as Hobart Gap. The chances were very good that Clinton could seize one or both of these doorways and descend on Morristown, where the American army's artillery and stores sat marooned because General Washington had neither horses nor the forage to feed them.

Fortunately for the Americans, Sir Henry Clinton had a fatal flaw as a general: a pathological, neurotic suspicion of his fellow generals. This was why he seldom committed a plan to writing. If anything went wrong, he would bear responsibility for the failure. So he preferred oral plans and orders that he called "hints."

This policy now left Crosbie in an impossible position. He had been told to reveal the plan only to those he thought "proper."[24] But he had no time to sort out the numerous generals now demanding to know the truth. Crosbie floundered and flapped and finally blurted out something vague. From it Knyphausen and company gathered that Sir Henry was going to raid the Chesapeake, leaving them on their own in New Jersey. The relieved Knyphausen invited Crosbie to join the expedition. Before the night was over, Crosbie found himself splashing through the marshes on Staten Island to board a New Jersey–bound flatboat.[25]

⌒

MEANWHILE, COLONEL von Wurmb and the men of the 1st Division were moving through the silent, empty streets of Elizabethtown toward its northwestern outskirts. They passed the charred hulks of the court-house and the Presbyterian church, burnt by earlier raiders, and swung west across a stone bridge over the narrow, muddy Elizabeth River. There they headed north on Galloping Hill Road toward Connecticut Farms.

At about 6:00 A.M. the head of the column approached Liberty Hall, Governor Livingston's mansion. Alone before the front door stood a solitary figure in white, the governor's daughter Susan. Colonel von Wurmb, who had a reputation for being as gallant in love as he was courageous in battle, cantered up the driveway to doff his hat and ex-change a few words with her. She begged him not to destroy Liberty Hall. Von Wurmb was an easy target for Susan's tear-filled eyes and plaintive voice. He not only vowed he had no intention of burning the house but said he would post a guard at the door to make sure no one looted it.

Colonel von Wurmb asked Susan if she could give him a small token of her esteem. She pointed to a trellis of bright red "blaze roses" beside the porch. The German colonel plucked one of these flowers, which still bloom in profusion in New Jersey, and put it in his hat. Softly, Susan told him she could not, as a good American, wish him victory, but she hoped that the flower would protect him from the bullets.[26]

Ahead of von Wurmb as he resumed the advance was a well-tilled countryside that more than justified New Jersey's nickname, the Garden of America. Flax and oats were eight inches high in the fields. Every farm had at least one sizable orchard of apple or cherry trees. Beside them were green and glowing stretches of lush pasture. Many of the farmhouses were built of red brick, testifying to the wealth derived from this fruitful soil.[27]

Sunlight filled the balmy June morning. Birds called sleepily from the fruit trees. The fertile fields stood empty and still. But not for long. A musket cracked, and a soldier stumbled out of Colonel von Wurmb's column, clutching his arm. A barefoot figure in loose, flapping clothes sprang from behind a haystack in a nearby pasture and bolted for the horizon. Cursing, the colonel ordered the flank companies of the 37th and 38th Regiments into the fields on either side of the column. One of the loyalist American guides trudging beside von Wurmb pointed up the road, where more figures in loose homespun were running toward an orchard. Before von Wurmb could decide what to do about them, a great echoing boom drifted across the green countryside. It was the Old Sow on Hobart Mountain, sounding the alarm and signaling the militia to report for duty.

Twice more the big mortar boomed. A moment later von Wurmb saw a huge blaze begin to glow on the mountaintop. The loyalist guide pointed to the northwest. There, atop the angular ridge known as Newark Mountain, another stupendous blaze leapt skyward. Yet another sprang up to the south, in the neighborhood of Mordecai's Gap. Colonel von Wurmb must have wondered where General von Knyphausen got the idea that these Americans were ready to surrender.[28]

In MORRISTOWN, the American army came to life with alacrity. George Washington had been writing a letter to his younger brother, Jack, when Colonel Dayton's message arrived sometime after midnight. He was advising Jack not to sell his land because the country's paper money was worthless. He condemned Congress, speculators, and the "disaffected" (loyalists) as contributors to this malaise.[29] The news of the British invasion put an abrupt end to the general's diatribe. He shrugged on his dark blue coat with its buff lapels and plain gilt buttons and began giving orders.

Alexander Hamilton and other aides tumbled from their beds. Drums rolled to awaken the 156 men of the Life Guards, who protected the commander in chief. In a moment the officer of the day and his staff were racing to Jockey Hollow, three miles away, where the army was encamped. Soon regimental drummers were thumping an early reveille. By 4:00 A.M. marching orders were written. Two days' provisions were issued with orders to cook them immediately.[30] Each man got forty rounds of ammunition—twenty fewer than the British allowance. But Americans were trained to aim and fire more carefully.

Aides feverishly scratched out letters. One of the first went to a man who shared Scotch Willie Maxwell's talent for leading militia: Major

General William Alexander, better known as Lord Stirling, thanks to his claim to a Scottish title. Washington's letter made clear that he too understood how to use militia. He told Stirling he did not yet know whether this was a foraging raid or an attempt to assault "our camp." In either case, the major general was to "collect the militia to give them all the opposition in our power." He told Stirling to sound the alarm as extensively as he could in his vicinity and to march the men he gathered to skirmish on the British left flank. Other letters went to commanders of Continental detachments in Paramus and elsewhere, ordering them to gather militia and march them to the battle zone, along with their regulars.

On his well-tilled farm in Morris County, Sylvanus Seeley, colonel of the eastern Morris County militia regiment, saddled his mare and rode for the rendezvous assigned to them, the town of Chatham, at the western foot of the Short Hills.[31] Frederick Freylinghuysen of nearby Somerset County started rounding up his regiment. In the little village of Lyons Farms, schoolmaster Darling Beach was preparing his morning lessons when he heard the alarm guns. He tacked a scribbled note, "School closed for the day," on the door of his schoolhouse and joined a half dozen other men racing for Elizabethtown.[32]

From Newark came another group of militiamen eager to avenge themselves for numerous British raids in the winter of 1780. They were led by Major Samuel Hayes, whom the militia called "Old Bark Knife." In their ranks was a husky black man, known only as Cudjo, formerly owned by a Newarker named Coe. Cudjo had entered the militia as a substitute for his master. He had fought so well at the battle of Monmouth that Coe gave him his freedom and an acre of farmland.

Inside Elizabethtown, the guns awakened other young men who were equally eager to fight. One of these was Jonathan Crane, the twenty-six-year-old son of Mayor Stephen Crane. His older brother William was a major in the New Jersey brigade. He had been badly wounded in the assault on Quebec in 1775.[33]

An unlikely combatant was Captain Nathaniel FitzRandolph of Woodbridge. He had just been released from a British prison where the sadistic provost marshal, William Cunningham, had starved and beaten him. Despite his physical weakness, FitzRandolph mustered his company and marched toward the sound of the guns.[34]

Elsewhere in Morris County, eighteen-year-old Ashbel Green seized his musket and rushed to the muster site. Although his father was a minister of the gospel, Green was wholly converted to the martial spirit. In the months before his sixteenth birthday, when he would be able to join his local militia company, he had spent hours drilling with a wooden gun.

About sixty militiamen gathered in an orchard up the Galloping Hill Road from Governor Livingston's mansion. These were the men Colonel von Wurmb spotted as he returned from his tête-à-tête with Susan Livingston. Among them was Jonathan Crane, the mayor's son. His house was only a few hundred yards away on the outskirts of Elizabethtown.

Muskets boomed in the morning sunshine, and deadly one-ounce balls whined through the summery air. Several militia bullets hit home. Red-coated figures toppled and lay still in the wet grass. Others stumbled to the rear, clutching shattered arms or legs. Not many men could stay in a fight after being hit by a musket bullet. But the rest of the light infantry companies kept coming, firing as they advanced.

As soon as their commanding officer saw they were fighting militia, he bellowed, "Fix bayonets." With a flash of burnished steel the sixteen-inch blades clicked into position on the sockets at the end of the forty-four-inch musket barrels. "Charge!" roared the captain.

Howling ferociously, the light infantrymen raced across the grass toward the orchard. Most of the militiamen ran for their lives. The British yell was as terrifying in its own way as an Indian war whoop. A few who had reloaded their muskets stayed to fire one more shot and then ran. A handful stood their ground. One of these was Jonathan Crane. As he frantically tried to reload for a third shot, a light infantryman sank his bayonet to the hilt into his chest. Two or three other militiamen died in the same swift, brutal way. If anyone tried to surrender, he met the same fate. At this point in the war, the British loathed militiamen far more than Continentals. The amateurs' fondness for sneak attacks and ambushes led the Royal Army to classify them as murderers.

The column resumed its march, with the flank companies sweeping the fields on both sides. In another quarter mile the British encountered New Jersey's Continentals. There were no more heroics of the sort that had ended in tragedy for Jonathan Crane and his militia company. The Continentals would fire a volley and immediately break and run for the next natural obstacle—an orchard or thicket or thorny hedge. The regulars knew how to manage a fighting retreat. A few men always held their fire when they fell back. They waited behind trees and fences while their friends ran past them. While the others reloaded, the first group blazed away at the oncoming redcoats.

But the red and blue column, its flankers spread through the fields ahead of it like the antennae of a huge insect, came steadily forward. The green slopes of the Short Hills grew closer. Just beyond them was Hobart Gap, the door to Morristown.

〜

IN THE village of Connecticut Farms, Scotch Willie Maxwell and the New Jersey brigade prepared for action. Halfway between the Short Hills and Elizabethtown, "the Farms," as it was called, was a pleasant place of about twenty-five houses scattered among pastures and orchards for over two miles on both sides of Galloping Hill Road. At the eastern border of the town was a ravine full of bushes and thickets. Scotch Willie posted some of his regulars in the center of this "defile," as he called it, and stationed militiamen on their flanks.[35]

While the fighting men checked their flints and cartridges, most of the Farms' civilians piled belongings into wagons and prepared to flee. Among these fugitives was the Reverend James Caldwell. As the "Rebel High Priest" of New Jersey, famed for his defiant sermons, he was near the top of the British wanted list. But he could not persuade his wife, Hannah, to join him. A cousin of the Ogdens in the New Jersey brigade and a fervent patriot, she insisted on staying, à la Susan Livingston, to prevent the British from burning their house. She had recently given birth to a child and feared that hours in a jouncing wagon might dry up her milk.[36] She assured her husband that God would protect her.

Unable to argue against such determination and faith, Caldwell left her and their younger children behind and rode west to rally the militia in Morris County.[37] As he departed, the firing on Galloping Hill Road grew closer. Soon the panting Continentals and militia who had been fighting the delaying action joined the men waiting in the ravine. It was about 8:00 A.M. Militiamen coming from the west side of the Short Hills reported that Washington's army had not yet left Morristown. That meant they could not reach the battlefield before noon. If they were going to stop the British short of Hobart Gap, it was up to the New Jersey Continentals and militia to do the job.[38]

The American position had one alarming defect. The Vauxhall Road forked from Galloping Hill Road and looped around the left flank of the American position, exposing the defenders to encirclement. Maxwell detached several companies to block this route. Meanwhile he assigned Major Aaron Ogden to work with the militia to harass the enemy's flanks along the Galloping Hill Road. The mixture of woods and orchards in the village gave them better cover than they had had in the open country beyond Elizabethtown.

More than a few militiamen dodged into empty houses and began firing from their windows. The British blasted back, and soon flying lead and shattered glass filled the air. A bullet struck one of the few civilians who stayed behind, a man named Ball, in the head as he watched the British come up the road. A few minutes later, the two British and two German regiments opened ranks and went up the hill to the defile in battle formation. There, Colonel von Wurmb sent his flankers and his two Jaeger companies swarming into the defile.[39]

A ferocious firefight erupted, swaying back and forth in the ravine, which soon became shrouded in gun smoke. In the eighteenth century, these shifts in momentum were called "drives." As attackers saw comrades falling around them, they tended to run out of steam. Similarly, defenders would melt toward the rear when their casualties rose. The action really consisted of a series of small combats between companies and platoons and even individuals.

For the next three hours the battle raged back and forth, with von Wurmb feeding in more and more men. He apparently thought he was only fighting militia and that applying pressure would eventually clear the road. It seems never to have occurred to him to send a regiment driving up the Vauxhall Road to threaten Maxwell's rear. Soon the whole four-hundred-man Jaeger corps had reached the scene, and von Wurmb fed them into the fight.

Toward the end of the morning, the Americans surged forward, militia and Continentals blending, to drive the British and Germans out of the ravine and back down Galloping Hill Road, where they met General Mathew and the 2nd Division of the army. In a few minutes the king's men surged forward again. This time Mathew led a flank attack up the Vauxhall Road, while the rest poured into the ravine. Soon their numbers and momentum had cleared this obstacle course of Americans. Among the dead left by the Jerseymen was young Moses Ogden, the ensign whose men had blasted General Stirling off his horse and wrecked the British timetable.

Now the Americans turned the rest of Connecticut Farms into a battleground, fighting from house to house. But the pressure from the oncoming British was soon impossible to withstand. The 3rd Division, containing the elite British Guards, arrived to join the fight, along with several German regiments. They were in a nasty mood. One of the German officers later wrote that they had had "two engagements" en route to Connecticut Farms. The militia were swarming up from Rahway River and down from Newark to harass their line of march.

The marchers would have had a much easier time of it if the 17th Dragoons had been with them. But the British quartermaster department did not get the horses across the water to the frustrated cavalrymen until 2:00 P.M.[40] Meanwhile the Americans slowly retreated to the western end of Connecticut Farms. There, Maxwell decided he now had enough militiamen—they were pouring in from western New Jersey—to counterattack. "The whole brigade," he later reported, "with the militia advanced to their right left and front with the greatest rapidity and drove their advance to the main body."[41]

But Knyphausen, knowing he still had numbers and training in his favor, declined to panic. He threw the Jaegers into the American center, and as the rebels recoiled—their advance had been slower than that of the men on the flanks—the Jaeger flank companies wheeled and poured a deadly blast of bullets into the American right, while two light infantry and two grenadier companies joined the attack in the center.[42]

Now it was the Americans' turn to be driven. Perhaps at this moment Captain Isaac Reeves of the Essex County militia went down with a bullet in his chest. His grieving men carried him out of the fight and over the Short Hills to Chatham, hoping to find a Continental Army doctor there. They arrived in the town just as General George Washington and his staff cantered down the main street. Washington spoke to the wounded man and ordered an army doctor to take care of him. But in a few hours he was dead.[43]

Many other Americans died in this British counterattack. But the militia used the heavily wooded hills around Connecticut Farms to filter back into the fight and snipe from behind houses and barns. By the time the fighting swirled around Hannah Caldwell's home, it had rubbed British nerves raw. Every house represented a potential ambush. The king's men had to check and clear each one as they fought past it to make sure no one would shoot them in the back.

Hannah Caldwell retreated to the rear of her house into a room with stone walls on three sides and only a single window. She realized there was a very good chance of musket bullets from either side flying wild. As she sat on the bed, her three-year-old son ran to the window to see the excitement. So did his nurse, a young girl named Abigail Lemmington.

Mrs. Caldwell urged both to get away from the window. Retreating, Abigail saw a short, squat soldier come around the back of the house and move toward the window. The light infantryman with two bullets in his musket probably caught a glimpse of Abigail as she moved away from the window. In the bright sunlight, he saw only a shadow. He didn't need to see more. He pulled his trigger, and the two bullets crashed through the window and struck Hannah Caldwell. She fell back on the bed, dead.

The rest of the British squad rushed the front door. They came thundering through the house, bayonets ready. It was army policy to kill anyone caught sniping from ambush. They found only a wailing Abigail

Lemmington, sobbing children, and Hannah Caldwell's bleeding corpse. That did not stop them from looting and smashing up the place.[44]

By this time the main battle line had reached the western edge of Connecticut Farms. Not far beyond it was a bridge over the Rahway River and the village of Springfield, which lay at the eastern base of the Short Hills. Second Lieutenant Samuel Seeley of the 1st New Jersey Regiment rallied his company to make a stand at the bridge. He stood erect, calmly pointing out targets among the oncoming Germans and British. A musket ball hit him in the shoulder. Blood soon soaked his shirt, but he refused to retreat. He continued to exhort his men to defend the bridge.[45]

The sheer weight of the British advance pressed the Americans back to the banks of the Rahway. Fearful of a rout, Maxwell ordered a retreat to the west side of the river. Lieutenant Seeley and his men were among the last to obey the order. It left the British in possession of Connecticut Farms—but still a long way from Hobart Gap.

Knyphausen's men had already paid a heavy price. The Jaegers alone had lost fifty-nine men, over 10 percent of their regiment.[46] Americans reported eighteen wagons on the road to Elizabethtown, filled with groaning wounded and silent dead. Knyphausen let his men take savage revenge on the Farms. They looted and smashed up every house, sparing not a window. They cut down no less than four hundred apple trees in one orchard and burned every house and the Presbyterian church.

The sight of the town in flames enraged the Americans on the other side of the Rahway River. Many swarmed across the bridge and began another round of savage skirmishing with Knyphausen's advance units. Scotch Willie Maxwell let them go. Even if they got chased back across the bridge, he now had something to fall back on. A messenger had just informed him that the Continental Army was in Chatham, and the Pennsylvania and Connecticut brigades were in possession of Hobart Gap. Up and down the American line went the word: "Washington is here." It gave the mostly militia skirmishers fresh nerve and energy.[47]

As the day dwindled, Knyphausen showed no interest in fighting his way across the Rahway. He seemed content to fend off the skirmishers and reduce Connecticut Farms to rubble. One reason was the exhaustion of many of his troops. Fully half of them had been up all night and had spent a long, hot day marching and fighting. The Americans were almost as worn out. Schoolmaster Darling Beach collapsed from heat stroke and had to be carried home unconscious to his distraught parents.[48]

Washington was soon conferring with Maxwell on the west side of the Rahway. The burning of Connecticut Farms angered him also. To support the militia, he sent his Life Guards,[49] picked troops, all over six feet, into action with them. They attacked the battered Jaegers just before sunset and sent them stumbling back to the main army. Knyphausen decided to retreat to high ground two and a half miles northwest of Connecticut Farms and give his men a night's rest. The militia continued to snipe at his picket guards until darkness fell.

Meanwhile, at a house owned by a man named Whitehead, Washington conferred with Maxwell and other generals. The American commander was worried. The militia and the New Jersey Continentals had fought the British and Germans to a standstill. But what about tomorrow? If willing to pay the price, Knyphausen had the manpower to batter his way through Hobart Gap. Even more grim was the possibility that the German general was acting under orders from Sir Henry Clinton, who might well arrive from Charleston tomorrow morning with his victorious army. This would give the British overwhelming numbers of regulars.

Unaware of the jealousy and noncommunication rampant in the British high command, Washington could only assume that Knyphausen would never have made such a daring move without explicit orders from Clinton. All of this added up, in Washington's mind, to a violent conclusion. The Americans had to attack Knyphausen at midnight and destroy him.[50] All the American generals at the table enthusiastically agreed with this decision. Orders went out to the infantry regiments and artillery. Militia regiments such as Sylvanus Seeley's were to take up blocking positions.

On the other side of the river, General von Knyphausen was having a very tense conference with Major William Crosbie. After a day of watching the Continentals and militia demonstrate they had no over-whelming wish to desert or surrender, Major Crosbie had an attack of second thoughts about revealing Sir Henry Clinton's plans.

If Knyphausen resumed his advance tomorrow, he was certain to bring on a general engagement with Washington's entrenched army. The result might be another Bunker Hill. If so, Major Crosbie's head would be figuratively, perhaps even literally, on the block. In a voice that no doubt strangled now and then, Crosbie revealed that Sir Henry was returning to New York with a different plan for invading New Jersey in his pocket.

Momentarily speechless, Knyphausen and everyone else in the British high command stood there, listening to the bark of muskets as their pickets exchanged fire with militiamen who still filtered through the woods to get in one last shot before darkness fell. There was no longer any reason to spend the night on this hill like sitting ducks. Why not retreat immediately?[51]

The strictest security was observed. Regiments were told to fall in and march one by one, lessening the chance of a deserter leaking the withdrawal to the Americans. It was, in the words of one lieutenant, "exceedingly dark." There was no moon, and thick clouds obscured the stars. A hot wind sighed through the trees, muffling the sound of march-ing feet. One grenadier company of the Guards marched away, and the company next to it did not know for fifteen minutes it had gone.

Officers sent men to the pickets to make sure they joined the re-treat. One squad, led by the lieutenant who disliked the pitch-black night, came back to discover the entire British army had vanished. While he hesitated, trying to decide what to do, a tremendous crash of thunder shook the ground, followed by a stupendous flash of lightning. Rain came down as if someone had opened a sluice in the sky. The agi-tated lieutenant and his men ran through the downpour like bewil-dered chickens, first north, then south. Still no army. Finally another lightning flash revealed the horses and cannons of the artillery.

But the army's ordeal was just beginning. The storm was one of the most violent anyone in the British army had ever seen in America. Ter-rified horses bolted off the road. General von Knyphausen's steed reared and flung the German commander into the mud on his back. Several times, the lightning was so bright, General Mathew said, "the whole army halted, being deprived of sight for a time."

At Liberty Hall, the crash of glass and the crunch of wood awakened Mrs. Livingston and her daughters. About ten drenched stragglers, drunk on army rum, burst into the front hall shouting, "Let's burn the Rebel house." The maid locked herself in the kitchen, and the three women bolted an upstairs bedroom door. One of the soldiers began battering it with his shoulder. Susan Livingston took a lamp, coolly flung open the door, and walked into the hail. The drunken man tried to grab her arm. She sidestepped, seized him by the collar, and sent him sprawling.

The drunken intruder looked up at her. Thunder still shook the house; lightning continued to streak the sky. "Gawd it's Mrs. Caldwell that we killed today!" he screamed. He fled downstairs. The courageous young woman followed him. She found a familiar face among his lurching companions, a loyalist who was an ex-Elizabethtown neighbor. She shamed him into ordering the rest of the men out of the house.[52]

At about 1:00 A.M. the last of the Royal Army trudged through Elizabethtown in the downpour and settled in soggy misery on Elizabethtown Point. There were no tents for the enlisted men, and few officers could find the baggage wagons that contained shelters for them. It was a sorry ending to what was to have been a glorious day.[53]

In the American camp, the thunderstorm caused intense frustration. It rendered an attack impossible. Eighteenth-century soldiers could not fire their muskets in the rain. Water dampened the powder in their priming pans and left them clicking fecklessly. A bayonet attack was out of the question because most militiamen did not have the weapon on their muskets. The downpour also made it all too probable that many of the militia would go home.

To Washington's relief, at daybreak scouts informed him that the enemy had vanished. A patrol captured a British soldier named Jeremiah Sullivan who had decided to forgo marching back to Staten Island. Later in the morning scouts reported the enemy were camped on Elizabethtown Point. The scouts estimated the number to be five hundred. Knyphausen was apparently trying to maintain a bridgehead in New Jersey. Washington immediately decided to attack it.

He gave Brigadier General Edward Hand of Pennsylvania three regiments of regulars and two brigades of militia, a total of about 2,500 men. He put Major General William Alexander—Lord Stirling—in overall command. The attack began with a small, deceptive victory. Hand's regulars captured a British picket, an officer and sixteen men of the 22nd Regiment, guarding the road from Elizabethtown. But Samuel Seeley's militia brigade encountered a hail of artillery fire as it advanced across swampy open ground toward the British camp. Hand rode to the front of his brigade and realized they were about to assault Knyphausen's entire army.

Hand's expedition was in serious danger of annihilation. He rushed word to Seeley to take a defensive position in some nearby woods and boldly paraded his Continentals across the front of the British lines as if daring them to come out and fight. This convinced the British he was trying to lure them into a trap. They were sure Washington's entire army, plus uncounted militia, awaited them in the streets of Elizabethtown.

Coolly, Hand ordered his regulars to retire and withdrew the two militia brigades in the same deliberate fashion.[54] It was a prime example of the importance of combining a regular's professionalism with the militia's ardor. Without him, the militiamen might have flung themselves at the British and been slaughtered.

Back in Elizabethtown, Hand regrouped and sent a swarm of skirmishers forward to harass the British from all sides. The British 22nd Regiment, which had advanced on the road to town, was soon in so much trouble it had to call on two German regiments for help. The Germans were soon in almost as much difficulty. One of their lieutenants reported "many wounded, killed and taken prisoners." There was "an astonishing number of Rebels, nearly all in bushes."[55]

When Washington learned Knyphausen's whole army was still on Elizabethtown Point, he rushed a letter to Lord Stirling with new orders. He was to stay on a strict defensive. Only if Knyphausen began to withdraw to Staten Island should Stirling consider an attack on his rear guard. The last thing Washington wanted was an all-out battle with Knyphausen in the open fields on Elizabethtown Point, where British superiority in artillery and bayonets could have "serious consequences."

Washington was in Connecticut Farms with most of the regulars. There he watched a weeping James Caldwell kneel beside his wife's body. That afternoon, after a brief service, friends, neighbors, and Continental officers walked beside the grieving minister to the open grave in the Connecticut Farms churchyard. The burnt-out ruins of the church were a more graphic sermon than anyone could have preached. After the funeral, James Caldwell took his two youngest children over the Short Hills to Chatham to leave them with his dead wife's sister. Then he rode away to spread the news of her murder throughout New Jersey.[56]

Enter the Outraged
Conqueror of Charleston

G eneral George Washington went back to the business of getting his army ready to meet another attack. He was more and more convinced that General Wilhelm von Knyphausen planned to make a second lunge for Morristown. He requested a careful head count of all the regulars "fit for action." He told militia general Nathaniel Heard to find "three or four very trusty horsemen" to patrol each of the passes through the barrier mountains. In Elizabethtown he replaced the impetuous Lord Stirling with the more cautious Baron Friedrich Wilhelm von Steuben.

The militia continued to skirmish fiercely with the British all around the perimeter of their camp. Along the Elizabeth River they dragged a cannon close enough to fire several rounds, one of which knocked the flagstaff out of the hands of a German color bearer.[1] The report of Hannah Caldwell's death guaranteed a high level of militia enthusiasm and a steady flow of volunteers.

After two days of stalemate, Washington grew even more worried about Knyphausen's intentions. He warned West Point commander General Robert Howe to be ready for a surprise attack. The German general might be trying to pin down the main American army while launching a surprise assault on this key fortress.

Proving himself more than a little prescient, Washington wrote, "'Tis probable Clinton with the whole or a part of the troops under his command is momently expected at New York." The British commander might be planning "to [push] immediately up the North River." The American commander rushed another express rider to General George Clinton and his New York brigade, sent north to fight loyalist and Indian forays from Canada.[2] This American Clinton was told to get back to West Point as soon as possible to frustrate his British counterpart.

Washington also tried to use the situation to recruit regulars to fill his understrength regiments. He complained to a Connecticut correspondent, "The country seems to be in an unaccountable state of security and to be sunk in the greatest supineness." He could only hope that the loss of Charleston and the "insulting manoeuvre" Knyphausen had just executed in New Jersey might arouse it. But he confessed it pained him to think only calamities could stir his countrymen.[3] Knyphausen's force was "inconsiderable" but still too large for the American army to meet in battle.

The Americans' aggressive sniping, patrolling, and cannonading kept the British and Germans under the illusion that they confronted a superior force. They got so jittery that they built a pontoon bridge from Elizabethtown Point to Staten Island to guarantee a rapid retreat. A German officer saw this precaution as justified: "the militia alone of the Rebel hordes, because of their imagined success, had grown in this short time to a force of seven thousand men. . . . It is inconceivable how these people, without being supplied with food, have stuck together and are as steadfast as the Continental troops."[4] The enemy was learning how committed militia could be when bolstered by a regular army.

On June 13 the weather turned rainy. Water poured through the makeshift huts the British troops had thrown up on Elizabethtown Point using their blankets. The army's morale drooped. Even in the rain, the militia managed to get off enough shots to kill or wound several men. In the absence of human targets, they fired at the British horses.[5]

Washington was doing his utmost to make their accommodations even more unpleasant. He ordered a militia brigadier to collect "all the horses and cattle (except for a few milch cows absolutely necessary for family use) within five miles of the water from Newark to Amboy." He would send the animals on to the Continental commissary. He was making sure that Knyphausen could not console himself with another grand forage.[6]

Washington rushed a letter to Major General Robert Howe at West Point, telling him that if the enemy tried another smash toward Morristown, "you may be useful to us by making a demonstration in your quarter." He told Howe to collect boats "sufficient for two thousand men" and to put the garrison "under moving orders with three days' provisions." Howe should also circulate the idea that the local militia might be called at any moment. The purpose was to give the enemy "some alarm." The commander in chief also recommended the dispatch of an "emissary" (a double agent) to New York to spread "these particulars."[7]

In his regular army, Washington had another worry: desertions. He issued strict orders against straggling from the area assigned to each regiment for camp. No one was to enter "the vicinity of the enemy" without orders. Anyone caught outside the chain of sentinels around the camp without permission would get thirty lashes. The general also forbade "transient persons" to pass through the encampment after dark. Those who tried were to be confined until morning.

Despite all this vigilance, a discouraging twenty men fled to the British lines. Only one, Thomas Brown of the 2nd New Jersey Regiment, was caught. He was condemned to death and hanged on June 16. James Thacher, the Massachusetts regimental surgeon who kept a vivid diary of the war, wasted no pity on him. He noted that Washington had pardoned him for a previous desertion attempt three weeks earlier.[8]

A lot of stragglers were not attempting to desert but searching for food. The regulars were not eating much better in the Short Hills than they had in Morristown. Private Joseph Plumb Martin of Connecticut told of going off guard duty with nothing to eat for forty-eight hours. In his desperation Martin cadged the liver of a slaughtered ox—the best cuts of the carcass had gone to the general officers. The thing was so tough, it almost killed him.[9]

By this time the British had been camping on Elizabethtown Point for twelve days. Washington became more and more concerned about a surprise attack. His best intelligence officer, Major Benjamin Tallmadge, who operated north of New York, reported his agents had picked up word that the British planned "some sudden movement . . . most probably up the North [Hudson] River."[10] This only increased Washington's uncertainty.

The arrival of Light Horse Harry Lee and his legion of green-coated cavalrymen cheered the American commander. They were among the few regiments in the American army with complete uniforms. Dr. James Thacher admired their elegant horses and martial appearance. Washington expected "important service" from them. They had been on their way south and had responded swiftly to the general's order to return. With them in his ranks, Washington need not worry about the British 17th Dragoons' carving up his militia regiments unopposed.[11]

But Lee's presence did not solve the commander in chief's other horse problem. Washington desperately wanted to move the army's artillery and stores in Morristown to the west side of the Delaware River. But he still faced a catastrophic shortage of horses and wagons. The quartermaster corps, harried by a stream of letters, scraped together every available horse in Morris County, but only a few of those irreplaceable guns got on the road.[12]

On Sunday, June 19, Washington got the news he had been dreading. Coast watchers in Monmouth County reported a large fleet sailing into New York Harbor. They counted no fewer than thirty-five ships passing the bar at Sandy Hook.[13] Sir Henry Clinton and his southern army, the conquerors of Charleston, had arrived.

A desperate Washington rushed a letter to the president of Congress, begging him to do something about his depleted army. "Not a single draft" from any of the states had joined the ranks, while the year's recruits numbered barely two hundred. "A very alarming scene may shortly open," Washington wrote. "It will be happy for us if we can steer clear of some grievous misfortune."[14]

⌒

THE AMERICAN commander might have felt a little better if he had known his British counterpart's state of mind. Consternation best describes Sir Henry Clinton's reaction on discovering that General von Knyphausen had invaded New Jersey.

In a fury, Clinton castigated this "ill-timed malapropos move." He had expected to find "Mr. Washington," as Clinton persisted in calling him, "in a state of unsuspecting security in his camp at Morristown and the bold persevering militia of that populous province quiet in their respective homes"; instead, "the whole country was now in arms."[15] Knyphausen blamed everything on the loyalists of New York, particularly William Franklin, who had assured him New Jersey was ripe for capitulation.[16]

For Clinton, the problem was what to do next. Reviewing the army on Elizabethtown Point on June 19, he found their situation "very unpleasant and mortifying." Meanwhile his Carolina troops were disembarking on Staten Island. They had been on the crowded ships for three weeks and needed to get their land legs again. No longer in love with his original plan to send two columns lunging toward Morristown from Amboy and Elizabethtown, Clinton pondered his options.[17]

There were other possibilities. West Point was a key to Washington's defensive strategy. He would move swiftly to defend it if he thought it under attack. A feint in that direction might lure the main American army out of the Short Hills into northern New Jersey, where Clinton could trap it between the Carolina army and Knyphausen's force. Or Knyphausen might manage to bull through the weakened defenses around Hobart Gap and reach Morristown.[18]

Washington was soon deluged with reports from spies warning him that Clinton was about to make a half dozen different moves. Perhaps the most worrisome came from a very reliable Staten Island spy, who said Clinton's army was advancing toward the Amboy ferry and British boats were assembling at the mouth of the Raritan River. That sounded like the start of a lunge toward Morristown.

In the American lines around the British camp in Elizabethtown, the situation suddenly deteriorated. Baron von Steuben asked to be relieved of his command. The undisciplined ways of the militia were driving the Prussian drillmaster crazy. The baron complained that he had found two of the advanced posts abandoned, the men gone home. The militia's overall numbers had dwindled to about five hundred—a desertion rate of 66 percent.[19]

To complete Washington's headaches, he learned from a friend in the New Jersey legislature that the local solons were about to draft militia to fill the gaps in the state's Continental regiments. To forestall resistance, they were to serve as full companies, under their own officers. An appalled Washington rushed a letter to Governor William Livingston, warning that such a law would unravel the regular army. The governor persuaded the politicians to abandon the idea. That left the ranks unfilled.

⌒

In New York, Sir Henry Clinton was at work on a plan even more ambitious than the strike against Morristown. He had learned from a spy in the American camp that the long-expected French fleet and expeditionary force would arrive in Rhode Island in about three weeks. The spy was none other than the hero of Saratoga, Major General Benedict Arnold. The widowed general had recently married beautiful twenty-year-old Peggy Shippen of Philadelphia, daughter of a family that included both patriots and loyalists. Lovely Peggy had secretly persuaded Arnold to switch sides, convincing him that he had a brighter future in a British uniform than he would ever have in the disintegrating American army.

Clinton decided to put the French on his military menu. He would execute his pincer movement in New Jersey, smash Washington's army in a day's hard fighting, and then put his men aboard transports and head for Rhode Island, where he would finish off the French in the same fashion. With no organized armed force left on the rebel side, the war would be over.

On June 22, Clinton ordered his Carolina army back on their transports to form the northern arm of his pincer. To help Knyphausen deal with the New Jersey militia, he assigned him the best loyalist regiment in the British army, the Queen's Rangers, commanded by a master of partisan warfare, Lieutenant Colonel John Graves Simcoe. Clinton also gave Old Knyp the 42nd Regiment, tough Scottish Highlanders fighting in America since 1776. These 800 experienced soldiers raised Knyphausen's strength to over 6,000.[20]

Meanwhile the Americans were devoting strenuous efforts to a new crisis. West Point was alarmingly short of food. Washington had organized a train of wagons loaded with enough flour to guarantee them the ability to withstand a siege. Taking the Pennsylvania and Connecticut brigades with him, he planned to personally escort the resupply to the fortress.

To replace the militia-maddened Baron von Steuben at Elizabethtown, Washington chose his most capable general, Nathanael Greene. His mission, Washington wrote, was "to cover the country and the public stores." He was referring to the magazines and artillery still sitting like beached whales in Morristown. He urged Greene to "use every precaution in your power to avoid surprise."[21]

Washington left two brigades of regulars with Greene. One was General William Maxwell's New Jersey brigade, which barely numbered 650 men. Brigadier General John Stark, the laconic, steely-eyed hero of Bunker Hill and Bennington, commanded the second, comprised of three skeleton regiments, one from Rhode Island, one from Connecticut, and the other from Massachusetts. The label "brigade" was almost a courtesy: the unit numbered only 461 men. Greene also retained Lee's Legion, about 400 men, half cavalry, half infantry. With a putative 1,500 militia, Greene had less than 3,000 rank and file.

Down on Elizabethtown Point, Simcoe's green-coated Queen's Rangers added new vigor to the British outposts. One of their lieutenants made a foray over the stone bridge across the Elizabeth River into American territory and retreated with the Americans in hot pursuit. In a wood just beyond the bridge, a company of the 17th Dragoons waited to cut the pursuers to pieces. But the Americans stopped on the safe side of the bridge, and the ambush failed to come off.

Undiscouraged, that night the Rangers teamed up with the Jaegers to attack another American outpost and bring in four prisoners. From them they learned that Washington had marched two nights ago for West Point and left the rest of the army and militia at Springfield. This was what the British wanted to know. Clinton's trap was ready to be sprung.[22]

Pondering their maps in their Staten Island headquarters, Clinton and Knyphausen noted a potential weakness in the American position. Clinton ran his finger up the Vauxhall Road on the right of the Galloping Hill Road to Springfield. One column would go up Vauxhall, which looped around the northeastern edge of Springfield before plunging through Hobart Gap. The other column would use the Galloping Hill route, which they had followed in their June 7 foray. Could the Americans, outnumbered two to one, defend both roads? Not likely. If the British broke through on either road, they could encircle the defenders of the other road and cut them to pieces at leisure.

What if Washington's army swung around the northern tip of the Watchung Mountains just west of Newark and struck at Knyphausen's flank to relieve the pressure on Springfield? Clinton smiled grimly. If the American commander tried it, the war might end tomorrow. He would have the 4,000-man Carolina army well up the Hudson River on transports, waiting for such a move. The moment Washington showed himself east of the mountains, these seasoned troops would come ashore to cut off his retreat. At the very least, if Washington did not try to help his cadres in Springfield, the British could look forward to smashing them up and wrecking the militia's morale for a long time to come.[23]

For a moment, Sir Henry must have been almost cheerful. There was a very good chance that he could be sitting in Newport in two weeks, waiting to inform the French commander when he landed that American resistance had collapsed. That meant Monsieur had two alternatives: surrender or die.

While these not-so-unrealistic dreams bemused the British high command, a very nervous American spy appeared in Nathanael Greene's headquarters in Bryant's Tavern, just west of Springfield on the road to Morristown. He insisted on seeing General Greene immediately and told an alarming story. He had slipped away from the British camp at 3:00 P.M., after learning that Clinton was planning a surprise attack on Washington's army as it marched to West Point.

They had hired him as a guide and ordered him to rendezvous with them on the road to Aquackanock (now Passaic) that night.

The more the man talked, the more Greene suspected that he was a double agent. Despite these doubts, common sense required that he warn Washington. In the letter he reported that Light Horse Harry Lee, whose horsemen were patrolling the shores of the Hudson, picking up information from everyone and anyone, thought the British would strike at West Point. Except for some minor skirmishing, all was quiet at Elizabethtown.

At 10:00 P.M., Greene wrote again. He was growing jittery. He now began to think the British might indeed strike at Washington, hoping to break through for a march to Morristown. Doubling back on his doubts, Greene now believed the spy was "sincere." Washington's force might well be the main target.[24]

Greene was probably right the first time. The spy's information stopped Washington's march to West Point, holding him in position to snap at the bait of Knyphausen's attack. But Greene did not change his mind enough to march his two thin brigades toward Washington, leaving the road to Morristown open. He kept them in the Short Hills above Springfield.

⌣

AT 5:00 A.M. on June 23, the British army, led by the Queen's Rangers and Skinner's Greens, also known as the New Jersey Volunteers, stormed out of the camp on Elizabethtown Point and swiftly overran all the advanced American positions inside Elizabethtown, capturing three cannons and a number of prisoners. The fleeing survivors warned Scotch Willie Maxwell's New Jersey brigade, camped just west of the town. What little resistance the Americans offered came from the outnumbered regulars. Baron von Steuben's warning that the militiamen were going home without waiting to be relieved had gone largely unheeded.

The fewer than five hundred militiamen on duty scattered as fast as their legs could carry them when they saw the whole British army coming. Maxwell covered the Galloping Hill Road with one of his

New Jersey Continental regiments and ordered Lee's Legion to cover the Vauxhall Road. The enemy, according to plan, had split into two columns and was using both roads. The Americans fell back, hard-pressed by the Rangers and the Greens.[25]

On the heights of Springfield, the Old Sow boomed, and the signal beacon blazed its fiery message into the dawn. But few militia responded. Everyone presumed that the men on duty would do the fighting. No one knew most of them had gone home. For the first hour, the situation looked far worse than it had on June 7.

At Bryant's Tavern, Nathanael Greene, exercising an independent command for the first time, ordered his men to rip up the planks on the two bridges across the Rahway River, one on the Galloping Hill Road, the other on the Vauxhall Road. Greene had positioned his infantry and artillery in echelons to force the British to make not one but a series of attacks. He ordered Elias Dayton's New Jersey Continental regiment and whatever militia he could gather to make a first stand in Connecticut Farms. As they fell back, the 2nd Rhode Island Regiment under Colonel Israel Angell would cover their retreat. These men from Greene's home state received the post of honor—defense of the Galloping Hill Bridge over the Rahway River.

The 2nd Rhode Island was down to 160 men but had a fighting record equaled by few American regiments. Its men had bled in every major battle of the war. In 1777 they had defended the Delaware River forts against weeks of bombardments and assaults by the British and Germans. The forty-year-old Angell was one of the coolest, most competent commanders in the American army.[26]

Behind Angell, on higher ground commanding a stone bridge over the west branch of the Rahway River, Greene posted portly Israel Shreve and his 2nd New Jersey Regiment. Behind them he positioned Major General Philemon Dickenson, finally on duty with his militia, and as many of his part-timers as showed up. To defend the Vauxhall Bridge, he dispatched Colonel Mathias Ogden and his 1st New Jersey Regiment. For a reserve, on the summit of the hills behind Bryant's Tavern, Greene placed Maxwell and the rest of the New Jersey brigade, plus John Stark with the two remaining regiments of his brigade.

In this painting by John Trumbull, General George Washington stands on the battlefield at Trenton the evening of January 2, 1777. The next day, Washington outwitted Cornwallis, as he would do with his British counterparts for most of the war. His confident and determined bearing throughout the war served him well against his opponents, both British and American.

Alexander Hamilton alluded perceptively to Roman general Quintus Fabius Maximus in a letter to General Washington, recognizing that Washington's cautious strategy would ultimately lead to victory.

The surprising victory at Bunker Hill convinced many in Congress that American enthusiasm was enough to defeat the British. General Washington spent years trying to convince doubters that the British could only be defeated in pitched battle by a regular, well-trained army.

In 1777, General Benjamin Lincoln played a crucial role in raising, organizing, and training a body of New England militia that operated effectively against General John Burgoyne's army in upstate New York.

After he married beautiful twenty-year-old Peggy Shippen of Philadelphia, General Benedict Arnold, American hero at the Battle of Saratoga and one of Washington's most talented officers, was convinced that he had a brighter future in a British uniform than he would ever have in a seemingly disintegrating American army.

General Horatio Gates, leading a group of disgruntled officers and with the support of some members of Congress, attempted to discredit and replace General Washington. Gates's battlefield leadership proved disastrous at the Battle of Camden, where he tried unsuccessfully to use militia like regulars.

By the end of the war, General Nathanael Greene emerged as General Washington's most gifted and effective general. His command of the Southern Campaign forced the British to retreat back into Virginia.

General Anthony Wayne's Pennsylvania troops were among General Washington's most valuable in battle. After the war, President Washington called on Wayne to lead the fledgling peacetime army to victory at the Battle of Fallen Timbers.

Telling anyone who would listen, General Charles Lee criticized General Washington's command of the army until he was relieved of command following his refusal to obey Washington's order to advance against the British at the 1778 Battle of Monmouth.

General Washington's strategy for victory was successful in the New Jersey campaigns of 1780. Washington's victory at the Battle of Springfield on June 23, 1780, dashed British ambitions in the state.

General Wilhelm von Knyphausen led the unsuccessful attempt to dislodge American positions at Springfield and ordered the British retreat, but not before burning down the town.

Henry Lee commanded a mixed infantry-cavalry unit known as "Lee's Legion." Lee's action in New Jersey earned the praise of Congress and Washington, and his famous nickname, "Light Horse Harry." Promoted to lieutenant colonel, Lee took his unit south where his cavalry proved invaluable in the style of warfare there.

At the turning-point Battle of Cowpens *(top)*, British forces, led by young Colonel Banastre Tarleton *(left)*, were defeated by an American force that included highly trained regulars and experienced militia under the brilliant command of General Daniel Morgan *(right)*.

This 1836 painting by Frenchman Auguste Couder *(above)* depicts General George Washington, standing in front of his headquarters tent, and Comte de Rochambeau at Yorktown, Virginia. Their combined forces of regulars and militia defeated Lord Cornwallis, who surrendered on October 19, 1781. In the John Trumbull painting *(below)*, General Benjamin Lincoln rides a white horse between rows of American *(right)* and French *(left)* troops as he extends his right hand to accept the British officer's sword. General George Washington, riding a brown horse, stayed in the background because Cornwallis himself was not present for the surrender.

At their camp near Newburgh on the Hudson River, a large group of disgruntled and angry (and unpaid) officers met to discuss mutiny on March 15, 1783. It was a perilous moment for the Continental Army and its commander, General George Washington. But Washington gave a stunning and moving speech that disarmed his officers and restored good order.

General George Washington met with many of his long-time officers on December 4, 1783, at Fraunces Tavern in New York City. In an emotional address, he told them that he would soon resign his commission and, "suffused with tears," thanked them all for their service and sacrifice.

After serving in the American Revolution, General Arthur St. Clair was the commander of American forces in the Northwest Territory in November of 1791 when his troops suffered a devastating defeat by Native Americans that triggered a response from President Washington that would lead to the formation of a standing army.

Leading the "Legion of the United States," the young nation's first army, General Anthony Wayne handily defeated a Native American force supported by the British at the Battle of Fallen Timbers on August 20, 1794, cementing General Washington's strategy of victory by means of a regular army.

Simultaneously, he rushed a messenger to Washington with the grim news. "The enemy are out on their march toward this place in full force, having received a considerable reinforcement last night." Greene might have felt a little more hopeful had he known that most of that reinforcement—five regiments—was staying behind to protect the British rear on Elizabethtown Point against roving militia. Even without these men, Knyphausen still outnumbered Greene five regulars to one.[27]

At Rockaway Bridge, eleven miles northwest of Morristown, Washington must have felt a twinge of anguish when Nathanael Greene's morning message arrived. He was too far away to come to his aid. At best he could fire his signal guns, order the men to cook two days' provisions, and get his half of the army on the road to Springfield as soon as possible. Ahead of him he sent one of his aides with a troop of cavalry to reconnoiter the roads from Elizabethtown to make sure the British were not coming in his direction.[28]

In Springfield, the civilians were panicky, with good reason. The charred ruins of the houses in Connecticut Farms provided stark warning of carnage to come. As in the Farms, Springfield's thirty-seven houses were scattered along Galloping Hill Road for several miles. Almost every house had an orchard and pasture lands nearby, as well as barns and other outbuildings.[29]

Some Springfielders were eager to fight. Joseph Tooker, an ensign in the militia, joined regulars at the defile in Connecticut Farms, while his wife threw the family silver down the well and hid blankets and other bedding in a nearby field of rye.[30] Other locals preferred to flee. George Ross, the town's glazier and shoemaker, abandoned almost 150 panes of glass and over two dozen boots and shoes. He also left behind his gun. Joseph Horton, the town silversmith, hid most of his wares but was unable to find any takers for "3 good guns."[31]

The civilian panic contrasted with the grim calm of the regulars. Massachusetts doctor James Thacher painted the scene at dawn in his diary. "At six o'clock . . . the alarm guns were fired and the drums . . . beat to arms, announcing the approach of the enemy; the whole army is instantly in motion, the scene to my contemplation is awfully sublime, yet animation and composure seem to pervade every countenance."[32]

Once more James Caldwell mounted his horse to arouse the militia. His inspiration was badly needed. The amateurs were already tired of the war. A farmer named Bishop in nearby Mendham was stacking wheat with the help of several hired men when the alarm guns boomed. He ran to get his musket. Not one of the hired men followed. They let him trot off alone to the rendezvous point.[33]

Most of the men who responded were young. Eighteen-year-old Ashbel Green showed up again to join the men of Colonel Sylvanus Seeley's Morris County regiment. So did sixteen-year-old Nathan Elmer, who wanted to be a cavalryman and groaned at the thought of marching his feet off again to get over the mountains to Springfield. Some were ex-regulars, like Samuel Elston, who had served a year in the Jersey line in 1776, fighting in Canada. He wore his red hair in a long ponytail hanging down his shoulders. His militia-mates called him "Carrot."[34]

Only a handful of Essex County militia joined Colonel Elias Dayton's Continentals at Connecticut Farms;[35] the amateurs no longer had any appetite for head-on clashes with the bayonet-wielding British regulars. But bands of militia were active along the British line of march. At its tail, in the very center of Elizabethtown, several militiamen sprang from behind a house and seized a wagon carrying the baggage of a lieutenant colonel of the Guards. They put a gun to the head of the Negro driver and quietly told him they would blow out his brains if he did not guide his horses into a nearby barn.[36]

The exploit made them local heroes but had no real impact on the juggernaut that was heading up the Galloping Hill and Vauxhall Roads toward Nathanael Greene and his men. The sun was rising steadily in the summery blue sky when the leading companies of Skinner's Greens and Queen's Rangers appeared at the eastern end of the Connecticut Farms defile. They paused to take a good look at Dayton's Continentals. A howl of mutual contempt leaped from hundreds of throats, followed by the ugly crash of musket fire.[37]

Virtually every man on both sides was American, and most were from New Jersey—a vivid depiction of the Revolution as a civil war. The Greens led the way up the slope of the defile, dodging Continental bullets, blasting back from behind trees and bushes, both sides fighting Indian-style. Despite their ferocity, the Greens made little real progress. Outnumbered, they soon began looking over their shoulders for the Queen's Rangers.

Colonel John Graves Simcoe coolly studied the situation for another minute and decided not to commit his men to the confused struggle in the defile. He ordered them to close ranks and follow him down the Galloping Hill Road without firing a shot.[38] Simcoe's maneuver achieved total surprise. Neither Dayton's regulars nor their supporting militiamen realized what was happening until the Rangers were in their rear.

Simcoe barked another order, and the Rangers wheeled left, opened ranks, and charged the militiamen, who were clustered in an orchard beside the road. The militia general in command took one look at what was coming and bellowed, "Retreat!" With the general leading the rout, the militiamen fled across the open fields, Ranger bullets whistling after them. They did not stop running until they had crossed the Rahway River.[39] Several Continentals, isolated by their sudden departure, flung down their guns and surrendered to the Rangers.

In the defile, Colonel Dayton realized his left flank had collapsed. He had no alternative to a swift retreat. But the Continentals' withdrawal contrasted starkly with the militia's flight. There was no panic, even though Skinner's Greens began a hot pursuit, whooping in triumph. Dayton took personal command of the rear guard. Musketry blasts kept the Greens at a respectful distance, while the head of the little column pegged shots at Simcoe's Rangers on the other side of the road.

Simcoe wisely ordered no pursuit. He realized Dayton's men were only the first line of the American defense and did not want his men tired out on a hot day before they reached the main body of Greene's army. He waited in the road for Knyphausen and the rest of the British army to reach him.

The German general soon arrived and sent the Rangers, the Greens, the Guards, and most of the British regiments up the Vauxhall Road, hoping to outflank the Americans defending the Galloping Hill Bridge over the Rahway. Knyphausen headed for this bridge with the Jaegers, two British regiments, and the German regiments. At the head of his column he placed the Jaegers and six cannons.[40]

Defending the bridge was the single skeletonized 2nd Rhode Island Regiment. Its men were not encouraged by the sight of the militia's racing headlong across the landscape, soon followed by the winded, sweat-soaked Continentals of Dayton's regiment, who passed through their ranks to the rear. Captain Stephen Olney, commanding one Rhode Island company, expected them to be annihilated. "I never had so much difficulty reconciling my mind to the fate contemplated," he later wrote. It looked like a suicide mission.

Knyphausen's six guns soon opened fire on the Rhode Islanders. To answer them, the Americans had a single cannon. For two hours, while the flanking column moved into position to attack the Vauxhall Bridge, the single American piece dueled the British guns at a range of 1,000 yards with little visible damage on either side. The Rhode Islanders remained stolidly indifferent to the balls hissing past them.

At 11:00 A.M., a messenger from the flanking column arrived. It was ready to attack. Knyphausen barked an order. His column came down the hill toward the Rhode Islanders around the bridge, the British regiments in the lead. With murderous accuracy, the single American cannon sent a ball smashing through their ranks, leaving a swath of dead and dying. The men broke for cover, wailing with fright. Their officers grimly reformed them, and they went forward again. This time the Americans fired a "ricochet," striking the ground just in front of the column, cutting an even deadlier swath. Again the men broke and had to be reformed. They came on a third time and got a blast of grapeshot. Once more the lone American gun shattered the British charge.

Knyphausen ordered his six guns to advance five hundred yards. At this range, they were exposed to American fire and took some casualties. But they swiftly decimated the American gun crew and smashed the gun. A final shot amputated both legs of the artillery captain in command of it.

Heartened, the British infantrymen renewed their charge. Blasts of Rhode Island musketry stopped them at the bridge, which the Continentals had stripped of its planks. A courageous British sergeant and two privates tried to get across on the runners and were shot into the water. The Jaeger commander, Colonel Johann von Wurmb, put a stop to these heroics. He sent his four hundred green-coated riflemen racing upstream and downstream, where they splashed across the shallow river unopposed and assaulted the Rhode Islanders' flanks. The British infantrymen opened their ranks and forded the river on either side of the bridge under cover of their artillery.[41]

A wild firefight exploded on the west bank of the Rahway, swirling around orchards, barns, and houses on Springfield's outskirts. Captain Olney ruefully admired the cool courage displayed by one Jaeger officer. "It seemed no ball would stop [him]; he came on, firing regularly." Olney was also leading a charmed life, as he walked up and down, encouraging his men. "The wind of their balls would at times shake the hair of my head," he said later.[42]

For almost a half hour, the Rhode Islanders fought five times their number to a standstill. Clouds of gun smoke shrouded the battlefield. The soldiers' faces were darkened by gunpowder. Their overheated muskets left the flesh of their hands raw.

Suddenly, from one end of the American line to the other, a cry went up: "Wadding. More wadding." Regulars added paper around the ball to steady it in the barrel and give the crude gun better aim. A frantic messenger raced to the rear. On the road he met James Caldwell. "I'll get you more wadding," the pastor said, putting spurs to his horse.

In minutes he rode back through the gun smoke and flung down dozens of hymnbooks. Isaac Watts, an English clergyman, had written most of the songs. "Give 'em Watts, boys," Caldwell roared and thundered back to the Springfield church for another load.[43]

The words created an instant local legend but did little for the Rhode Islanders. More and more of them crumpled under British fire at point-blank range. Other pockets succumbed to bayonet charges. A bullet smashed Stephen Olney's arm. He calmly tied a handkerchief around the wound and walked from tree to tree, telling his men he "thought it best to retreat." Carrying a half dozen badly wounded men with them, they fell back minutes before the 37th Regiment stormed down a road in their rear to cut them off.[44]

With one out of four men dead or wounded, the Rhode Islanders retreated to a second bridge over another branch of the Rahway. Here they found the 2nd New Jersey Regiment and some New Jersey militia waiting with guns primed and ammunition pouches full. This branch of the river was little more than a creek. The British charged across it and began another firefight with these fresh troops. The Americans slowly gave ground. General Greene's battle plan did not call for last stands on the low ground along the river. He planned to do his serious fighting on the steep slopes of the Short Hills, beyond the town limits of Springfield.

The 38th British Regiment tried to work its way around the American flank. Suddenly it caught a blast of fire from a swarm of militiamen who had gathered unnoticed on this part of the battlefield. Simultaneously about thirty Continentals fired from the window of a stone house. The British recoiled, with two dozen dead and wounded. But the wide-ranging Jaegers then caught the militia from all sides and sent them fleeing into the middle distance, dragging their wounded with them.

British artillery now fired on the 2nd New Jersey. The British and Jaegers swarmed its flanks. General Greene sent orders to retreat to the high ground. The Americans would have to abandon most of Springfield to the enemy.

A few minutes after he gave this order, Greene sent a pessimistic report to Washington. He vowed to dispute the British attempt to crash through Hobart Gap "as far as I am capable." But he worried about the second British column fighting its way across the Vauxhall Bridge. The Vauxhall Road snaked into the hills to join the Galloping Hill Road at Hobart Gap. If the British broke through at the bridge, they would cut off Greene's retreat. "The militia to our aid are few," he wrote. "And that few are so divided as to render little or no support."[45]

While Greene worried, Major Henry Lee was playing Horatio at the Vauxhall Bridge. He scattered his men in small parties through the nearby fields and woods to present less tempting targets for the British artillery. He had only the men of his legion, most of them fighting as dismounted cavalrymen, and a detachment of regulars under Captain George Walker from the 1st New Jersey Regiment—in all about six hundred soldiers. On his flank hung a sizable but indeterminate number of militia under the command of Brigadier General Nathaniel Heard. Neither group had artillery.[46]

Major General Edward Mathew's largely British column spent an hour bombarding Lee's position. When Knyphausen's cannon boomed at 11:00 A.M., signaling the attack, the New Jersey Volunteers and the Queen's Rangers surged forward, wading the river on both sides of the bridge. For several minutes an all-American civil war raged again, replete with howls of defiance and roars of detestation. Muskets boomed, and ex-neighbors spilled each other's blood.

As the rest of the British column poured over the bridge, Lee ordered a slow retreat. Firing steadily, the regulars and militia fell back to the upper branch of the Rahway River. Like Greene, Lee positioned his small force in echelons so they could concentrate their fire on the road. Colonel Simcoe countered this tactic by ordering the Queen's Rangers into an attacking line.

While the New Jersey Volunteers skirmished with the militia, Simcoe's men fought their way through a thicket-filled gully in a series of short, deadly hand-to-hand struggles. Soon they were pouring bullets into Lee's left flank. For a moment a rout seemed imminent.[47]

At this point, Greene's aide, Lieutenant Colonel Francis Barber, galloped up, saw what was about to happen, and rushed back to headquarters for reinforcements. Greene ordered Brigadier General Stark's two regiments forward on the double with a cannon. They arrived just as Lee's men gave up the defense of the road and scrambled up the slopes of the Short Hills. The sight of another four hundred regulars deploying on this high ground with an artillery piece brought the British attack to an abrupt halt. Only the Queen's Rangers tried to advance—until the cannon left two mangled corpses in their ranks.[48]

To continue up the Vauxhall Road meant running a gauntlet of musket fire and grapeshot. Attacking the regulars on the heights would be an even costlier move. A jittery General Mathew, unnerved by the growing swarm of militia on his right flank and concerned about the possible reappearance of Washington and the rest of the American army, decided to take a road that forked from Vauxhall back to the center of Springfield.

It took some time for Mathew to get Simcoe and his men back on the road to serve as his rear guard. Meanwhile the British column stood in the road, a very tempting target. Most of the Americans in the hills fired high, but many bullets whizzed so close that one colonel of the Guards, Cosmo Gordon, reportedly advanced to the rear on his hands and knees behind a stone fence[49]—an unforgiveable breach of conduct for an eighteenth-century officer. Gordon wound up defending himself before a court-martial board. He was acquitted, but his reputation was ruined.

In Springfield, General Knyphausen ordered General Mathew to clear the heights of snipers so the army could regroup, eat dinner, and decide what to do next. The German general could see no sign that he had broken the spirit of the American army. Moreover, he had to assume that the militia were rallying by the thousands from west of the Short Hills. Simcoe's Rangers and the New Jersey Volunteers skirmished briskly with a mixture of militia and Continentals while the regulars dined.

Seeing some militia moving into swampy ground by the river, Simcoe took a company of the Queen's Rangers into the same morass and stationed them in a thicket. They waited until the militia, led by Captain Nathaniel FitzRandolph, were within point-blank range, then rose and poured a volley in their faces. A dozen men went down. The survivors dragged the dying FitzRandolph out of the swamp and carried him home.[50]

Dozens of other wounded men were being carried to the rear. The young militiaman Ashbel Green saw pools of blood on the dusty road down the mountain to Chatham. Angry, he and his friends implored their officers to let them attack the British. They also wanted to know where Washington and the rest of the American army was hiding.

Washington was marching for Chatham, carefully keeping the mountains between him and the British army. He did not show the slightest desire to come around Newark Mountain and fall on Knyphausen's rear. He simply did not have enough men to give free rein to his aggressive instincts.

Even if he had made the move, Sir Henry Clinton was not poised to pounce on him. Admiral Marriot Arbuthnot had done a beautiful job of sabotaging Clinton's plan. He had marched his Carolina army across Staten Island to Cole's Ferry, where he expected to find transports waiting to take them up the Hudson River. Instead he found an empty harbor. Without bothering to tell Sir Henry, the admiral had decided to take his fleet to sea. After choleric complaints from Clinton, the transports finally returned. But it was dark by the time they ferried the army up the river, and a disgusted Clinton abandoned his pincer movement.[51]

General Knyphausen also decided to abandon his arm of the pincer. Rather than the boom of cannons, spurts of smoke and flames in Springfield announced his intentions. In a half hour, the town was an inferno. Some men in Greene's army, seeing their homes in flames, went berserk and started down the mountain in a suicidal attack. Their friends restrained them.[52]

Soon fire wreathed the Presbyterian church—with American wounded inside. A German soldier, Stephan Popp, noted in his diary that the wounded men's pleas for life were moving but did them no good. Only four houses belonging to known British sympathizers were spared. Everything else—barns, sheds, outbuildings—was put to the torch. "Not even a pig-sty was left standing," Popp wrote in his diary.[53]

Covered by the smoke billowing from Springfield, Knyphausen began his retreat. The Royal Army moved in two divisions, one on the Vauxhall Road with the Queen's Rangers as the rear guard, the other on the Galloping Hill Road with the Jaegers protecting its rear. Swarms of infuriated militiamen stormed after them. Nathanael Greene ordered two regiments of regulars to join them.

The Jaegers, low on ammunition and bitter about their losses earlier in the day, made only halfhearted attempts to defend their column. Militiamen raced past them to bushwhack the regulars along the line of march. Soon at least fifteen bodies lay by the side of the road, and the column was moving at a most undignified trot.[54] Passing Liberty

Hall, Cosmo Gordon received a bullet in a part of his anatomy genteelly described in the *Royal Gazette* as his "upper thigh."

On the Vauxhall Road, the Queen's Rangers exacted a heavy toll from the pursuing militiamen. The Rangers' riflemen were all crack shots. Brigadier General Heard ordered his men to stay at a safer distance.[55] One of the pursuers, Ashbel Green, was disgusted with Heard's caution. He and his friends called the brigadier a coward—typical of how militia criticized their officers. Years later, Green admitted that Heard's prudence probably saved his life.[56]

As Knyphausen's column hurried through Elizabethtown toward the Point and safety, the disheartened Jaegers in his rear came apart. "There were only 300 riflemen [left] with whom I had to sustain a violent attack from all sides by all sorts of militiamen," Colonel von Wurmb later recalled. He had lost another ten men along the road and was forced to ask Knyphausen to relieve his exhausted soldiers.[57]

In a wood near the crossroads where General Stirling had become a casualty on June 7, the 37th Regiment fought a brief, savage battle with Essex County militiamen. The amateurs finally retreated,[58] clearing the road for the second column, which soon joined Knyphausen on Elizabethtown Point. At midnight the German general led his weary men over the bridge of boats to Staten Island.

The invasion of New Jersey was over. The adventure had cost the British and Germans 307 dead and wounded.[59] We can glimpse the effect on their morale from a single line in a report Colonel von Wurmb sent home to Hesse-Cassel: "I regret from the depths of my heart that the great loss of the Jaegers took place to no greater purpose."[60]

Even more costly to the British was the impression their two advances and retreats left on the Americans in New Jersey. With the revolutionary cause teetering, a British victory could well have been decisive. The aura of defeat Knyphausen left behind him revived the spirits of thousands of waverers.

Ashbel Green, like most militiamen, was exhausted by a hot day's marching and fighting. When the last British soldier had reached the security of Elizabethtown Point, he and many friends sought shelter for the night in nearby houses. The next day he trudged home, "almost fatigued to death."

His route led him over the battlefield. For the first time he saw "the yet unburied corpses of the victims of war." Two or three dead British "stripped as naked as when they were born" lay on the western side of Springfield Bridge. Young Green realized these were "daring and determined soldiers"—the men who had charged across the runners of the bridge and "met instant death as soon as they reached the other side."

Looking around him in the morning sunlight, Green saw nothing but "gloomy horror—a dead horse, a broken carriage of a fieldpiece, a town laid in ashes, the former inhabitants standing over the ruins of their dwellings, and the unburied dead, covered with blood and with the flies that were devouring it." Filled with melancholy, he was ready to ask, "Is the contest worth all this?"

Just west of Springfield he saw George Washington on horseback coming down the road at a gallop, accompanied by a single dragoon escort. Something about how the tall Virginian sat his bay horse, the big hands in absolute control, communicated new purpose, new resolution, to the young militiaman's troubled soul.[61]

THE BATTLES of Springfield and Connecticut Farms reminded many in the American army of the fighting that had convulsed Massachusetts in April 1775. The rush of militia to the battle from all parts of New Jersey made one man exclaim, "It was Lexington repeated!"[62] Others did not view the outcome—the two British retreats—as victories. Hotheaded aide Alexander Hamilton was in despair. "Would you believe it," he wrote to a friend, "a German baron at the head of 5000 men, in the month of June insulted and defied the main American army with the Commander in Chief at their head with impunity and made them tremble for the safety of their magazines forty miles in the country."[63]

Colonel Ebenezer Huntington of Connecticut wrote to his father even more vehemently about the weakness of the Continental Army, denouncing his "cowardly countrymen who flinch at the very time when their exertions are wanted. . . . I despise my country. I wish I was not born in America."

George Washington took a larger view of the failed invasion. In his general orders he praised the regulars and militia extravagantly. He told the president of Congress that the militia particularly "deserve everything that can be said. They flew to arms universally and acted with a spirit equal to any thing I have seen in the course of the war."[64] He could have added—but was wary of boasting—that they had given dramatic proof that militia would fight hard if supported by an army to look the enemy in the face.

Looking back on the battle of Springfield, which is barely mentioned in most histories of the Revolution, it is easy to see why some writers have romanticized the militia. From young plowboys to substantial farmers like Sylvanus Seeley and Nathaniel FitzRandolph, they raced from peaceful homes to bullet-filled fields. We tend to forget Washington's bitter, hungry, ragged Continentals, who stood up to the British Sunday punches while the militiamen jabbed on the enemy's flanks. The devotion of these regulars is much harder to understand than the response of the militia, who were fighting virtually on their own doorsteps to protect their wives and children, farms and houses. Only those who saw what the regulars endured could really appreciate them. "I cherish those dear ragged Continentals, whose patience will be the admiration of future ages and glory in blooding with them," wrote one of Washington's aides.[65]

The war was far from over, but peace settled over most of New Jersey after the battle of Springfield. The enemy still conducted numerous raids along the shore but left the men and women of the interior mostly untroubled. A line from the diary of Sylvanus Seeley gives us a glimpse of this lovely quiet—and the way it was preserved. On July 12 his younger brother, Lieutenant Samuel Seeley, declared himself recovered from the wound he had received at Connecticut Farms. He was ready to return to the harsh life of the Continental soldier once more. Militia Colonel Sylvanus Seeley wrote in his diary, "Samal Seeley went for camp. Plowd my corn."[66]

CHAPTER 9

How Much Longer Can Fabius Last?

N ew Jersey had been rescued. The Continental Army's precious artillery and stores remained intact at Morristown.
But what about the rest of the barely breathing nation
General George Washington was defending? The Marquis de Lafayette
provided the first hint of hope in six months when he returned to
America with welcome news: the French were sending a large fleet and
army to rescue their struggling ally. Washington used the report to try
to browbeat Congress into making a major effort to recruit more men
for the army. "This is the time for America by one great exertion to put
an end to the war; but for this purpose the necessary means must be
furnished. The basis of everything else is the completion of the Continental battalions to their full establishment."[1]

July, with its celebration of the fourth anniversary of independence,
brought no improvement. Of the thousands of men Congress had
promised to find for Washington, not more than thirty had reported
for duty. Worse, the troops in the ranks still suffered from shocking
neglect. On July 6, 1780, Washington wrote to his brother-in-law Fielding Lewis that anyone at a distance would find it hard to believe that
his soldiers "should be five or six days together without meat; then as
many without bread, and once or twice . . . without either."[2]

The news from South Carolina grew worse every day. Civil government had collapsed. Governor John Rutledge had fled the state. The
British were marching into the backcountry, setting up forts staffed by
a mix of regulars and loyalist militia volunteers. They aimed obviously

for total domination. There was talk of a peace treaty that would return South Carolina and Georgia to the empire.

In Congress South Carolina's delegates pleaded for help. The frazzled legislators decided to send a general who had, they believed, proven his ability to snatch victory from looming defeat. Soon Washington learned that General Horatio Gates had become the new commander in the south.

⌒

IF GATES succeeded, few doubted that Congress would ask him to take charge of the entire Continental Army, which had accomplished so little in the past two years. Washington, determined to avoid any hint of disapproval, gave Gates the two best regiments he had left in his army—the men from Maryland and Delaware—commanded by a burly professional soldier who had come to America with Lafayette, Baron Johann DeKalb.

The Marylanders and Delawareans had been on their way to Charleston when the city surrendered. They continued to advance cautiously, their progress delayed by an acute shortage of food. When Gates joined them on July 25, 1780, he brought with him about 1,500 Virginia and North Carolina militiamen, about 250 cavalry, and a baggage train nearly a mile long. The new commander emanated confidence. He had heard reports of victories over British outposts by South Carolina partisan bands. He seemed to think this activity would intimidate the British and permit him to set up a strong base camp in or near the town of Camden, on the border between North and South Carolina.

To his deputy adjutant general, Colonel Otho Holland Williams, Gates revealed how much of this confidence rested on fantasy. He estimated that he had 7,000 men. Williams asked each regiment to report its exact strength. Some quick addition revealed a total force of only 3,052 men. Gates casually dismissed this vital number. "Sir," he said, "it will be enough for our purpose." To another officer, Gates remarked that he expected to have breakfast the following morning in Camden, "with Cornwallis at my table." The Saratoga victory had apparently rendered Gates susceptible to delusions of grandeur.[3]

General Gates was also oblivious of the existence of Banastre Tarleton. This newly promoted lieutenant colonel had already demonstrated a terrifying ability to strike suddenly and ferociously where the Americans least expected him. On May 6, 1780, at Lenud's Ferry, he surprised and virtually destroyed the American cavalry, forcing many officers and men to leap into the Santee River to escape.[4]

After Charleston surrendered, only one unit of regular American troops remained in South Carolina, the 3rd Virginia Continentals commanded by Colonel Abraham Buford. They had been marching to Charleston when the city surrendered. Buford was ordered to retreat to North Carolina. Lord Cornwallis sent Tarleton and his legion in pursuit. Covering 105 miles in fifty-four hours, Tarleton caught up with the Americans at Waxhaws, on the Carolina border. The 380 Virginians were largely new recruits, few of whom had seen action before. Their commander, Buford, was a fool and a coward. Tarleton and the legion charged from front, flank, and rear. Buford ordered his men to hold their fire until the saber-swinging dragoons were on top of them. The American line was torn to fragments. Buford wheeled his horse and fled. Tarleton reportedly sabered an American officer as he tried to raise a white flag. Other Americans screamed for quarter, but some kept firing. A bullet killed Tarleton's horse, and he crashed to the ground. This, he later claimed, aroused his men to a "vindictive asperity." Thinking their leader had been killed, they bayonetted or sabered dozens of Americans who had already thrown down their guns and surrendered.

At Waxhaws 113 Americans perished, and 203 were captured; of the latter, 150 were so badly wounded that the British left them on the battlefield. Throughout the Carolinas, word of the massacre—as the Americans called it—passed from settlement to settlement. The slaughter, dubbed "Tarleton's quarter," did not inspire much trust in British benevolence among those urged to surrender.[5]

⌒

CORNWALLIS HAD taken command of British forces in the south when Henry Clinton returned to New York. He was in Camden, setting up a base from which he hoped to launch an attack on North Carolina. Several regimental commanders, notably William Smallwood, head of the Maryland regiment, disputed Gates's assumption that his superior numbers and the partisan activity elsewhere in South Carolina would force the British to retreat.[6] On August 16, 1780, the two armies met at dawn. Gates ordered his militia into the front line, on the left. His Continentals, the Marylanders and Delawareans, he placed in the center and on the right. Did Gates know he was fighting the battle in a way that directly challenged General Washington on the use of militia? One can only conclude that he did. Gates was gambling on a victory that would not only wipe out the humiliations he had suffered at Valley Forge, when he allowed others to push him for commander in chief, but enable him to heap scorn on Washington's pretensions as a thinking general.

After a brief artillery duel, Cornwallis ordered a bayonet charge. As the howling regulars emerged from the gun smoke, most of Gates's militia fled without firing a shot. Wheeling, the British assaulted the 1,200 Continentals from the flank and front. At first the regulars stood their ground, and the battle seesawed. Then Cornwallis unleashed Banastre Tarleton's six-hundred-man British Legion. Their savage shouts and whirling sabers proved too much for regimental pride and military discipline to endure. The Continentals disintegrated and fled.

Far ahead of them, on the fastest horse he could find, was their commander, General Horatio Gates. He did not stop fleeing for two days and nights, finally halting at Hillsboro, North Carolina, 180 miles from Camden. There he set up a camp of sorts and welcomed the survivors who staggered in his ruinous wake. The retreat forever destroyed his reputation as a general.[7]

In New York, ecstatic loyalists ran an ad in one of their newspapers: "Lost: A Whole Army," signed Horatio Gates, "late commander of the Southern Army." It declared that Charles Thomson, secretary to the Continental Congress, promised to pay "Three Millions of Paper Dollars" to anyone who could help him find the missing army. This was first-class mockery. It not only demolished Gates's reputation but satirized Congress's pretensions of financing the war with its make-believe money.[8]

⌣

OUTSIDE BRITISH-HELD New York, General Washington faced another disappointment. The exhilarating news brought by Lafayette in the spring—that France was sending an army and a fleet—dwindled to another form of mockery when the French arrived in Newport. Their army consisted of barely 5,000 men, at least a fifth of them unfit for duty after the long voyage. The escorting fleet was too small to cope with the British squadron patrolling off Newport's harbor. Washington's recurrent dream of a successful attack on New York was indefinitely postponed.

On September 20, 1780, Washington journeyed to Hartford, Connecticut, to confer with the French commander, Lieutenant General Jean Baptiste Donatien de Vimeur, Comte de Rochambeau. The revelation that Washington had barely 3,000 men in his army rendered the stocky Frenchman almost speechless with shock. Rochambeau called Washington's proposal for an attack on New York "a fantasy of expiring patriotism." The two men could only agree to write to their governments, asking for the reinforcements needed to strike an effective blow at the enemy.

⌣

ON THE way back from Hartford, Washington decided to stop at West Point, where Major General Benedict Arnold had recently become commander. Washington hoped that Arnold's leg wound, suffered at the climax of the battle of Saratoga, had healed sufficiently to permit him to assume a more active role in the Continental Army. The commander in chief did not know that while he conversed with Rochambeau, General Arnold was having a traitorous conversation with Major John Andre, adjutant general of the British army. It was the culmination of Arnold's romantic brainwashing by his beautiful young wife, Peggy Shippen. Arnold had agreed to betray West Point to the British in return for £20,000 and a general's commission in the Royal Army.

Things went disastrously wrong for the plotters after they sealed this bargain. American militia captured Andre when he attempted to return to New York and forwarded the incriminating papers they had found in his boot to General Arnold at West Point. Realizing his treachery had collapsed, Arnold fled down the Hudson River to a British sloop. When Washington saw Andre's papers, he realized their import. "Arnold has betrayed us!" he gasped. "Whom can we trust now?"[9]

CONGRESS, ITS Fabian hostility mollified, humbly asked Washington to appoint a new commander in the south. If Arnold's treason had not accidentally come to light, the commander in chief might have chosen him. Instead, Washington reluctantly named the general he valued most as a confidant and advisor: Nathanael Greene. In introducing Greene to Congressman John Mathews of South Carolina, he wrote, "I think I am giving you a general, but what can a general do, without men, without arms, without clothing, without stores, without provisions?"[10]

It was neither the first nor the last of Washington's attempts to shock Congress into helping him and his generals maintain an army to look the enemy in the face. For the moment, he could do nothing more in his part of the continent. Would Nathanael Greene be able to apply his strategy of victory to rescue the south?

On November 19, 1780, the two men began a correspondence that would reveal the appalling difficulties Greene was about to confront and his remarkable grasp of Washington's approach to the war. It would also display Greene's penetrating insights into his situation and his readiness to add nuance to the strategy. Writing from Richmond, Greene told Washington that both Congress and the Virginia legislature were crucial to his hopes of success. "I must request, therefore, in the most earnest manner that your Excellency continue to animate both these bodies with your opinion and recommendations." Otherwise, he was "very apprehensive the langour that is too apt to seize all public bodies will lull them into a state of false security; and the affairs of the southern Department will and must go to ruin." Greene added a suggestion as daring as it was radical. "It has been my opinion for a long time that personal influence must supply the defects of civil Constitution; but I have never been so fully convinced of it as on this journey. I believe the views and wishes of the great body of the people are entirely with us. But remove the personal influence of a few, and they are a lifeless and inanimate mass, without direction or spirit to employ that means they possess for their own security." These words reveal the crucial nature of Washington's leadership, north and south.[11]

CHAPTER 10

A Plan So Daring Even
Daniel Morgan Feared the Worst

O n December 2, 1780, Major General Nathanael Greene arrived in Charlotte, North Carolina, where Horatio Gates was trying to reorganize the remnants of the army shattered at Camden. The numbers were not encouraging. Of 1,482 soldiers present and fit for duty, 949 were Continentals; the rest were militia. Worse, as Greene told his friend the Marquis de Lafayette, if he counted as fit for duty only those soldiers who were properly clothed and equipped, he did not have eight hundred men. The camp had provisions for only three days. There was scarcely a horse or a wagon in sight and not a dollar of hard money in the military chest.[1] In a December 7, 1780, letter to General George Washington, Greene wrote, "Nothing can be more wretched and distressing than the condition of the troops, starving with cold and hunger—without tents and equipage. Those of the Virginia line are literally naked, and a great part totally unfit for any kind of duty, and must remain so until clothing can be had from the Northward. I have written to Governor Jefferson not to send forward any more until they are well cloathed and properly equiped."[2]

On December 3, Brigadier General Daniel Morgan arrived in the American camp. It was the first encouraging news General Greene had heard since his arrival. This huge, muscular man was a living legend. He had fought ferociously in the 1775 invasion of Canada, leading a charge into the heart of Quebec City, although the British outnumbered him four or five to one. Finally trapped, he had surrendered his sword to a Catholic priest rather than give anyone in a British uniform the satisfaction of capturing him.

Exchanged, Morgan and his riflemen had played crucial roles in winning both battles of Saratoga. He had rejoined Washington's army during the ordeal of Valley Forge but, angered by Congress's failure to promote him, resigned his colonel's commission in 1779. The disaster at Camden and the threat of England's new southern strategy had persuaded him to discard his personal grievances. Congress had responded by making him a brigadier general. Studying his maps and knowing Morgan's ability to inspire militia and command light infantry, Nathanael Greene began to think the "Old Wagoner," as Morgan liked to call himself (he had worked as a wagon master during the French and Indian War), was the key to frustrating British plans to conquer North Carolina. Lord Cornwallis and the main British army were now at Winnsborough, South Carolina, about halfway between the British base at Camden and their vital backcountry fort at Ninety Six. An early mapmaker had named the fort and surrounding settlement in the course of measuring distances on the Cherokee Path, an ancient Indian travel route from the mountains to the ocean. The British general commanded 3,324 regulars, four times the number of Greene's motley army, all presumably well trained and equipped. Spies and scouts reported that he was preparing for a winter invasion of North Carolina, which had, if anything, more loyalists than South Carolina. There was grave reason to fear that they would volunteer at the sight of a British army and take that state out of the shaky American confederacy.[3]

To delay, if not defeat, this potential disaster, Greene divided his pathetic army and gave more than half of it to Daniel Morgan. The Old Wagoner would march swiftly across the front of Cornwallis's army into western South Carolina and operate on his left flank and in his rear, threatening the enemy's posts at Ninety Six and Augusta, disrupting British communications, and, most importantly, encouraging the militia of western South Carolina to return to the fight. "The object of this detachment," Greene wrote in his instructions to Morgan, "is to give protection to that part of the country and spirit up the people."[4]

This hope that the regulars would inspire a substantial turnout of the militia obviously reflected the thinking of America's Fabius, George Washington. On February 2, 1781, he told Greene that he based his orders on "just military principles." But neither Greene nor Morgan nor the commander in chief realized they were setting the stage for another climactic battle in which the strategy of victory would rescue the Revolution from looming defeat.[5]

General Lord Cornwallis had no intention of letting General Greene get away with his ingenious maneuver. Cornwallis had an answer to Daniel Morgan. His name was Banastre Tarleton.

〜

AFTER HELPING to smash the American army at Camden with another devastating charge, Tarleton was ordered to pursue Thomas Sumter and his partisans. Pushing his men and horses at his usual pace despite the tropical heat of August, he caught up with Sumter's men at Fishing Creek. Sabering a few carelessly posted sentries, the British Legion swept down on the Carolinians as they lay about their camp, weapons stacked, half of the men sleeping or cooking meals. Sumter leaped on a bareback horse and imitated General Gates and Colonel Abraham Buford, fleeing for his life. Tarleton's men killed or captured virtually the entire American force of 450 men. When the news was published in England, Tarleton became a national hero. In his official dispatches, Lord Cornwallis called him "one of the most promising officers I ever knew."[6]

But Sumter immediately began gathering a new band of partisans, and Francis Marion and his raiders repeatedly emerged from the lowland swamps to harass communications with Charleston and punish any loyalist who declared for the king. Tarleton did not understand this stubborn resistance and liked it even less. A nauseating bout with yellow fever deepened his saturnine mood. Pursuing Marion along the Santee and Black Rivers, Tarleton ruthlessly burned the farmhouses of "violent rebels," as he called them. "The country now is convinced of the error of insurrection," he wrote to Cornwallis. But Tarleton failed to catch "the damned old fox," Marion.

The British Legion had scarcely returned from this exhausting march when it was ordered out once more in pursuit of Sumter. On November 9, 1780, Sumter and his new band of partisans had fought the British 63rd Regiment, backed by a troop of legion dragoons, at Fishdam Ford on the Broad River and mauled them badly. "I wish you could get three legions and divide yourself in three parts," Cornwallis wrote Tarleton. "We can do no good without you."[7]

Once more the legion marched for the backcountry. As usual, Tarleton's pace was preternaturally swift. On November 20, 1780, he caught Sumter and his men as they prepared to ford the Tyger River. But this time Tarleton's fondness for headlong pursuit got him into serious trouble. He had left most of his infantry far behind and pushed ahead with fewer than two hundred cavalry and ninety infantry riding two men to a horse. Sumter had close to 1,000 men and attacked, backwoods style, filtering through the trees to pick off foot soldiers and horsemen. Tarleton ordered a bayonet charge. The infantry was so badly shot up that Tarleton had to charge with the cavalry to extricate it, exposing his dragoons to deadly rifle fire from other militiamen entrenched in a big log tobacco house known as Blackstock's. The battle ended in a bloody draw. Sumter was badly wounded, and his men abandoned the field to the green-coated dragoons, slipping across the Tyger River in the darkness. Without their charismatic leader, Sumter's militia went home.[8]

"Sumter is defeated," Tarleton reported to Cornwallis, "his corps dispersed. But my Lord I have lost men—50 killed and wounded." The lieutenant colonel was finding the war more and more disheartening and infuriating. Deepening his black mood was news from home. His older brother had put him up for Parliament from Liverpool. The voters had rejected him. They admired his courage, but the American war was no longer popular in England.[9]

While Cornwallis remained at Winnsborough, Tarleton returned from Blackstock's and camped at various plantations south of the Broad River. During his projected invasion of North Carolina, Cornwallis expected Tarleton and his legion to keep the dwindling rebels of South Carolina dispersed in their homes. Thus the British commander would have no worries about the British base at Ninety Six, the key to the backcountry. The district around Ninety Six was the breadbasket of South Carolina; it was also heavily loyalist. But a year of partisan warfare had weakened morale. The American-born commander of the fort, Colonel John Henry Cruger, had recently warned Cornwallis that the loyalists "were wearied by the long continuance of the campaign . . . and the whole district had determined to submit as soon as the rebels should enter it." The mere hint of a threat to Ninety Six and the order it preserved in the vicinity sent flutters of alarm through British headquarters.[10]

THERE WERE flutters aplenty when Cornwallis heard from spies that Daniel Morgan had crossed the Broad River and was marching on Ninety Six. Simultaneously came news that Colonel William Washington, commander of Morgan's seventy-man cavalry detachment (the remnant of the regiment Tarleton had smashed during the siege of Charleston), had routed a group of loyalists at Hammond's Store, then forced another group to abandon a fort not far from Ninety Six. At 5:00 A.M., on January 2, 1781, Lieutenant Henry Haldane, one of Cornwallis's aides, rode into Tarleton's camp and told him the news. Close behind Haldane, a messenger brought a letter from Cornwallis: "If Morgan is . . . anywhere within your reach, I should wish you to push him to the utmost."

Haldane rushed an order to Major Archibald McArthur, commander of the first battalion of the 71st Regiment, which was not far away, guarding a ford over the Broad River that guaranteed quick communication with Ninety Six. McArthur was to place his men under Tarleton's command and join him in a forced march to rescue the crucial fort.[11]

Tarleton obeyed with his usual speed. His dragoons ranged far ahead of his little army, which now numbered about seven hundred men. By the end of the day he concluded that there was no cause for alarm about Ninety Six. Morgan was nowhere near it. But his scouts reported that Morgan was definitely south of the Broad River, urging militia from North and South Carolina to join him.

Tarleton's response to this challenge was almost inevitable. He asked Cornwallis for permission to pursue Morgan and either destroy him or force him to retreat over the Broad River again. There, Cornwallis and his army could devour him.

The young cavalry commander outlined the operation in a letter to Cornwallis on January 4. Realizing that he was all but giving orders to his general, he tactfully added, "I feel myself bold in offering my opinion [but] it flows from zeal for the public service and well grounded enquiry concerning the enemy's designs and operations." If Cornwallis approved the plan, Tarleton asked for reinforcements: a troop of cavalry from the 17th Light Dragoons and the infantrymen of the 7th Regiment of Royal Fusiliers, who were marching from Camden to reinforce Ninety Six.

Cornwallis approved the plan, including the reinforcements. As soon as they arrived, Tarleton began his march. January rain poured down, swelling every creek and turning the roads into quagmires. Cornwallis, with his larger army and heavy baggage train, began a slow advance up the north bank of the Broad River. As the commander in chief, he had more to worry about than Tarleton. Behind him was another British general, Alexander Leslie, with 1,500 reinforcements. Cornwallis feared that Greene or Marion might strike a blow at them. The British general assumed that Tarleton was as mired by the rain and blocked by swollen watercourses as he was. On January 12, Cornwallis wrote to Leslie, then delayed by even worse mud in the lowlands, "I believe Tarleton is as much embarrassed with the waters as you are." The same day, Cornwallis reported to another officer, the commander in occupied Charleston. "The rains have put a total stop to Tarleton and Leslie." On this assumption, Cornwallis decided to halt and wait for Leslie to reach him.

But Tarleton had not allowed the August heat of South Carolina to slow his pace. He held the January rains in equal contempt. His scouts reported that Morgan's army was at Grindal's Shoals on the Pacolet River. To reach the Americans, Tarleton had to cross two smaller but equally swollen rivers, the Enoree and the Tyger. Swimming his horses and floating his infantry across on improvised rafts, he surmounted these obstacles and headed west, deep into the South Carolina back-country. He did not realize that his column, which now numbered over 1,000 men, was becoming more and more isolated. He assumed that Cornwallis was keeping pace with him on the north side of the Broad River, cowing the rebel militia there into staying home.[12]

⌒

NOR DID Tarleton realize that this time, no matter how swiftly he advanced, he was not going to take the Americans by surprise. He was being watched by forty-one-year-old Andrew Pickens, who was fighting with a hangman's noose around his neck. The Cherokees called him Skyagunsta, the Wizard Owl. They both feared and honored him as a battle leader who had defeated them repeatedly on their home ground. Born in Pennsylvania, Pickens had come to South Carolina as a boy. In 1765 he had married the beautiful Rebecca Calhoun and settled on Long Canes Creek in the Ninety Six district. Pickens was no speech-maker, but everyone recognized this lean, slender man, who was just under six feet tall, as a leader. When he spoke, people listened. One acquaintance declared he was so deliberate that he seemed at times to take each word out of his mouth and examine it before uttering it.

Pickens had inspired hundreds of men to join him in repelling the Cherokee Indians' British-inspired assaults on the backcountry in 1776. They soon carried the war into the red men's country, totally defeating them. By 1779 Pickens was a colonel commanding one of the most dependable militia regiments in the state. When the loyalists, encouraged by the British conquest of Georgia in 1778, began to gather and plot to punish their rebel neighbors, Pickens led four hundred men to assault them at Kettle Creek on the Savannah River. In a fierce hour-long fight, he whipped them, although they outnumbered him almost two to one.[13]

After Charleston surrendered, Pickens's military superior in the Ninety Six district, Brigadier General Andrew Williamson, was the only high-ranking official left in South Carolina. The governor, John Rutledge, had fled to North Carolina, the legislature had dispersed, and the courts had collapsed. Early in June 1780, Williamson called together his officers and asked them to vote on whether they should continue to resist. Only eight officers opposed immediate surrender. In Pickens's regiment, which Williamson urged in a speech to stay in the fight, only two officers and four enlisted men favored resistance. The rest saw no hope of stopping the British regular army's advancing toward them from captured Charleston. Without a regular army of their own to match the British, they could envision only destruction of their homes and desolation for their families if they resisted. It was another graphic example of how militia reacted when there was no regular army to look the enemy in the face.

Andrew Pickens was among the realists who accepted the surrender terms offered by the British. At his command, his regiment of three hundred men stacked their guns at Ninety Six and went home. As Pickens understood the terms, he and his men were paroled on their promise not to bear arms against the king. They became neutrals.

The British commander of Ninety Six, Colonel John Henry Cruger, seemed to respect this stance. Cruger treated Pickens with great deference. The motive for this delicate treatment became visible in a letter Cruger sent to Cornwallis on November 27. "I think there is more than a possibility of getting a certain person in the Long Canes settlement to accept of a command," Cruger wrote. "And then I should most humbly be of opinion that every man in the country would declare and act for His Majesty."[14]

It was a tribute to Pickens's influence as a leader. He was also a man of his word. Even when Sumter, the Georgian Elijah Clarke, and other partisan leaders demonstrated that many men in South Carolina were ready to keep fighting, Pickens remained peaceably at home on his plantation at Long Canes. Tales of Tarleton's cruelty at Waxhaws and of British and loyalist vindictiveness in other districts of the state undoubtedly reached him. But he and his men had suffered no acts of injustice. The British were keeping their part of the bargain, and he would keep his.

Then Cornwallis's aide, Lieutenant Henry Haldane, appeared at Ninety Six and summoned Colonel Pickens. He offered him a colonel's commission in the royal militia and a promise of protection. There were also polite hints of a monetary reward for switching aides. Pickens agreed to ride down to Charleston and talk the whole thing over with the British commander there. Partisan warfare in the Ninety Six district, stirred by the arrival of Nathanael Greene to take command of the remnant of the American regular army, delayed the visit. Greene urged the wounded Sumter and Clarke to assemble their men and launch a new campaign. Sumter wrote to Pickens, urging him to break his parole, call out his regiment, and march with him to join Greene. Pickens refused to leave Long Canes.

∽

IN DESPERATION, the rebels came to Pickens. Elijah Clarke led a band of Georgians and South Carolinians to the outskirts of Long Canes on their march to join Greene. Many men from Pickens's old regiment broke their paroles and joined them. Clarke ordered Major James McCall, one of Pickens's favorite officers and one of the two who had refused to surrender at Ninety Six, to kidnap Pickens and bring him before an improvised court-martial board. Accused of preparing to join the loyalists, Pickens calmly admitted that the British were making him offers. So far he had refused them. But even if his former friends made good on their threat to court-martial and hang him, he could not break his word of honor to remain neutral.[15]

The frustrated Georgians and South Carolinians let Pickens go home. On December 12, Colonel Cruger sent a detachment of regulars and loyalist militia to attack the interlopers. The royalists surprised the rebels and routed them, wounding Clarke and McCall and dispersing the survivors. Most of the Georgians drifted back to their home state, and the Carolinians straggled toward Greene in North Carolina.

The battle had a profound effect on Andrew Pickens. Friends and former comrades in arms had been wounded, humiliated. He still hesitated to take the final step and break his parole. His strict Presbyterian conscience and soldier's sense of honor would not permit it. But he went to Ninety Six and told Colonel Cruger that he could not accept a commission in the royal militia. Cruger sighed and revealed what he had been planning since he started wooing Pickens. In a few days, on orders from Cornwallis, the loyalist colonel would publish a proclamation permitting no one to remain neutral. It would require everyone around Ninety Six to come to the fort, swear allegiance to the king, and enlist in the royal militia.[16]

Pickens said his conscience would not permit him to comply. A British threat of punishment for his refusal would violate his parole, and he would consider himself free to join the rebels. One British officer, who had become a friend and admirer of the resolute Pickens, warned, "You will campaign with a halter around your neck. If we catch you, we will hang you."

Pickens decided to take the risk. He rode about Long Canes calling out his regiment. The response was somewhat discouraging. Only about seventy men turned out. Coordinating their movements with Colonel Washington's raid on the loyalists at Hammond's Store, they joined the American cavalry and rode past Ninety Six to Morgan's camp on the Pacolet.

The numbers Pickens brought with him were disappointing. But he and his men knew the backcountry intimately. They were the eyes and ears Morgan's little army desperately needed. Morgan immediately asked Pickens to send his horsemen ranging in all directions to guard against a surprise attack by Banastre Tarleton.[17]

The Wizard Owl and his men mounted their horses and rode away to begin their reconnaissance. General Morgan soon knew enough about the enemy force coming after him to fear for the survival of his army. Daniel Morgan might call Banastre Tarleton "Benny" for the entertainment of young militiamen, but he had been fighting the British for five years. He was as close to being a professional soldier as any American of his time. He knew Banastre Tarleton was no joke.

⌒

NOT LONG after realizing that he was Tarleton's target, Morgan almost casually announced a decision to concentrate his cavalry and infantry at the Thompson plantation on Thicketty Creek. It was a carefully disguised retreat. The march to Thicketty Creek put an additional ten miles between him and the aggressive British cavalry leader. Behind the mask of easy confidence Morgan wore for his men lay a very worried general.

Morgan began sending messengers to the men of western Georgia, South Carolina, and North Carolina, urging them to turn out and support him. The response was disheartening. Pickens, as we have seen, failed to muster more than a fraction of his old regiment. From Georgia came only a small detachment of about one hundred men under the command of Major James Jackson and John Cunningham. With their leader, Elijah Clarke, out of action from his wound at Long Canes, the Georgians were inclined to stay home. Sumter, although almost recovered from his injury, sulked on the north side of the Broad River. He felt General Greene had sent Morgan into his sphere of command without properly consulting him.[18]

Morgan had focused his highest hopes on North Carolina, thus far relatively untouched by the British. Brigadier General William Davidson, a former Continental officer whom Morgan had known at Valley Forge, commanded the militia in the backcountry. An energetic, committed man, popular with the militia, Davidson had been expected to muster from 600 to 1,000 men. Instead, Morgan got a letter from him with the doleful report, "I have not ninety men." On December 28, Davidson rode into Morgan's camp, bringing only 120 men. He said that he hoped to have another 500 mustered at Salisbury in the next week and rode off to find them, leaving General Morgan muttering in dismay.[19]

Morgan had eagerly accepted this independent command because he thought at least 2,500 militiamen would join his 300 Continentals. With an army that size, he could have besieged or even stormed the British stronghold at Ninety Six. His present force seemed too small to do the enemy any damage. But it was large enough to give its commander numerous headaches, in addition to the major worry of annihilation by the enemy. Food was very scarce. The country around his line of march had been plundered and fought over for so long, the farms and barns had nothing left to requisition. On December 31, in a letter to Greene, Morgan predicted that in a few days, supplies would be "unattainable."[20]

What to do? The only practical move Morgan could see was to march his feeble army into Georgia. The British outpost at Augusta was weaker and more isolated than Ninety Six. Even here, Morgan was extremely cautious. "I have consulted with General Davidson and Colonel Pickens as to whether we could secure a safe retreat, should we be pushed by a superior force. They tell me it can be easily effected," he wrote to Nathanael Greene, asking for his approval of this plan.

Morgan's hesitation grew out of his keen understanding of the average militiaman: He wanted to come out, fight, and go home as soon as possible. He did not want to fight if the regular army that was supposed to look the enemy in the face seemed more interested in showing the enemy its back. "Were we to advance, and be constrained to retreat the consequences, would be very disagreeable," Morgan told Greene, speaking as one general to another. The militia, he was saying, would go home.[21]

⌁

GREENE WAS equally nervous about Morgan. The southern commander told Morgan of the arrival of General Leslie in Charleston with reinforcements. This news meant the British would almost certainly advance soon. "Watch their motions very narrowly and take care to guard against a surprise," he wrote. Greene vetoed Morgan's expedition into Georgia. He did not think Morgan was strong enough to accomplish much. "The enemy . . . secure in their fortifications, will take no notice of your movement," he predicted. Convinced that Cornwallis would soon strike at his half of the army, Greene did not want Morgan in Georgia if this threat materialized. Ignoring Morgan's worries about feeding his men, Greene told him to stay where he was, on the Pacolet River or "in the neighborhood," and await an opportunity to attack the British rear when that army marched into North Carolina.

Morgan replied with a lament. He reiterated his warning that "forage [for the horses] and provisions are not to be had." He insisted there was "but one alternative, either to retreat or move into Georgia." A retreat, he warned, "will be attended with the most fatal consequences. The spirit which now begins to pervade the people and call them into the field, will be destroyed. The militia who have already joined will desert us and it is not improbable but that a regard for their own safety will induce them to join the enemy."[22]

That last line provides grim evidence of the power of the British policy of forcing everyone to serve in the loyalist militia. But Nathanael Greene remained adamant. He reported to Morgan more bad news, which made a march into Georgia even more inadvisable. Another British general, with 2,500 men, had landed in Virginia and was attacking that vital colony, upon which the southern army depended for many of its supplies. Sending some of the army's best troops deeper south made no sense, when Virginia might call on Greene and Morgan for aid. Almost casually, Greene added, "Col. Tarleton is said to be on his way to pay you a visit. I doubt not but he will have a decent reception and a proper dismission."

This was a strange remark from a worried general. Other letters Greene wrote around this time indicate that he had received a number of very conflicting reports about Tarleton's strength and position. The American commander was also unsure about British intentions. He assumed that Cornwallis and Tarleton were moving up the opposite sides of the Broad River in concert. Since the main British army under Cornwallis had all but stopped advancing, Greene thought Tarleton had stopped too and that Morgan was in no immediate danger.[23]

∽

MUCH AS he dreaded the thought of a retreat, Morgan was too experienced a soldier not to prepare for one. He sent the officer acting as his quartermaster across the Broad River with orders to set up magazines of supplies for the army. The officer returned with dismaying news. General Sumter had refused to cooperate with this request and directed his subordinates to obey no orders from Daniel Morgan.[24]

Adding to Morgan's supply woes was a Carolina military custom. Every militiaman brought his horse to camp with him. This meant that Morgan had to find forage for over 450 horses (counting William Washington's cavalry horses), each of which ate twenty-five to thirty pounds of oats and hay a day. "Could the militia be persuaded to change their fatal mode of going to war," Morgan groaned to Greene, "much provision might be saved; but the custom has taken such deep root that it cannot be abolished."

Bands of militiamen constantly left the army to hunt for forage. This practice made it impossible for Morgan to know how many men he had at his disposal. In desperation, he ordered his officers, both Continental and militia, to call the roll every two hours. This measure only gave him more bad news. On January 15, after retreating from the Pacolet to Thicketty Creek, he reported to Greene that he had only 340 militia with him. Worse, he did not expect "to have more than two-thirds of these to assist me, should I be attacked, for it is impossible to keep them collected."

A personal problem made Morgan feel even more like a military Job. The incessant rain and the damp January cold had awakened an illness that he had contracted fighting in the Canadian winter of 1775, a rheumatic inflammation of the sciatic nerve in his hip. It made riding a horse agony.[25] In his tent on Thicketty Creek, where he had rendez-voused with William Washington and his seventy cavalrymen, Morgan all but abandoned any hope of executing the mission on which Greene had sent him. "My force is inadequate," he wrote. "Upon a full and mature deliberation I am confirmed in the opinion that nothing can be effected by my detachment in this country, which will balance the risks I will be subjected to by remaining here." It would be best, Morgan told Greene, if he were recalled with his little band of Continentals and Andrew Pickens or William Davidson left to command the backcountry militia. Without the regulars to challenge them, the British would be less likely to invade the district, and under Pickens's leadership the rebels would be able to keep "a check on the disaffected"—the Tories—"which," Morgan added mournfully, "is all I can effect."[26]

When he wrote these words on January 15, Morgan remained unaware of what was coming at him. From the reports of Pickens's scouts, he had begun to worry that Tarleton might have more than his 550-man British Legion with him. With the help of Washington's cavalry, he felt confident that he could beat off an attack by the legion. But what if Tarleton had been given additional men? "Col. Tarleton has crossed the Tyger at Musgrove's Mill," Morgan told Greene. "His force we cannot learn."

Into Morgan's camp galloped more scouts from Andrew Pickens. They brought news that made Morgan revise the last sentence of his letter. "We have Just learned that Tarleton's force is from eleven to twelve hundred British." The last word, "British," was the significant one: 1,200 regulars, trained troops, saber-swinging dragoons and bayonet-wielding infantry like the men who had sent the militia running for their lives at Camden and then cut the Continentals to pieces. General Daniel Morgan could see only one alternative: retreat.

Until he got this information on the exact numbers and composition of Tarleton's army, Morgan, it seems, toyed with the possibility of ambushing the British as they crossed the Pacolet. He left strong detachments of his army at the most likely fords. At the very least, he may have wanted to make the crossing a bloody business for the British, perhaps killing some of their best officers, even Tarleton himself. If he could repulse or delay Tarleton at the Pacolet, Morgan hoped he could gain enough time to retreat to a ford across the upper Broad, well out of the reach of Cornwallis, on the other side of the river. Pickens had kept Morgan well informed of the sluggish advance of the main British army. He knew they were far to the south, a good thirty miles behind Tarleton.

North of the Broad, Morgan reasoned they could easily meet up with the five hundred North Carolina militia promised by William Davidson. If Tarleton continued the pursuit, they could give battle on the rugged slopes of King's Mountain, where the British Legion cavalry would be useless.[27]

Morgan discussed this plan with the leaders of the militiamen who were already with him. They did not have much enthusiasm for it and warned Morgan that at least half the militia, especially the South Carolinians, would be inclined to go home rather than retreat across the Broad River. In the backcountry, men perceived rivers as dividing lines between districts. Most of the South Carolina men in camp came from the south side of the Broad. Moreover, with Sumter hostile, they could not count on persuading many men on the other side of the river to join them.[28]

∽

IN THIS discussion, the militia leaders likely mentioned the Cowpens grazing ground as a good place to fight Tarleton on the south side of the river. The name was familiar to everyone in the backcountry. The militia had assembled at that spot before the battle of King's Mountain the previous fall. Messengers could be sent into every district within a day's ride to urge laggards to join them there.

Morgan mulled over his alternatives while his men guarded the fords of the Pacolet. As dusk fell on January 15, Tarleton and his army appeared on the south bank of the river. He saw the guards and wheeled, marching up the stream toward a ford near Wofford's Iron Works. On the opposite bank, Morgan's men kept pace with him, step for step. Then, with no warning, the British disappeared into the night. Retreating? Making camp? No one knew. Venturing across the swollen river to follow was too risky. The British Legion cavalry always guarded Tarleton's flanks and rear.

On the morning of January 16, a militia detachment miles down the river in the opposite direction made an alarming discovery. Tarleton was across! He had doubled back in the dark and marched most of the night to cross at Easterwood Shoal. He was only six miles from Morgan's camp on Thicketty Creek. Leaping on their horses, the guards galloped to Morgan with the news.

Morgan's men were cooking breakfast. The general charged out of his tent to roar orders at them. Prepare to march immediately! The men grabbed their half-cooked cornmeal cakes and stuffed them into their mouths. The militia and the cavalry ran for their horses, the wagoners hitched their teams, the Continentals formed ranks, and the column got under way. Keeping his options open, Morgan pressed forward, ignoring the agonizing pain in his hip, demanding more and more speed from his men. He headed northwest, toward the Cowpens, on the Green River Road, a route that would also take him to the Island Ford across the Broad River, about six miles beyond the Cowpens.

All day the men slogged along the slick, gooey roads, Morgan at the head of the column setting a relentless pace. His rheumatic hip tormented him. Behind him, the militiamen were expending "many a hearty curse" on him, one of them later recalled. As Nathanael Greene and other American generals often wryly observed, in the militia every man considered himself a general. They deemed retreat cowardly.[29]

But Brigadier General Daniel Morgan was responsible for their lives and those of his Continentals, some of whom had marched doggedly from battlefield to battlefield for over four years. In the company of Delaware Continentals serving beside the Marylanders in the light infantry brigade, a lieutenant named Thomas Anderson had kept track of the miles he had marched since they headed south in May 1780. By January 16, 1781, the total was 1,435. No matter what the militia thought of him, Daniel Morgan was not going to throw such men away in a battle simply to prove his courage.[30]

Seldom has anyone better exemplified the difference between the professional and the amateur soldier. In his letters urging militiamen to join him, Morgan had warned against the futility of fighting in small detachments. He had asked them to come into his camp and subject themselves to "order and discipline . . . so that I may be enabled to direct you . . . to the advantage of the whole."

In the same letters, Morgan had made a promise to these men. "I will ask you to encounter no dangers or difficulties, but what I shall participate in." If he retreated across the Broad River, he would expose the men who refused to go with him to Tarleton's policy of extermination by fire and sword. Those who did accompany him, on the other hand, would be abandoning their families, their friends, and their homes to the saturnine young lieutenant colonel's vengeance.

This conflict between prudence and his promise raged in Morgan's mind as his army toiled along the Green River Road. It was hard marching. The road dipped into hollows and looped around small hills. Swollen creeks cut across it. The woods were thick on both sides. As dusk's shadows lengthened, the Americans emerged from the forest onto what looked, at first glance, like a flat, relatively treeless meadow. As Morgan led his men farther, he noted that the ground rose gradually to a slight crest, then dipped and rose to another slightly higher crest. Oak and hickory trees dotted the more or less rectangular area, but there was practically no underbrush. This was the Cowpens, a place where backcountry people used to pasture their cattle and prepare them for the drive to market.

In the distance, Morgan could see the Blue Ridge Mountains, which rise from the flat country beyond the Broad River like a great rampart. They were forty miles away. If they could reach them, the army would be safe. But militia scouts brought in grim news. The Broad River was rising. Crossing at Island Ford in the dark would be a difficult business. The ford was still six miles away, and the men were exhausted from their all-day march. But if they rested at Cowpens and tried to cross the river the next morning, Banastre Tarleton, that soldier who liked to march by night, would be upon them, ready to slash them to pieces.

Perhaps this report helped Daniel Morgan make his decision. One suspects he almost welcomed the news that his army was, for all practical purposes, trapped, with no alternative but to fight. Daniel Morgan had enough of the citizen-soldier in him to dislike retreating almost as much as the average militiaman.

The more Morgan studied the terrain around him, the more he liked it. The militia leaders were right. This was the best place to fight Tarleton. Sitting on his horse, looking down the slope to the Green River Road, Morgan noted how the land fell off to the left and right toward several creeks. The Cowpens was really a long, narrow tableland, surrounded by marshy ground, which would make it difficult for Tarleton to execute any sweeping flank movements with his cavalry. That was not Tarleton's style, anyway. He was more likely to come straight at the Americans with his infantry and cavalry in a headlong charge. Daniel Morgan had met similar British charges at Saratoga. Experience had taught him ways to handle such an assault—tactics that twenty-six-year-old Banastre Tarleton had probably never seen.

Now the important thing was to communicate the will to fight. Turning to his officers, General Morgan said, "On this ground I will beat Benny Tarleton or I will lay my bones."[31]

CHAPTER 11

Downright Fighting

"Eleven to twelve hundred British," Daniel Morgan had written. Ironically, as Morgan ordered another retreat from this formidable foe, the British were barricading themselves in some log houses on the north bank of the Pacolet River, expecting an imminent attack from the Americans. Their spies had told them that Morgan had 3,000 men, and Banastre Tarleton was taking no chances. After seizing this strong point, only a few miles below Morgan's camp, he sent out a cavalry patrol. They soon returned, reporting that the Americans had "decamped." Tarleton immediately advanced to Morgan's abandoned campsite, where his hungry soldiers were delighted to find "plenty of provisions which they had left behind them, half cooked."

Nothing stirred Tarleton's blood more than a retreating enemy. Some have compared British soldiers, famed for their tenacity in war, to the bulldog. Tarleton was more like a bloodhound. A fleeing foe meant the chance of an easy victory. It was not only instinct; it was part of his training as a cavalryman.[1]

"Patrols and spies were immediately dispatched to observe the Americans," Tarleton later recalled. He ordered the British Legion dragoons to follow Morgan until dark, then turn the job over to "other emissaries"—loyalists. Tarleton had about fifty with him to act as scouts and spies. Early that evening, January 16, 1781, probably at around the time Morgan was deciding to fight at the Cowpens, a party of loyalists brought in a militia colonel who had wandered out of the American line of march, perhaps in search of forage for his horse. Threatened with instant hanging, the man talked. He told Tarleton that Morgan hoped to stop at the Cowpens and gather more militia. But the captive said that Morgan then intended to get across the Broad River, where he thought he would be safe.

The information whetted Tarleton's appetite. It seemed obvious to him that he should "hang upon General Morgan's rear" to cut off any militia reinforcements that might show up. If Morgan tried to cross the Broad, Tarleton would be in a position to "perplex his design," as he put it—a stuffy way of saying he could cut him to pieces. Around midnight, other loyalist scouts brought in a rumor of more American reinforcements on their way—a "corps of mountaineers." This sent a chill through the British, even through Tarleton. It sounded like the return of the Blue Ridge Mountain men who had helped destroy the loyalist army at King's Mountain. Tarleton saw more and more clearly that he should attack Morgan as soon as possible.[2]

At 2:00 A.M. on January 17, Tarleton called in his sentries and ordered his drummers to rouse the men from their sleep. Leaving thirty-five baggage wagons and seventy Negro slaves with a one-hundred-man guard commanded by a lieutenant, he marched his groggy men down the Green River Road, the same rutted route Morgan had followed to Cowpens the previous day. The British found the marching even harder in the dark. The ground, Tarleton later wrote, was "broken, and much intersected by creeks and ravines." Ahead of the column and on both flanks, scouts prowled the woods to prevent an ambush.

Describing his march, Tarleton also gave a precise description of his army. Three companies of light infantry, supported by the infantry of the British Legion, formed his vanguard. The light infantry were all crack troops who had been fighting in America since the beginning of the war. One company, from the 16th Regiment, had participated in some of the swift surprise attacks for which light infantry was designed. It had been part of the British force that killed and wounded 150 Americans in a night assault at Paoli, Pennsylvania, in the fall of 1777. It had been part of another force that virtually wiped out the 3rd Continental Dragoons at Tappan, New Jersey, the following year. The light infantry company of the 11th Regiment had a similar record, having also been part of the light infantry brigade that the British organized early in the war.

With these two companies of regulars marched another company of light infantry whose memories were not so grand: the green-coated men of the Prince of Wales Loyal American Volunteers. In the war since 1777, these northern loyalists had seen little fighting until they sailed south in 1780. After the fall of Charleston, Lord Cornwallis had divided them into detachments and used them to garrison small posts, with disastrous results. In August 1780 at Hanging Rock, Thomas Sumter had attacked and virtually annihilated one detachment. Francis Marion mauled another at Great Savannah around the same time. The British army had cashiered the regiment's colonel for cowardice at Hanging Rock. It was hardly a brilliant record. But the men of this company of light infantry, supposedly the boldest and best of the regiment, might eagerly seek revenge for their lost comrades.

Behind the light infantry marched the first battalion of the Royal Fusiliers of the 7th Regiment, one of the oldest in the British army, with a proud history stretching back to 1685. Known as the City of London Regiment, it had been in America since 1773. The war had started out badly for its men. Divided into detachments to garrison three forts along the Canadian border, all but ninety of them had been captured in the 1775 American invasion of Canada. The ninety who remained, however, had played a vital part in repulsing the December 31, 1775, attack on Quebec, which wrecked American plans to make Canada the fourteenth colony. Among the 426 Americans captured was Daniel Morgan. Few, if any, of the men in Tarleton's ranks had been in that fight. The battalion's 167 men were all new recruits. When they arrived in Charleston early in December, the British commander there had written to Cornwallis, describing them as "so bad, not above a third can possibly move with a regiment."[3]

The British government was having problems recruiting men to fight in America. It had never been easy to persuade Englishmen to join the army and endure its harsh discipline and low pay. Now, with the war growing more and more unpopular, army recruiters were scouring the jails and city slums. Lord Cornwallis had decided to use these new recruits as garrison troops at Ninety Six. Tarleton, as we have seen earlier, had borrowed them for his pursuit. Although the 7th's motto was "Nec Aspera Terrent" (hardships do not frighten us), these men must have found it unnerving, little more than a month after a long, debilitating sea voyage, to be marching through the cold, wet darkness, deep in the backwoods of South Carolina, to their first battle.

Undoubtedly worsening the Fusiliers' morale was their officers' low opinion of Banastre Tarleton. The commander of the regiment, Major Timothy Newmarsh, had stopped at a country house for the night about a week before, during the early stage of the pursuit, and indiscreetly voiced his fears for the safety of the expedition: he was certain of defeat because almost every officer in the army detested Tarleton, who had been promoted over the heads of men who had been in the service since before he was born.

Behind the Royal Fusiliers trudged a two-hundred-man battalion of the 71st Scottish Highlanders who probably did not find the night march through the woods quite as forbidding as the city men of the Fusiliers. But at least half of these men were relatively new recruits who had arrived in America little more than a year before. The rest were veterans who had been campaigning in the rebellious colonies since 1776. They were commanded by Major Archibald McArthur, a tough veteran who had served with the Scottish Brigade in the Dutch Army, considered one of the finest groups of fighting men in Europe.

Between the 71st and 7th Regiments plodded some eighteen blue-coated royal artillerymen, leading horses that carried two brass cannons and sixty rounds of round shot and case shot (also known as grapeshot, because each "case" contained smaller, bullet-size projectiles that scattered when fired). These light guns were considered an important innovation when introduced into the British army in 1775. Because they could be dismantled and carried on horses, they could be moved over rough terrain where ordinary artillery and its cumbersome ammunition wagons could not go. The two guns Tarleton had with him could also be fitted with shafts that enabled four men to carry them around a battlefield, if the ground was too muddy or rough to move them on their carriages. With the shafts added, they bore a distinct resemblance to grasshoppers, and this was what the artillerymen, fond of nicknaming their guns, called them.

The grasshoppers added to Tarleton's confidence. They could hurl their three-pound round shot almost 1,000 yards. There was little likelihood that Morgan had any cannons with him. The British had captured all the artillery of the southern American army at Camden. The guns with Tarleton may indeed have been two of these pieces, themselves originally seized from the British when the field army commanded by General John Burgoyne surrendered at Saratoga in 1777.[4]

Behind the infantry and artillery rode the cavalry of the British Legion and a 50-man troop of the 17th Dragoons, giving Tarleton about 350 horsemen. In scabbards dangling from straps over their shoulders they carried the fearsome sabers that could lop off a man's arm with a single stroke. The legion cavalry were, relatively speaking, amateurs, animated only by their courage and belief in the loyalist cause. The 17th Light Dragoons were regulars to the core, intensely proud of their long tradition. Their brass helmets displayed a death's-head and below it a scroll with the words "Or Glory." They and their officers disdained the British Legion.

Despite their large reputation among the Americans, the legion had several times exhibited cowardice unthinkable to a 17th Dragoon. When the British advanced into Charlotte, North Carolina, in the fall of 1780, a handful of backcountry riflemen had opposed them. Tarleton was ill with yellow fever, and his second in command, Major George Hanger, had ordered the legion cavalry to charge the Americans. The dragoons had refused to budge. Not even the exhortations of Lord Cornwallis himself stirred them until the infantry had dislodged the riflemen from cover. They apparently remembered the punishment they had taken at Blackstock's, when Tarleton's orders had exposed them to these sharpshooters.

∽

As DAWN turned the black night sky to charcoal grey, Tarleton ordered a select group of cavalry to the front of his infantry. They soon collided with American scouts on horseback and captured two, who told them that Morgan and his men were only a few miles away. Tarleton immediately ordered two troops of the legion cavalry, under one of his best officers, Captain David Ogilvie, to reinforce his vanguard. Captain Ogilvie galloped into the murky dawn. Within a half hour, one of his troopers came racing back with unexpected news. The Americans were not retreating! They were drawn up in an open wood in battle formation.

Tarleton halted his army and summoned his loyalist guides. They instantly recognized the place where Morgan had chosen to fight. The Cowpens was familiar to everyone who had visited or lived in the South Carolina backcountry. They gave Tarleton a detailed description of the battleground. The woods were open and free of swamps. The Broad River was about six miles behind the American position.

The Americans' battle site was, Tarleton decided, made to order for their destruction. In fact, America could not produce a place more suitable to his style of war. His bloodhound instinct dominant, Tarleton assumed that Morgan, having run from him for two days, was still only trying to check his advance and gain time to retreat over the Broad River. Morgan had failed to stop him at the Pacolet. He would fail even more disastrously here.

With six miles of open country in the Americans' rear, Tarleton looked forward to smashing Morgan's ranks with an infantry attack and then unleashing his legion horsemen to hunt down the fleeing survivors. Tarleton never dreamt that Daniel Morgan was planning a fight to the finish.

⌒

WHILE TARLETON'S troops spent most of the night marching along the twisting, dipping Green River Road, Daniel Morgan's men had been resting at the Cowpens and listening to their general's battle plan. First Morgan outlined it for his officers; then he went from campfire to campfire, explaining it to his men. The plan rested on the terrain at

Cowpens and on Morgan's knowledge of Tarleton's battle tactics. Morgan probably told his men what he repeated in later years: he expected nothing from Tarleton but "downright fighting." The young Englishman was going to come straight at them in an all-out charge.

To repel that charge, Morgan adopted tactics he had himself helped to design at Saratoga. The little army he commanded at the Cowpens bore a similarity to the men he led in northern New York. Like his old rifle corps, his militia were crack shots. But they could not stand up against a British bayonet charge. Rifles took too long to load and fire and were not equipped with a bayonet.

Before Saratoga, the British had killed American riflemen by the dozen. But at Saratoga, Morgan had worked out close tactical cooperation with a brigade of American light infantry, commanded by Henry Dearborn. His riflemen exacted a fearful toll in their opening volleys but depended on Dearborn's infantry, whose muskets did have bayonets, to keep the British from charging them. In later phases of the fighting at Saratoga, Morgan's riflemen had harassed the British flanks, while the regular infantry engaged the enemy from the front. Morgan's plan envisioned doing all these things with his mixture of militia and regulars at Cowpens.[5]

He had complete confidence in his Continentals. No regiments in the British army had a prouder tradition than these men from Maryland and Delaware. They and their comrades in arms had demonstrated their heroism on a dozen battlefields. Above all, Morgan trusted their commander, Lieutenant Colonel John Eager Howard of Maryland. At the battle of Germantown in 1777, he had led his 4th Maryland Regiment in a headlong charge that drove the British light infantry in panicky flight from their battle line back to their tents. After the American defeat at Camden, Howard had rounded up the survivors of his own and other regiments and led them on a three-day march to Charlotte, North Carolina, through swamps and forests to elude British pursuit. Someone asked what they had eaten during that time. "Some peaches," Howard said.[6]

Morgan was equally sure of the steadiness of the ex-Continentals who comprised the bulk of his two companies of Virginia six-month militiamen. He told them that he was going to station them on either side of the Maryland and Delaware regulars, on the first crest of the almost invisibly rising slope that constituted the Cowpens. A professional soldier would consider this the "military crest" of the hill, because it was the high ground from which to mount the best defense. Behind this crest, the land sloped off to a slight hollow and then rose to another slightly higher hump of earth, which was the geographical crest of the hill. Here Morgan posted William Washington and his eighty dragoons. To make them a little more of a match for Tarleton's 350 horsemen, he issued a call for volunteers to serve with Washington. About forty-five men stepped forward. Morgan gave them sabers and told them to obey Washington's orders.

This part of Morgan's battle plan entailed nothing unusual or brilliant. Selecting the most advantageous ground for his infantry and keeping Washington's cavalry out of the immediate reach of Tarleton's far more numerous horsemen simply made good tactical sense. Morgan demonstrated his genius in his plan for the militia. At Camden, Horatio Gates had tried to use the militia like regulars, positioning them in his battle line side by side with the Continentals. They swiftly demonstrated that they could not withstand a British bayonet charge.

Morgan decided he would use his militia as he had used his riflemen at Saratoga. He put the backwoodsmen under the command of Andrew Pickens and carefully explained what he wanted them to do. They were going to form a line about 150 yards ahead of Howard and the Continentals. They were to hold their fire until the British were within "killing distance." Then they were to get off two or three shots and retreat behind the Continentals, who would carry on the battle while the militiamen reformed and came back into the fight on the British flanks.

A select group of riflemen, considered the best shots in the army, were to advance another hundred yards on both sides of the Green River Road and begin skirmishing with the British as soon as they appeared. Sumter had used this tactic at Blackstock's to tempt Tarleton into a reckless charge that cost him heavy casualties.

His plan complete, Daniel Morgan did not retire to his tent, in the style of more autocratic generals, to await the moment of battle. He understood the importance of personal leadership. Above all, he knew how to talk to the militia. He, like them, was a man of the frontier. Although crippled by his rheumatism, he limped from group to group, while they cooked their suppers and, afterward, as they smoked their pipes, telling them how sure he was that they could whip "Benny." Sixteen-year-old Thomas Young was among the men who had volunteered to serve in the cavalry with William Washington. He remembered how Morgan helped them to fix their sabers, joked with them about their sweethearts, told them to keep up their courage, and assured them that victory was certain.

"Long after I laid down," Young recalled, "he was going among the soldiers encouraging them and telling them that the Old Wagoner would crack his whip over Benny in the morning, as sure as they lived."

"Just hold up your heads, boys, give them three fires and you will be free," Morgan told the young militiamen. "Then when you return to your homes, how the old folks will bless you and the girls will kiss you."

"I don't believe he slept a wink that night," Young later said.[7]

Many of these young militiamen had something else to motivate them: a fierce resentment of the way the British and loyalists had abused, and in some cases killed, their friends and relatives. Loyalist militia had shot down Thomas Young's brother, John, in the spring of 1780 in an attack on the Youngs' militia regiment. "I do not believe I had ever used an oath before that day," Young said. "But then I tore open my bosom and swore that I would never rest until I had avenged his death."[8]

Another South Carolinian, seventeen-year-old James Collins, had fought under Sumter and other militia leaders since the fall of Charleston. He remembered with particular anger the swath of desolation left by loyalists when they plundered rebel Americans on the south side of the Broad River. "Women were insulted and stripped of every article of decent clothing they might have on and every article of bedding, clothing or furniture was taken—knives, forks, dishes, spoons. Not a piece of meat or a pint of salt was left. They even entered houses where men lay sick of the small-pox . . . dragged them out of their sick beds into the yard and put them to death in cold blood in presence of their wives and children. We were too weak to repel them."

Collins and his friends had joined Sumter, only to encounter Tarleton at Fishing Creek. "It was a perfect rout and an indiscriminate slaughter," he recalled. Retreating to western South Carolina, Collins described how they lived, before Morgan and his regulars arrived to confront the British and loyalists. "We kept a flying camp, never staying long in one place, never camping near a public road . . . never stripping off saddles." When they ate, "each one sat down with his sword by his side, his gun lying across his lap or under the seat on which he sat." It soon became necessary "for their safety," Collins said, to join Morgan. At Cowpens, men like James Collins were literally fighting for their lives.[9]

Equally desperate—and angry—were men like Joseph Hughes, whose father had died at loyalist hands. Hughes had been living as an "out-lyer," hiding in the woods near his home with a number of other men loyal to the American cause. One day he ventured out to visit his family. As he approached the house, three loyalists sprang out the door with leveled guns, shouting, "You damned Rebel, you are our prisoner!" Hughes wheeled his horse and leaped the gate to escape in a hail of bullets.

At the Cowpens, Hughes, though still in his teens, received command of a company of militia. Probably by his side was his close friend, William Kennedy, considered one of the best shots in South Carolina. His prowess with the rifle had discouraged rebel loyalists from venturing into the settlement at Fair Forest Shoal. His gun had a peculiar crack that his friends recognized. When they heard it, they often said, "There is another Tory less."

The men who had turned out to fight for Andrew Pickens had no illusions about what would happen to them if captured. Like their leader, they had violated their paroles and were liable to instant execution if caught. On the night of January 16, Lord Cornwallis, in his camp at Turkey Creek on the other side of the Broad River, demonstrated what else would happen to their families. He wrote out an order for Colonel Henry Cruger at Ninety Six. "If Colonel Pickens has left any Negroes, cattle or other property that may be useful . . . I would have it seized accordingly and I desire that his houses may be burned and his plantations as far as lies in your power totally destroyed and himself if ever taken instantly hanged." Cruger executed the order the moment he received it. His men hurried Rebecca Pickens and her children into the January cold to watch their house, barns, and other outbuildings become bonfires.[10]

The one hundred Georgians in Morgan's army were all veterans of numerous battles, most of them fought under Elijah Clarke's command. With their leader wounded, Major James Jackson now commanded them. Morgan had relied on Jackson to rally them. Like most of Morgan's men, he was young, only twenty-three. He had fought Tarleton at Blackstock's, where he had ducked bullets to seize the guns of dead British to continue the fight when his men ran out of ammunition. In one respect, Jackson was unusual. Born in England, he arrived in America in 1774 and, it seems, became an instant Georgian, right down to his extreme pugnacity and prickly sense of honor. He had recently quarreled with the rebel lieutenant governor of Georgia, challenged him to a duel, and killed him. Morgan appointed Jackson brigade major of the militia, making him Pickens's second in command.

At least as formidable as Jackson's Georgians were the 140 North Carolinians under Major Joseph McDowell. They had fought in numerous battles in the summer of 1780 and scrambled up the rugged slopes of King's Mountain to destroy the loyalist army entrenched there.

∽

WELL BEFORE dawn, Morgan sent cavalry under a Georgian, Joshua Inman, to reconnoiter the Green River Road. They collided with Tarleton's advance guard and hastily retreated. Into the Cowpens they pounded to shout the alarm. Morgan seemed to be everywhere on his horse, rousing the men. "Boys, get up, Benny's coming!" he shouted. Militia and Continentals quickly bolted down cold hominy they had cooked the night before. Morgan ordered the baggage wagons to depart immediately for a safe place, about a mile in the rear of the battlefield. The militiamen's horses were tied to trees, under a guard, closer to the rear of the battle line.[11]

Morgan rode down to the picked riflemen who would open the fight and told them he had heard a lot of tall tales about who were better shots, the men of Georgia or Carolina. Here was their chance to settle the matter and save their country in the bargain. "Let me see which are most entitled to the credit of brave men, the boys of Carolina or those of Georgia," he roared. By positioning Georgians on the left of the road and Carolinians on the right, Morgan shrewdly arranged to make this competition highly visible.

To Pickens's men Morgan made a full-fledged speech, reminding them of what the British had already done to their friends and many of their families. He pounded his fist in his hand and told them this was their moment of revenge. He also praised the courage with which they had fought the British in earlier battles, without the help of American regulars or cavalry. Here they had the support of veterans in both departments. He had not the slightest doubt of victory, if they obeyed their orders and displayed their manhood.

To his Continentals, Morgan made an even more emotional speech. He called them "my friends in arms, my dear boys" and asked them to remember Saratoga, Monmouth, Paoli, Brandywine. "This day," he said, "you must play your parts for honor and liberty's cause." He restated his battle plan, reminding them that after two or three rounds, the militia would retreat under orders. They would not be running away. They would be falling back to regroup and harry the enemy's flanks.

A Delaware soldier watching Morgan's performance said that by the time he was through, every man in the army was "in good spirits and very willing to fight."

᠁

THE BLOOD-RED rising sun crept above the trees along the slopes of Thicketty Mountain to the east. The men stamped their feet and blew on their hands to keep warm. It was very cold, but the air was crisp and clear. The mighty ramparts of the Blue Ridge Mountains were visible forty miles away—much too distant for a refuge now, even if the swollen Broad River did not lie between them and Morgan's men.

Suddenly the British army emerged from the woods along the Green River Road. The green-coated dragoons at their head slowed and then stopped. So did the red-coated light infantrymen behind them. An officer in a green coat, undoubtedly Banastre Tarleton, rode to the head of the column and studied the American position.

On his horse behind the American Continentals, Daniel Morgan roared one last question to his men. "Are you ready to fight?"

"Yes!" they shouted.

⌒

BANASTRE TARLETON soon found that his position at the head of the column was hazardous. The Georgia and Carolina riflemen drifted toward him through the trees on either side of the road. Their rifles popped, and bullets whistled very close to Lieutenant Colonel Tarleton's head. He turned to the fifty British Legion dragoons commanded by Captain Ogilvie and ordered them to "drive in" the skirmishers. With a shout the dragoons charged. The riflemen rested their weapons against convenient trees and took steady aim. Again the long barrels blazed, and blue flame leaped from the firing pans of the rifled guns. Dragoons cried out and pitched from their saddles; horses screamed in pain. The riflemen flitted back through the open woods, reloading as they ran, a trick that constantly amazed the British. Each man carried four or five bullets in his mouth. Some whirled and fired again, and more dragoons crashed onto the cold brown grass of the Cowpens. In a minute or two the riflemen were safely within the ranks of Pickens's militiamen. The dragoons recoiled from this array of fire power and cantered back toward the British commander. They had lost fifteen of their fifty men.

Tarleton meanwhile continued studying the American army. At a distance of about four hundred yards, he could identify Pickens's line of militiamen, whose numbers he guessed to be about 1,000. He estimated the Continentals and Virginia six-months militiamen in the second line at about 800. Washington's cavalry on the crest behind the Continentals he put at 120, his only accurate figure.

Tarleton was not in the least intimidated, even though his estimates doubled Morgan's actual strength. He was supremely confident that his regular infantry could sweep the militia and riflemen off the field, leaving only the outnumbered Continentals and cavalry to deal with. The ground looked level enough to repeat the Waxhaws rout. In his self-confidence and growing battle fever, Tarleton did not even bother to confer on a tactical plan with Major Timothy Newmarsh of the Royal Fusiliers or Major Archibald McArthur of the 71st Highlanders. He simply ordered them to form a line of battle.

The infantrymen were told to drop their heavy packs and blanket rolls. The light infantry companies were ordered to file to the right, until they were extended as far as the flank of the militia facing them. The green-coated legion infantry was ordered into line beside them. Next came a squad of blue-coated artillerymen, with their brass grasshopper.

The light infantrymen and British Legion foot soldiers were now told to advance one hundred yards, while the Fusiliers of the 7th Regiment moved into line on their left. The other grasshopper was placed in the center of this regiment, no doubt to bolster the courage of the raw recruits. The two guns began hurling round shot and grapeshot into the woods through which the riflemen were again filtering to potshot the tempting red and green targets.

On each flank of the line, Tarleton posted a captain and fifty dragoons, more than enough, he thought, to protect his infantry from a cavalry charge. Finally, Tarleton ordered the 71st Highlanders to form a line about 150 yards in the rear of the 7th Regiment, slightly to their left. These veteran Scots and two hundred cavalry were his reserve, to be committed to the fight when most needed.

The army was ready. Everywhere Tarleton looked, he later recalled, he saw "the most promising assurance of success." The officers and men were full of fire and vigor. Every order had been obeyed with alacrity. There was no sign of weariness, although the men had marched half the night. They had been chasing these Americans for two wearying weeks.

They knew that defeating them here would end the war in South Carolina. To ensure that end, Banastre Tarleton issued a cruel order: they were to give no quarter, take no prisoners.

The order might have made some gruesome sense with regard to the militiamen. The British regarded them generally as criminals, fighting in direct violation of the law as laid down by his majesty's officers in numerous proclamations. Killing them would save the trouble of hanging them. But an order to give no quarter to Morgan's Continentals blatantly violated the rules of war under which both sides had fought for the past five years. It offered a graphic glimpse of the rage that continued American resistance was igniting in Englishmen like Banastre Tarleton.

One British officer in the battle later said that Major Timothy Newmarsh was still posting the officers of the Royal Fusiliers, the last regiment to move into the line, when Tarleton ordered the advance to begin. With a tremendous shout, the green- and red-coated line surged forward.

From the top of the slope, Morgan called on his men to reply. "They give us the British halloo, boys," he shouted. "Give them the Indian whoop." A howl of defiance leaped from nine hundred American throats. Simultaneously, the Georgians and North Carolinians opened fire from behind the big trees. Some of the new recruits of the 7th Regiment revealed their nervousness by firing back. Their officers quickly halted this tactical violation. British infantry fired by the volley, and the riflemen were out of musket range anyway. Rifles outshot muskets by 150 yards.

Daniel Morgan watched the riflemen give the British infantry "a heavy and galling fire" as they advanced. But the sharpshooters made no pretense of holding their ground. Morgan had ordered them to fall back to Pickens's militia and join them for serious fighting. On the British came, their battle drums booming, their fifes shrilling, the two brass cannons barking. The artillerymen apparently did not consider the militiamen an important target. They blasted at the Continentals on the crest. Most of their balls whizzed over the heads of the infantrymen and came dangerously close to Colonel William Washington and his horsemen. He led his men to a safer position, on the slope of the geographic crest, behind the right wing of the main American line.

Andrew Pickens and his fellow colonels, all on horseback, urged the militiamen to hold their fire, aim low, and pick out "the epaulette men"—the British officers with gold braid on the shoulders of their red coats. It was no easy task to persuade these militiamen not to fire while those sixteen-inch British bayonets approached, glistening wickedly in the rising sun. The closer they got, the more difficult it would be to reload their clumsy muskets and get off another shot before the British were on top of them. But the musket was a grossly inaccurate weapon at more than fifty yards. This was the "killing distance" for which Pickens and Morgan wanted the men to wait. The steady fire of the grasshoppers, expertly served by the British artillerymen, made the wait even more harrowing.

Then came the moment of truth. "Fire," snarled Andrew Pickens. "Fire," echoed his colonels up and down the line. The militia muskets and rifles belched flame and smoke. The British line recoiled as over four hundred iron and pewter bullets hurtled into it. Everywhere, officers, easily visible at the heads of their companies, went down. It was probably here that Major Timothy Newmarsh of the Royal Fusiliers, who had been so pessimistic about fighting a battle under Banastre Tarleton's command, fell with a painful wound. But confidence in their favorite weapon, the bayonet, and the knowledge that they were confronting militia quickly overcame the shock of this first blow. The red and green line surged forward again.

Thomas Young, sitting on his horse among William Washington's cavalry, later recalled the noise of the battle. "At first it was pop pop pop [the sound of the rifles] and then a whole volley," he said. Then the British regulars fired a volley. "It seemed like one sheet of flame from right to left," Young said.[12]

But the British were not trained to aim and shoot. Their volley firing was designed more to intimidate than to kill. It made a tremendous noise and threw a cloud of white gun smoke over the battlefield. Most of the bullets went high over the heads of the Americans. Decades later, visitors to Cowpens found bullets in the trees as much as thirty feet above the ground.

Out of the cloud of gun smoke the British regulars came, bayonets leveled. James Collins was among those militiamen who decided that perhaps the two shots requested by General Morgan were more than they could manage. "We gave the enemy one fire," he recalled. "When they charged us with their bayonets we gave way and retreated for our horses."

Most of the militiamen hurried around the American left flank, following Andrew Pickens and his men. A lesser number may have found the right flank more convenient. The important thing, as far as they were concerned, was to escape those British bayonets and reach the position where Morgan had promised them that John Eager Howard's Continentals and Washington's cavalry would protect them.

Watching from the military crest, William Seymour, sergeant major of the Delaware regiment, thought the militia "retreated in very good order, not seeming to be in the least confused." Thus far, Morgan's battle plan was working smoothly.[13]

Tarleton ordered the fifty dragoons on his right flank to pursue Pickens and the bulk of the militiamen. If, as he later claimed, the English commander had seen William Washington and his 120 cavalry at the beginning of the battle, this order was an incomprehensible blunder. With two hundred cavalrymen in reserve, awaiting a summons to attack, Tarleton sent fifty horsemen to face twice their number of mounted Americans. He may have assumed that Morgan was using standard battle tactics and regarded Washington's cavalry as his reserve, which he would not commit until necessity required it. The young British commander never dreamt that the Old Wagoner had made a solemn promise to the militiamen that he would protect them from the fearsome green dragoons at all costs.

As the militia retreated, Tarleton's cavalrymen thundered down on them, their murderous sabers raised. "Now," thought James Collins, "my hide is in the barn." A wild melee ensued, with the militiamen dodging behind trees, parrying the slashing sabers with their gun barrels. "They began to make a few hacks at some," Collins said, "thinking they would have another Fishing Creek frolic." As the militiamen dodged the swinging sabers, the British dragoons lost all semblance of a military formation and became "pretty much scattered," Collins said.

At that moment, "Col. Washington's cavalry was among them like a whirlwind," Collins exultantly recalled. American sabers sent dragoons keeling from their horses. "The shock was so sudden and violent, they could not stand it, and immediately betook themselves to flight," Collins said. "They appeared to be as hard to stop as a drove of wild Choctaw steers, going to Pennsylvania market." Washington's cavalrymen hotly pursued them, and "in a few moments the clashing of swords was out of hearing and quickly out of sight."

Thomas Young, one of the South Carolina volunteers in this ferocious cavalry charge, was riding a "little tackey"—a very inferior horse—which put him at a considerable disadvantage. When he saw one of the British dragoons topple from his saddle, he executed "the quickest swap I ever made in my life" and leaped onto "the finest horse I ever rode." Young said the American charge carried them through the fifty dragoons, whereupon they wheeled and attacked them in the rear. On his new steed he joined Washington's pursuit of the fleeing British.

Despite William Washington's victorious strike, many militiamen decided that Cowpens was unsafe, leaped onto their horses, and departed. Among the officers who took prompt action to prevent further panic was young Joseph Hughes. Although blood streamed from a saber cut on his right hand, he drew his sword and raced after his fleeing company. Outrunning them, he whirled and flailed at them with the flat of his blade, roaring, "You damned cowards halt and fight—there is more danger in running than in fighting." Andrew Pickens rode his horse among other sprinters, shouting, "Are you going to leave your mothers, sisters, sweethearts and wives to such unmerciful scoundrels, such a horde of thieves?"

On the battlefield from which they had just retreated, volley after volley of musketry thundered and cannons boomed. The Continentals and the British regulars were slugging it out. Daniel Morgan rode up to the milling militiamen, waving his sword and roaring in a voice that outdid the musketry. "Form, form my brave fellows. Give them one more fire and the day is ours. Old Morgan was never beaten."

Would they fight or run? For a few agonizing moments, the outcome of the battle teetered on the response of these young backwoodsmen.

⌐

ON THE other side of the crest behind which Morgan and Pickens struggled to rally the militia, Banastre Tarleton was absorbed in pressing home the attack with his infantry. He seems to have paid no attention to the rout of his right-wing troop of cavalry. Nor did any of his junior officers in the British Legion attempt to support the fleeing dragoons with reinforcements from the two-hundred-man cavalry reserve. At this point in the battle, Tarleton badly needed a second in command with the confidence to make on-the-spot decisions. One man cannot be everywhere on a battlefield. Unfortunately for Tarleton, Major George Hanger, his right-hand man in the leadership of the British Legion, was in a hospital in Camden, slowly recovering from yellow fever.

With the militia out of their way, the British infantry had advanced on the Continentals and begun blasting volleys of musketry at them. The Continentals blasted back. Clouds of gun smoke enveloped the battlefield. Tarleton claimed that the fire produced "much slaughter," but it is doubtful that men on either side could see what they were shooting at after the first few rounds. The British continued to fire high, hitting very few Continentals.

To Tarleton, the contest seemed "equally balanced," and he judged it the moment to throw in his reserve. He ordered Major McArthur and the 71st Highlanders into his battle line to the left of the Royal Fusiliers. This gave Tarleton over 700 infantrymen in action to the Americans' 420. Simultaneously, Tarleton ordered the troop of cavalry on the left to form a line and swing around the American right flank.

These orders, shouted above the thunder of musketry and the boom of the three-pound cannon, were promptly obeyed. On the crest of the hill, Lieutenant Colonel John Eager Howard saw the British threat developing. Men outflanked and taking bullets from two sides are in grave danger of being routed. Howard ordered the ex-Continentals in the Virginia militia on his right to "change their front" to meet this challenge. This standard battlefield tactic requires a company to wheel and face the flanking enemy.

A battlefield is a very confusing place, and the Virginians, although mostly trained soldiers, were not regulars who had lived and drilled together over the previous months and years. Their captain shouted the order given to him by Colonel Howard, and the men wheeled and began marching toward the rear. The Maryland and Delaware Continentals, seeing this strange departure and noting that it was done in perfect order and with the utmost deliberation, assumed that they had missed an order to fall back. They wheeled and followed the Virginians. On the opposite flank, the other company of Virginians repeated this performance. In sixty seconds the whole American line was retreating.[14]

Behind the geographical crest of the hill, Daniel Morgan and Andrew Pickens had managed to steady and reorganize the militia. Morgan galloped back toward the military crest on which he assumed the Continentals were still fighting. He was thunderstruck to find them retreating. In a fury, he rode up to Howard and cried, "Are you beaten?"

Howard pointed to his unbroken ranks and told Morgan that soldiers who retreated in that kind of order were not beaten. Morgan agreed and told him to stay with the men; he would ride back and choose the place where the Continentals should turn and rally. The Old Wagoner spurred his horse ahead of the infantrymen toward the geographical crest of the hill, about fifty paces behind their first line.

On the British side of the battlefield, the sight of the retreating Continentals revived hopes of an easy victory. Major McArthur of the 71st rode up to Tarleton and urged him to order the cavalry reserve to charge and turn the retreat into a rout. Tarleton claims that he sent this order to the cavalry, now at least four hundred yards from the vortex of the battle. Perhaps he did. The cavalry very probably would have obeyed, had the instruction arrived in time. The dragoons of the British Legion liked nothing so much as chopping up a retreating enemy.[15]

But events now occurred with a rapidity that made it impossible for the cavalry to respond. The center of Tarleton's line of infantry surged up the slope after the Continentals, bayonets lowered, howling for American blood. With almost half their officers dead or wounded by now, the infantrymen had lost all semblance of military formation. At almost the same moment, the 71st Highlanders, whose weight, had they joined the charge, would probably have been decisive, received an unexpected blast of musketry from their flank. Andrew Pickens and the militia had returned to the battle. The backwoodsmen blazed at the kilted Scotsmen, the riflemen among them concentrating on the screen of cavalrymen. The cavalry fled, and McArthur's men found themselves fighting a private war with the militia.

Far down the battlefield, where he had halted his pursuit of the British cavalry, William Washington saw what was happening. He sent a horseman racing to Morgan with a terse message. "They are coming on like a mob. Give them another fire and I will charge them."

Thomas Young, riding with Washington, never forgot the moment. "The bugle sounded," he said. "We made a half circuit at full speed and came upon the rear of the British line shouting and charging like madmen."

Simultaneously, Morgan reached the geographical crest of the slope, with the Continentals only a few steps behind him. He roared out an order to turn and fire. The Continentals wheeled and threw a blast of concentrated musketry into the faces of the charging British. Officers and men toppled. The line recoiled.

"Give them the bayonet," bellowed John Eager Howard. With a wild yell, the Continentals charged. The astonished British, assailed from front and rear, panicked. Some of them, probably the raw recruits of the Royal Fusiliers, flung themselves face down on the ground begging for mercy. Others, Thomas Young recalled, "took to the wagon road and did the prettiest sort of running away."

Tarleton, astonished and appalled, sent an officer racing to the British Legion cavalry to order its men to form a line of battle about four hundred yards away, on the right of the road. He rode frantically among his fleeing infantrymen, trying to rally them. His first purpose was "to protect the guns." To lose a cannon was a major disgrace in eighteenth-century warfare. The artillerymen were the only part of the British center that had not succumbed to the general panic. They continued to fire their grasshoppers, while the infantrymen threw down their muskets or ran past them helter-skelter. Part of the artillery's tradition was an absolute refusal to surrender. Artillerymen lived by the code of victory or death.

Once the Continentals had passed the surrendering infantry, the cannon became their chief target. Like robots—or very brave men—the artillerymen continued to fire until every man except one had been shot down or bayoneted. Lieutenant Colonel Howard, seeing one gun crew wiped out, shouted to one of his captains to seize the cannon. Another captain joined him in a footrace. Both carried the only weapon American officers used in battle, a long pike with a spear tip, called an espontoon. The second officer won the race by converting his espontoon into a vaulting pole. Plunging the spear tip into the ground, he made a great leap over the dead bodies of the artillerymen and captured the gun.

The last survivor of the other gun crew was the man who thrust the match into the touchhole. An American infantryman called on him to surrender this tool. The artilleryman refused. As the infantryman raised his bayonet to kill him, Howard rode up and blocked the blow with his sword. A man that brave, the colonel said, deserved to live. The artilleryman surrendered the match to Howard.

Up and down the American line on the crest of the hill rang an ominous cry: "Give them Tarleton's quarter." Remembering Waxhaws, the regulars and their Virginia militia cousins were ready to massacre the surrendering British. But Daniel Morgan, the epitome of battle fury while the guns were firing, was a humane and generous man. He rode his horse into the shouting infantrymen, ordering them to let the enemy live. Junior officers joined him in enforcing the order.

Discipline as well as mercy made the order advisable. The battle was not over. The 71st Highlanders were still fighting fiercely against Pickens's militiamen. Banastre Tarleton was riding frantically toward his legion cavalry to bring them into the battle. But the militia riflemen were back on the field, and Tarleton was their prime target. Bullets whistled around him as he rode. Several hit his horse. The animal crashed to the ground. Tarleton sprang up, his saber ready. Dr. Robert Jackson, assistant

surgeon of the 71st Regiment, galloped to the distraught young lieutenant colonel and offered him his horse. Tarleton refused. For a moment he seemed ready to die on the chaotic battlefield with his men.
Dr. Jackson helped to change his mind. He sprang off his horse and
shouted, "Your safety is of the highest importance to the army."

Tarleton mounted Jackson's horse and rode to rally his dragoons.
Jackson fastened a white handkerchief to the end of his cane and
strolled toward the all-but-victorious Americans. No matter how the
battle ended, he wanted to stay alive to help the wounded.[16]

Looking over his shoulder at the battlefield, Tarleton clung to a
shred of hope. An all-out charge by the cavalry could still "retrieve the
day," he said later. The Americans were "much broken by their rapid
advance."

But the cavalrymen of the British Legion had no appetite for another encounter with the rifles of Andrew Pickens's militia. "All attempts to restore order, recollection [of past glory] or courage, proved
fruitless," Tarleton said. No fewer than two hundred British Legion
dragoons wheeled their horses and galloped for safety in the very teeth
of Tarleton's harangue. Fourteen officers and forty dragoons of the 17th
Regiment obeyed his summons and charged with him toward the all
but disintegrated British battle line. They hoped chiefly to save the cannon and rescue some small consolation from the defeat.

They never got there. Instead, they collided with William Washington's cavalry, which had wheeled after its assault on the rear of the infantry and begun a pursuit of the scampering redcoats, calling on them
to surrender and sabering those who refused. Washington shouted an
order to meet the British charge. Most of his horsemen, absorbed in
their pursuit of the infantry, did not hear him. Washington, leading the
countercharge, did not realize he was almost unsupported. The burly
Virginian, remembering the humiliation of his defeat at Lenud's Ferry
in the fall of 1780, had a personal score to settle with Banastre Tarleton.
He headed straight for him.

Tarleton and two officers accepted Washington's challenge. The Virginian slashed at the first man, and his saber snapped at the hilt. As the
officer stood up in his stirrups, his saber raised for a fatal stroke,

Washington's black bugle boy rode up and fired a bullet into the Englishman's sword arm. The second officer assaulted Washington and was about to make a similar stroke when the sergeant major of the 3rd Continental Dragoons arrived to parry the blow and slash this assailant's sword arm. Tarleton made a final assault. Washington parried his blow with the hilt of his broken sword. From his saddle holsters, Tarleton drew two pistols in swift succession and fired them at Washington. One bullet wounded Washington's horse.

By this time Tarleton saw that the battle was totally lost. The American riflemen were running toward his horsemen, and their bullets were again whistling close. Pickens's militia and Morgan's Continentals were methodically surrounding the 71st Highlanders. Summoning his fifty-four gallant supporters, Tarleton galloped down the Green River Road a defeated man.

On the battlefield, the Highlanders were trying to retreat. But Morgan's Continentals and Washington's cavalry were now between them and safety. Through the center of their line charged Major James Jackson and some of his Georgians to try to seize their standard. Bayonet-wielding Scotsmen were about to kill Jackson when Howard and his Continentals broke through the 71st's flank and saved him. Howard called on the Highlanders to surrender.

Major McArthur handed his sword to Andrew Pickens, as did almost every other officer who was still alive. Pickens passed the major's sword to James Jackson and ordered him to escort McArthur to General Morgan. Jackson took him to Colonel Washington instead.

Captain Duncasson of the 71st's grenadiers surrendered his sword to Lieutenant Colonel Howard. When Howard remounted, the captain clung to his saddle and almost unhorsed him. "I expressed my displeasure," Howard recalled, "and asked him what he was about." Duncasson told Howard that Tarleton had issued orders to give no quarter, and they thus did not expect any. The Maryland and Delaware Continentals were approaching with their bayonets still fixed. He was afraid of what they might do to him. Howard ordered a sergeant to protect the captain.

Around the American main position, a happy chaos raged. In his exultation, Morgan picked up his nine-year-old drummer boy and kissed him on both cheeks. Major Jackson, having delivered Major McArthur, noticed that a Continental sergeant seemed to have charge of a cask of wine, from which he was distributing drinks to his friends. A wounded militiaman, propped against a tree, asked Jackson to get him a swig of it. Jackson asked for a cup, and the sergeant haughtily informed him that General Morgan had told him to guard the wine, which meant it was not available to militiamen. The fiery-tempered Jackson called for his Georgia friends, and they chased the sergeant away with kicks and curses. The sergeant ran to Morgan, who came roaring after Jackson, his huge fists ready to strike a knockout blow. Jackson hastily explained what the sergeant had been doing. Morgan made the sergeant get down on his knees in front of Jackson and beg his pardon.

Others were off on even more curious adventures. Volunteer cavalryman Thomas Young joined a half dozen riders who decided to pursue prisoners and possible loot down the Green River Road. They must have embarked on this adventure shortly after most of Tarleton's cavalry had deserted him and before Tarleton himself quit the battlefield, following his encounter with William Washington.

"We went about twelve miles," Young said in his recollections of the battle, "and captured two British soldiers, two negroes and two horses laden with portmanteaus. One of the portmanteaus belonged to a paymaster . . . and contained gold." The other riders decided this haul was too good to risk on the road and told Young to escort the prisoners and the money back to the Cowpens.

Young had ridden several miles when he collided with Tarleton and the fifty-four troopers and officers who had joined him for his last charge. Abandoning his captures, Young tried to escape. He darted down a side road, but his horse was so stiff from the hard exercise on the battlefield that the British overtook him.

"My pistol was empty so I drew my sword and made battle," the courageous young militiaman said. "I never fought so hard in my life." But he was hopelessly outnumbered. In a few clanging, cursing seconds, one saber split a finger on his left hand; another slashed his sword arm. A third blade raked his forehead, and the skin slipped over his eyes, blinding him. A saber tip speared his left shoulder, a blade sank deep into his right shoulder, and a final blow hammered the back of his head. Young clung to his horse's neck, half conscious.

He was battered and bleeding, but his courage saved his life. With the somewhat peculiar sense of sportsmanship that the British bring to war, they took him off his horse, bandaged his wounds, and led him back to the main road, where they rejoined Tarleton and the rest of his party. One of the Tory guides who had led the British through the backcountry to the Cowpens recognized Young and announced he was going to kill him. He cocked his gun. "In a moment," Young said, "about twenty British soldiers drew their swords, cursed him for a coward wishing to kill a boy without arms and a prisoner, and ran him off."

Colonel Tarleton ordered Young to ride beside him and asked many questions about Morgan's army. He was particularly interested in how many dragoons Washington had. "He had seventy," Young said, "and two volunteer companies of mounted militia. But you know, they [the militia] won't fight."

"They did today," Tarleton replied.[17]

⌒

ON THE battlefield at the Cowpens, surgeons Robert Jackson of the 71st Regiment and Richard Pindell of the 1st Maryland Regiment were doing their limited best to help the wounded of both sides. Sixty-two Americans and two hundred British needed medical attention, which consisted largely of extracting a bullet if possible, then bandaging the wound and giving the sufferer some opium or liquor, if available. The battle had also cost the British 110 dead, including ten officers. Only twelve Americans had perished. But the number of prisoners, 502, underscored the totality of the American victory.

Even as prisoners, the British, particularly the Scots, somewhat awed the Americans. Joseph McJunkin said they "looked like nabobs in their flaming regimentals as they sat down with us, the militia, in our tattered hunting shirts, black-smoked and greasy."

Other Americans were not content to inspect their exotic captives. William Washington and Andrew Pickens, in a terse conference, agreed they still had a good chance of catching Tarleton. But they needed enough men to overwhelm his fifty-four-man squadron. Washington changed his wounded horse for a healthy mount and rounded up his scattered dragoons. Pickens summoned some of his own men and ordered James Jackson to follow him "with as many of the mounted militia as he could get."

Down the Green River Road they galloped, sabers in hand. But Tarleton the cavalryman was not easy to catch. He rode at his usual horse-killing pace. A few miles above William Thompson's plantation on Thicketty Creek, they found the expedition's thirty-five baggage wagons, most of them belonging to the 7th Regiment, abandoned. The fleeing cavalry of the British Legion had told the one-hundred-man guard of the defeat. The officer in command had set fire to all the baggage that would burn, cut loose the wagon horses, mounted his infantry two to a horse, and ridden for the safety of Cornwallis's army. Abandoned with the baggage were some seventy black slaves. A short time later, a party of loyalists, fugitives from the Cowpens battlefield, reached the baggage train and began to loot it. They were not long at this work before Tarleton and his heartsick officers and troopers came thundering down the road. Asking no questions about loyalty, they cut down the looters without mercy.

Tarleton was riding for Cornwallis's camp but had more than safety on his mind. He assumed the British commander was just across the Broad River at King's Mountain in a position to rescue the five hundred men Morgan had taken prisoner. Perhaps Tarleton met a loyalist messenger or a scout somewhere along the road; at any rate, he heard from someone, "with infinite grief and astonishment," that the main army was twenty-five miles away at Turkey Creek.

This news meant a change of route. The British decided they needed a guide. Near Thicketty Creek they stopped at the house of a man named Goudelock, known as a rebel. But Tarleton probably put a saber to his throat and told him he would be a dead man if he did not lead them to Hamilton's Ford across the Broad River. Goudelock's terrified wife watched this virtual kidnapping of her husband.

About a half hour after Tarleton and his troopers departed to the southeast, Washington, Pickens, and their dragoons and volunteer militia troopers rode into Goudelock's yard. They had stopped to extinguish the fires the British started in the baggage wagons and to collect some of the slaves the enemy had abandoned. The Americans asked Mrs. Goudelock if she had seen the British fugitives. Yes, she said. What road did they take? they eagerly asked. Mrs. Goudelock pointed down the Green River Road to Grindal's Shoals on the Pacolet.

Like a great many people in every war, she was more interested in personal survival than national victory. If the Americans caught up to Tarleton, a bloody struggle would certainly result, and her husband might get killed. Mrs. Goudelock preferred a live husband to a dead or captured British cavalry commander.[18]

The Americans galloped for the Pacolet. Not until they had traveled twenty-two miles on this cold trail did they turn back. By then, it was much too late. Tarleton was safely across the Broad River at Hamilton's Ford. But the American pursuit helped save the captured volunteer cavalryman Thomas Young. When Tarleton and his men, guided by the reluctant Mr. Goudelock, reached the ford, it was almost dark. Someone told them the river was "swimming." Someone else, probably a loyalist scout, rode up to tell them that Washington and the American cavalry were after them.

Considerable confusion ensued, as Tarleton and his officers conferred about whether to flee down the river to some other ford, attempt to swim the river in the dark, or stand and fight. Everyone stopped thinking about Thomas Young and another prisoner, a Virginian whom the British had scooped up along the road. The two Americans spurred their horses into the darkness, and no one noticed they were gone.

Tarleton crossed the Broad River that night and spent the next morning collecting his runaway dragoons and other stragglers before riding down to Cornwallis's camp at Turkey Creek. The British commander had already heard the bad news. Some of the legion cavalry had drifted into the camp the previous night. But Tarleton, as the field commander, had to make a detailed report.

According to Joseph McJunkin, whose father had been taken prisoner by the British and was an eyewitness, Cornwallis grew so agitated that he plunged his sword into the ground in front of his tent and leaned on it while he listened to the details of the disaster. By the end of Tarleton's account, he was leaning so hard on the hilt that the sword snapped in half. He threw the broken blade on the ground and swore he would recapture the lost light infantry, fusiliers, and highlanders.

The British commander exonerated Tarleton of all culpability for the defeat at the Cowpens. "You have forfeited no part of my esteem, as an officer," he assured Tarleton. Cornwallis blamed the loss on the "total misbehavior of the troops." But he confided to Francis, Lord Rawdon, the commander at Camden, "The late affair has almost broke my heart." It also shattered his plan for an easy conquest of North Carolina.[19]

ON THE same morning that Tarleton made his doleful report, William Washington and Andrew Pickens returned to the Cowpens. On their ride back, they collected several dozen—some versions make it as many as one hundred—additional British soldiers straggling through the woods. At the battlefield they found only the two surgeons caring for the wounded and a handful of Pickens's militia guarding them. Daniel Morgan, knowing Cornwallis would make a determined effort to regain the 530 prisoners, had crossed the Broad River on the afternoon of the battle and headed northwest toward Gilbert Town, North Carolina. Pickens and Washington caught up to him there, and Morgan gave Pickens charge of the prisoners, with orders to head for an upper ford of the Catawba River. Decoying Cornwallis, Morgan led his Continentals toward a lower ford of the same river. In an exhausting five-day march, often in an icy rain, both detachments got across this deep, swift-running river ahead of the pursuing British. The prisoners were now beyond Cornwallis's reach. They were soon marched to camps in Virginia, where the men Morgan had helped to capture at Saratoga were held.

This final retreat, a vital maneuver that consolidated the field victory at the Cowpens, worsened Morgan's rheumatism. He warned Nathanael Greene that he would have to leave the army. "I grow worse every hour," he wrote. "I can't ride out of [faster than a] walk." As the rain continued to pour down, Morgan had to abandon his tent and seek the warmth of a private house. By the time the Old Wagoner departed for Virginia, he was in such pain that he had to ride in a litter.[20]

CHAPTER 12

Fight, Get Beat, Rise and Fight Again

Among the most gratifying tasks of Nathanael Greene's career as a general was writing to General George Washington on January 24, 1781. "I have the satisfaction to transmit your Excellency the copy of a letter which I at this moment received from Brigadier General Morgan announcing the total defeat of Lieutenant Colonel Tarleton's detachment. The victory was compleat, and the action glorious. The brilliancy and success with which it was fought, does the highest honor to the American arms and adds splendor to the character of the General and his officers. I must beg leave to recommend them to your Excellency's notice, and doubt not but from your representation Congress will receive pleasure from testifying their approbation of their conduct." He sent with these words a copy of General Daniel Morgan's report on the battle of Cowpens.[1]

The victory had an exhilarating effect on the morale of Nathanael Greene's half of the southern army. Greene ordered a celebration and praised Morgan extravagantly in the general announcement of the triumph. A friend on Greene's staff sent a copy to Morgan, adding, "It was written immediately after we heard the news, and during the operation of some cherry bounce" (a potent mixture of rum and cider). To Francis Marion, Greene wrote, "After this, nothing will appear difficult."

Greene sounded a very different note in a second letter he wrote to Washington on January 24. He told the commander in chief,

I am exceeding unhappy that our wretched condition will not permit our improving it [the victory at Cowpens] to the best advantage. I shall do all I can but our prospects are gloomy. Our force is small and dayly declining. We have no clothing or provisions but what we collect from day to day. . . . I hope your Excellency will repeat your letters to Congress upon the necessity of filling the Army and forming Magazines of provision and forage. . . . Above half the pleasure that results with the victory is lost in the apprehension that it will [relax] the preparations for the support of the war. I wish your Excellency to place this event in its true point of light to Congress; that if it stands alone, it will be of no consequence but if properly improved upon, it may have the most salutary effects.[2]

∽

WHEN MORGAN reported his growing physical helplessness, Greene rode from Cheraw, South Carolina, and took personal command of the Old Wagoner's half of the army. It was a risky trip through a heavily loyalist countryside, accompanied only by a few cavalrymen. The southern commander immediately called a council of war, asking Morgan and the other top officers whether they thought he should fight Lord Cornwallis. All doubted the army's ability to survive a battle with the victor of Camden.

Greene decided to retreat north, toward Virginia, where there was hope of supplies; Morgan favored marching deeper into South Carolina in the hope that the news of Cowpens would inspire the local militia to join their ranks. Morgan growled that he could not be responsible for the disasters he foresaw if Greene retreated north. "Neither will you," Greene snapped. "For I shall take the matter upon myself."[3] Greene was skeptical of councils of war. He had seen them argue good battle plans to death, as General Double Trouble had done at Monmouth.[4]

∽

AROUND THIS time Greene temporarily took heart from a letter in which Congressman John Mathews of South Carolina told him that news of Cowpens "seems to have had a very sensible effect on *some folks*." A majority of Congress had decided "something must to be done in that department. . . . They seem at present to be well disposed to give it every possible aid." Talk subsided of abandoning Georgia and South Carolina in a peace treaty.[5]

Alas, this optimism soon faded. The bankrupt Congress and the even more bankrupt southern state governments could do little to raise new Continental regiments. Greene was soon telling his friend, Congressman James Varnum of Rhode Island, that his army was in "a deplorable condition and not withstanding this little success, must inevitably fall prey to the enemy if not better supported. . . . Depend upon it, the Southern states must fall, unless there is established a well appointed army for their support." Here Greene enunciated yet again the absolute necessity to the strategy of victory of a trained army to look the enemy in the face. His statement refutes once and hopefully for all the notion that the United States won the revolution using guerrilla tactics.[6]

Greene's words also reflected the realities of the war he was fighting. On his dangerous ride to take command of Morgan's half of the army, he found no evidence that Cowpens had created a surge of enthusiasm among the militia. "The people have been so harassed for eight months past and their domestick matters in such distress that they will not leave home," he glumly concluded. The few who volunteered were willing to serve only for the shortest permissible time, which meant they were of "no use."[7] From his sickbed, Daniel Morgan wrote a despairing letter to Virginia governor Thomas Jefferson, describing the southern army retreating from Cornwallis, "our men almost naked," still too weak to fight him. "Great God what is the reason we can't have more men in the field?" Morgan wrote. "How distressing it must be to an anxious mind to see the country overrun and destroyed for want of assistance."[8]

From the viewpoint of the average militiaman, Cowpens had changed little. Banastre Tarleton was soon back in action at the head of the British cavalry. Lord Cornwallis, vowing revenge, had stripped his army of all forms of comfort to toughen the troops unto victory. He created a huge bonfire into which he threw his bed, his china, his extra uniforms—and asked his men to imitate his example. Even their supply of rum vanished in the conflagration. His field army began marching as much as thirty miles a day, which Greene had to match if he hoped to survive.[9]

Greene's reunited army had fewer than 1,500 Continentals and about six hundred militia. The latter were poorly armed and inadequately clothed for a winter campaign. In a February letter to George Washington, Greene wrote, "The miserable situation of the troops for want of clothing has rendered the March the most painful imaginable, several hundreds of the soldiers tracking the ground with their bloody feet. Your feelings for the suffering soldiers had you been here, must have been pained upon the occasion."[10]

For days at a time, they marched in cold, drenching rain. Cornwallis remained grimly on their trail. Greene saw he was hoping to trap him against the Dan River, which flowed between North Carolina and Virginia. Once more, Greene decided to split his army. He ordered Colonel Otho Holland Williams of the Maryland brigade to take command of some seven hundred light troops and maneuver between the Americans and the British, who were marching in roughly parallel lines. Williams's actions convinced Cornwallis that Greene planned to cross the river at one of the upper fords. Instead, Greene successfully crossed downriver. From the safety of the northern bank, Greene ordered Williams to cross and join him. In four frantic days of marching, Greene had slept only about four hours.

⌒

IN THE south, with partisan leaders such as Thomas Sumter and Francis Marion already active and state governments virtually nonexistent, Greene had to take a more direct approach to bolstering his army. In a series of letters, he urged all the guerrilla leaders to join his force and give battle to Cornwallis in North Carolina. "The salvation of this country don't depend on little strokes nor should the great business of establishing a permanent army be neglected to pursue them," Greene told Sumter. "Partisan strokes in a war are like the garnish of the table, they give splendor to the army and reputation to the officers but they afford no national security. . . . It is not a war of posts but a contest for states."

This may well be the best summary of George Washington's strategy of victory that anyone has written, including the commander in chief. Preaching this credo was especially valuable in the dismembered states of the south. The egotistic Sumter declined to heed it, but other partisans were convinced, and Greene soon had more than 4,000 men in his army. For the first time, he felt ready to challenge Cornwallis for control of North Carolina.

Cornwallis, meanwhile, marched slowly back to Hillsboro, North Carolina. Still determined to add the state to conquered Georgia and South Carolina, he issued a proclamation inviting all loyal subjects to respond to the king's standard. Soon, no fewer than six hundred loyalists had assembled under Colonel John Pile. Marching briskly toward Hillsboro, they saw dozens of green-uniformed dragoons coming toward them. Assuming them to be Tarleton's men, they called out, "God save the King!"

Unfortunately for the loyalists, these horsemen belonged to Light Horse Harry Lee's Legion. They instantly charged the loyalists, who were trapped on the road between two rail fences. In a few minutes, 90 loyalists were dead and another 150 lay slashed and bleeding. The panicky survivors fled in all directions.[11]

Ironically, Tarleton was camped only a mile away. He roused his horsemen and prepared to pursue Lee's men. But a letter from Lord Cornwallis changed his mind. Spies had informed his lordship that Greene's army had crossed the Dan and was ready to challenge him for control of North Carolina. Tarleton raced back to Cornwallis's army and was soon skirmishing with American dragoons in Greene's advance guard.

AT FIRST Cornwallis was inclined to retreat to Wilmington on the coast of North Carolina. Spies warned him that Greene's army was almost twice the size of his force. During the days and nights of ruthless marching, Cornwallis had lost four hundred men to desertion. He had barely 2,000 men in his ranks.

For a week, Cornwallis maneuvered, hoping to break away. But then, seeing that Greene was determined to make him fight, he opted to accept the challenge. He was fairly sure that most of Greene's army were militia. Memories of their cowardly performance at Camden probably influenced his decision. Another factor was his army's dwindling supplies. His men were weary of attempting to live off the land and eager to revenge themselves on these elusive Americans.

From his sickbed in Virginia, Daniel Morgan sent Greene some tough advice. If he could persuade his militia to fight, he would defeat Cornwallis. If they ran away, his lordship would cut "you and your regulars to pieces." Morgan's answer to this problem: station some of the best Continentals behind the militia's line "with orders to shoot the first man who ran away." Greene decided not to take this advice. He wanted to keep as many militia as he could on his side of the contest whether he won or lost.[12]

～

AT DAWN on March 14, 1781, Greene marched his men a dozen miles to the tiny town of Guilford Court House. He had paused there on his retreat to the Dan River and had a good grasp of the local geography. The British were only ten miles away. There was little doubt that Cornwallis would attack the next morning. This gave Greene the better part of the day to lay out his battle lines.

New Garden Road was a narrow thoroughfare that ran down the center of the battlefield. Behind rail fences on both sides of the road, Greene positioned 1,000 North Carolina militia. Few if any had any previous battle experience. Greene told them that he hoped that they would stand long enough to deliver two or three good volleys. Then they could retire with honor.

Two or three hundred yards behind this uncertain battle line stood a line of Virginia militia, many of them Continental Army veterans. Five hundred yards behind this line lay the heart of Greene's army, two regiments of regulars from Maryland and Delaware and two from Virginia. On the flanks he positioned the cavalry of William Washington and Light Horse Harry Lee.

ON MARCH 15, 1781, the British army approached. Harry Lee spurred his horse in front of the North Carolina militia. Waving his saber, the cavalryman roared, "My brave boys, your lands, your lives and your country depend on your conduct this day—I have given Tarleton hell this morning and I will give him more of it before night." Lee and his legion had skirmished with Tarleton, commander of the advance guard. Nothing quite approaching hell had occurred, beyond a few casualties on both sides. But Lee was ready to say almost anything to stiffen the spines of the militia.

Soon the jittery volunteers in the first line were staring at the scarlet uniforms and brilliant banners of the British army. When they were about four hundred yards away, American artillery began the battle by firing into the British ranks. The British responded with quickly unlimbered six-pounders. Neither side sustained much damage. Then the British began their advance. Greene had chosen his position shrewdly. The enemy would have to approach across an open field. Dense woods lined both sides of this access route.

The scarlet line stretched nearly a mile. Bayonets lowered, the British troops emitted a savage howl and broke into a trot. Not until they were forty yards from the Americans did they realize that the militia were resting their guns on a rail fence. As one British sergeant later said, "They were taking aim with the nicest precision."

With a blast of flame and smoke, the militia fired. One eyewitness said that half the Highlander Regiment "dropt on the spot." A North Carolina militiaman thought the dead and dying enemy resembled "the stalks of a wheatfield after a harvester had passed through it with his cradle." For a moment the British hesitated, seemingly stunned and confused. Lieutenant Colonel James Webster, commander of the Royal Welsh Fusiliers, rode to the head of his regiment and shouted, "On my brave fusiliers!" The regiment surged forward, bayonets lowered.

Most of the North Carolina militia ran. One disgusted officer said his men "dispersed like a flock of sheep, frightened by dogs." Only on the flanks, where Greene had stationed detachments of Maryland and Delaware veterans, did resistance persist. But soon they too joined the militia's headlong retreat.[13]

The British now had to struggle through woods and gullies to get to Greene's second line of defense, the Virginia militia. In this rough terrain, the battle degenerated into a series of isolated skirmishes, frequently marked by hand-to-hand combat. General Greene was on horseback in the midst of the Virginians, sharing the risks, shouting orders and encouragement.

But the British were equally determined. Cornwallis rode to the front of the line on a dragoon's horse, having lost his own steed to American bullets. A sergeant warned him that if he went a few more yards, the enemy would surround him and cut him to pieces. He retreated to the protection of the 23rd Regiment, which was drawn up in nearby woods, preparing to attack. After about half an hour, the Virginians began to give way, and parts of the British line started assaulting Greene's Continentals on a hilltop not far from the courthouse.

The 5th Maryland Regiment, composed almost entirely of new recruits, broke and fled without firing a shot. The British surged forward, hoping to outflank the American position on the hilltop. William Washington's cavalry checked them for several minutes. But they were too few to have any sustained impact. Soon the hilltop was a mass of men fighting hand to hand.[14]

At this point Lord Cornwallis emerged from the woods and decided that his attacking men were in danger of being engulfed. He ordered the lieutenant in command of his artillery to fire grapeshot into the melee. He knew that the deadly balls would kill British as well as Americans. The gambit had its hoped-for effect. The 1st Maryland Regiment, the bulwark of Greene's defensive plan, began to come apart.

The British 23rd and 71st Regiments rallied and charged with devastating effect.

What to do? A hotheaded general, or one who did not understand Washington's strategy of victory, could easily have ordered a fight to the finish. But Nathanael Greene knew exactly how to proceed. Before the battle began, he had selected a route of retreat. He ordered Colonel Otho Williams to pass the word to the commanders of the regiments.

Williams soon reported that the retirement was progressing with "good order and regularity." At first, Cornwallis ordered his army to pursue the retreating Americans. But Greene had one of the Virginia Continental regiments ready to provide an aggressive rear guard. After a few miles Cornwallis abandoned the chase. His battered army was in no condition to continue fighting, having lost over five hundred men, a quarter of its strength. The British retained dubious possession of the battlefield—victors in name only.

As he had after Cowpens, Greene reported the outcome of Guilford Court House to General Washington. The commander in chief's response revealed how desperate the situation was becoming in the north as well as the south. "Although the honors of the field did not fall to your lot, I am convinced you deserved them. . . . The consequences if you can prevent the dissipation of your troops, will no doubt be fortunate." Then came the grim news. "Every support that is in my power to give you from this Army shall cheerfully be afforded—but if I part with any more troops, I must accompany them, or have none to command."

Determined to close on an upbeat note, Washington turned to a letter from his stepson, Jack Custis, who was serving in the Virginia Assembly at Richmond. He told Greene that in a recent letter Custis had written, "General Greene has by his conduct gained universal esteem, and possesses in the fullest degree the confidence of all ranks of people."[15]

A letter from Greene crossed this one in the mail, with equally warm words for Washington. "Virginia has given me every support I could wish or expect since Lord Cornwallis has been in North Carolina and nothing has contributed more to this than the prejudices of the people in favor of your Excellency, which has been extended to me from the friendship you have been pleased to honor me with."[16]

⌒

WITH HIS army decimated, Cornwallis had no alternative but retreat to the North Carolina coast. Instead of following him, Greene made one of the most daring decisions of the war. As he explained it to Washington in a long letter on March 29, 1781, he had abandoned all hope of reinforcements from the north. Maryland had not raised a man and Virginia only a handful. North Carolina was equally barren of recruits. "In this critical and distressing situation, I am determined to carry the war immediately into South Carolina. The enemy will be obliged to follow us or give up their posts in that state. . . . All things considered, I think the movement is warranted by the soundest reasons, both political and military. The maneuver will be critical and dangerous and the troops exposed to every hardship. But as I share it with them, I hope they will bear up under it with that magnanimity which has already supported them, and for which they deserve everything of their country."[17]

On April 22, Washington replied that the project of "endeavoring to transfer the war [to South Carolina] has many favorable sides." One of the best and least expected was Cornwallis's reaction. Instead of pursuing Greene, he marched his battered army into Virginia and took command of the British troops already there. His lordship had decided the south would never be pacified until Virginia was subdued. This conclusion contained more than a little truth. If Cornwallis triumphed in Virginia, he could return to South Carolina and obliterate Greene's achievements there. It soon became apparent that a great deal depended on General Washington's almost invisible northern army. No one else had the ability to challenge Cornwallis's strategy.[18]

CHAPTER 13

From Mutiny and Despair to
Improbable Victory

I n the north, the total collapse of the Continental currency forced
General George Washington to distribute his army all over
New Jersey and lower New York. He set up a headquarters in
New Windsor, near Newburgh in the Hudson River valley. The abandonment of a formal winter camp enabled him to feed the Continentals better but prevented him from exercising the personal leadership
that had steadied morale at Valley Forge and Morristown.

Worse in some ways was the feeling among the troops that the war
was lasting much too long. On January 1, 1781, the Pennsylvania Continentals who were camped at Morristown decided to declare an end to
their participation in this seemingly eternal contest. At 9:00 P.M. that
night they mutinied, killed two captains who tried to stop them, and
began a march on Philadelphia to collect their back pay from the bankrupt Continental Congress.

General Anthony Wayne, a fellow Pennsylvanian, summoned the
soldiers of the New Jersey Continental line and blocked their departure. While both sides brandished loaded guns, Wayne rushed messengers to Washington and to Congress. The politicians reacted with raw
panic and prepared to flee Philadelphia again. But Washington insisted
that under no circumstances should Congress cut and run. The politicians would have to stay and face these angry men lest the soldiers take
out their grievances on the citizens of Philadelphia in an orgy of

looting and violence. Washington prepared to rush to Morristown to appeal to the Pennsylvanians—until his staff warned that if he left the regiments camped with him at New Windsor, they very well might mutiny as well.

For the next six days General Wayne and two colonels pleaded and argued with the Morristown mutineers. General Sir Henry Clinton, watching from New York, sent two agents, who guaranteed the mutineers back pay and total forgiveness if they joined the British army. Instead, the mutineers decided to prove that they were not "Arnolds." They turned the spies over to Wayne, who promptly hanged them.

Finally Wayne persuaded the mutineers to put down their guns in return for a promise from the government of Pennsylvania of back pay, better food, and the discharge of half the men who had served three years. The other half would receive furloughs until April. An appalled Washington learned that the Pennsylvania Continental line, one of his strongest brigades—over three-quarters of its men were pugnacious Irish Americans—had ceased to exist.[1]

A FEW weeks later the New Jersey Continental line mutinied for the same reasons. This time Washington decided he could not afford to settle for another semi-surrender. He seized four of the ringleaders and executed two of them. As he watched them go to the gallows, he realized the Continental Army, the crucial ingredient in his strategy of victory, was nearing collapse. In his personal diary, Washington wrote a cry of soldierly despair. "Instead of having magazines filled with provisions, we have a scant pickings scattered here and there in different states. . . . Instead of having the regiments completed, scarcely any state has an eighth part of its quota in the field. . . . Instead of having the prospect of a glorious offensive campaign before us we have a gloomy and bewildered prospect of a defensive one."[2]

America's Fabius was close to confessing, at least to himself, that his strategy of victory might soon become a formula for humiliating defeat—a probability underscored by a raid that Benedict Arnold launched in Virginia. With 2,000 men under his command, the traitor, now a

British brigadier, sailed boldly up the James River to Richmond, routed the few militia that turned out, and sent Governor Thomas Jefferson and his wife and children fleeing into the countryside. Arnold proceeded to burn the city's public buildings and its tobacco warehouses. Also up in smoke and flames went tons of supplies for Nathanael Greene's southern army. Next came a march upriver to Westham, where Arnold burned the foundry in which Virginia made its muskets.

Retreating to the coast, Arnold set up a base in Portsmouth and burned the state shipyard as well as many ships and even larger quantities of tobacco. Once more he brushed aside the scattering of militia who turned out to oppose him. A desperate Governor Jefferson begged General Washington for his "personal aid." He could think of no other way to persuade the state's militia to turn out. Washington politely declined to rush to Virginia in person—a precedent that would have him scampering up and down the continent to little or no avail.

Doing his best with his pathetic handful of Continentals, Washington ordered the Marquis de Lafayette and 1,200 regulars to Virginia, hoping this would inspire the French army and navy to send help from Newport. The Comte de Rochambeau and his admiral promised to join the battle, but when the French squadron encountered a British fleet, it sailed hastily back to Newport.

Washington ordered Lafayette to advance into Virginia anyway, hoping his regulars would inspire a militia turnout. But the numbers remained so heavily in favor of the British that no such happy event occurred. Worsening matters for the marquis was Lord Cornwallis's decision to center the coming campaign on Virginia. Even when a revived Pennsylvania line led by General Anthony Wayne reinforced Lafayette, their numbers remained so pathetic that he could do nothing but retreat. "I am not even strong enough to get beaten decently," Lafayette groaned to Washington.[3]

⌇

IN NEW York, meanwhile, the commander in chief was hearing more grim news. Congress, almost totally under the influence of the French ambassador, the suave Duke de la Lucerne, told him that France and other European nations were planning to convene a peace conference in Vienna. France was running out of money and had lost all faith in her American allies. The French foreign minister had persuaded Austria and Russia to help France evade her treaty of alliance with America. At the peace conference the Americans would be urged to accept a truce with England. Each side would claim the territory its armies controlled. For the British that would include all of Georgia and South Carolina and possibly North Carolina and Virginia, where they were now flexing their military muscles virtually unchallenged. George III could also claim northern New York, where a loyalist and Indian guerrilla war continued to rage. Even more probable would be their claim to New York City and its environs, including Long Island, where they had ruled for six years.

The French had no illusions about what they were really doing: abandoning America to eventual reconquest. A desperate Washington clung to the dwindling hope that General Rochambeau would obtain enough reinforcements to join him in an attack on New York City. But Rochambeau gloomily reported that instead of a promised 6,000-man expansion of his army, he was to receive only another 600 recruits.

In May 1781 the two generals met in Wethersfield, Connecticut, to discuss their next move. Washington reiterated his desire to attack New York. Rochambeau said that their combined force—considerably less than 10,000 men—could not crack the city's formidable defenses. The Frenchman suggested a campaign in Virginia to help Lafayette, who could only watch helplessly while Cornwallis rampaged through the state, burning and looting. Washington confessed that his mostly northern soldiers would likely mutiny if he marched south. When he held out for a strike at New York, Rochambeau became so angry, he came close to insulting Washington to his face.

⌒

As an American, Washington had no authority over the French fleet, either in Newport or in the West Indies. Neither did Rochambeau, but he knew the admirals of both fleets personally. Without telling Washington, he wrote to the commander of the West Indies fleet, François

Joseph Paul, Comte de Grasse, that Washington's army was too weak to attack New York. Virginia looked like a far better target. The enemy was "making his strongest efforts" there. By bringing his fleet into Chesapeake Bay, de Grasse could perhaps render them "the greatest service." The general also advised the comte to bring troops and money. "The Americans were at the end of their resources."[4]

To mollify Washington, Rochambeau agreed to unite their two armies at Dobbs Ferry on the Hudson River. The crisp white uniforms of the French awed the Americans, while the mixture of humanity in Washington's ranks amazed the French. One in every seven soldiers was black; boys of fifteen fought next to grey-haired men of sixty. For a month the two armies maneuvered around New York, probing the British defenses. They were not encouraged by the blasts of musketry and cannon fire whenever they approached a British strong point.

∽

IN SOUTH Carolina General Nathanael Greene was giving battle to the British garrisons there. Though the British won victory after victory, heavy casualties forced them to abandon one interior post after another, including the crucial fort at Ninety Six. "We fight, get beat, rise and fight again," Greene said, in another classic formulation of George Washington's strategy.[5]

Greene also recognized the crucial nature of Cornwallis's campaign in Virginia. The southern commander corresponded frequently with Lafayette, urging him to avoid a general action in which he might be annihilated. Such a defeat could have fatal consequences for the revolution in Virginia—and free Cornwallis to do a wrecking job on Greene's conquests in South Carolina.

∽

ON AUGUST 14, 1781, a messenger from the French admiral in Newport informed Washington and Rochambeau that Admiral de Grasse was coming to America from the French West Indies with twenty-nine warships and 3,000 troops. But his destination was the Chesapeake, not New York.

Washington decided he had no alternative but to march south. He—and everyone else—was unaware of another drama unfolding inside the British army. General Sir Henry Clinton, infuriated by General Lord Cornwallis's decision to invade Virginia, angrily ordered his second in command to retreat to the coast, set up a base, and ship half his army to New York. Without a moment's delay he should return with the other half of the army to the Carolinas, where Nathanael Greene was wreaking havoc on British garrisons. Cornwallis sullenly obeyed. He chose the tobacco port of Yorktown for the base, then nastily informed Clinton that he could not return any of his troops to New York because fortifying the place would take several months.[6]

∽

IN NEW YORK Washington began dealing with another problem: persuading Sir Henry Clinton not to attack the allied army on the march south. He rushed orders to build ovens in New Jersey to give the impression that he was creating a base camp for an attack on Staten Island. When he and Rochambeau crossed the Hudson and began the march south, Washington brought along thirty large flatboats on wheels, again suggesting plans to attack New York. On August 18 he ordered a detachment to advance on Sandy Hook, as if he were thinking of capturing the British fort there to make it easy for the French fleet to enter New York Harbor.

British brigadier Benedict Arnold asked General Clinton for 6,000 men, promising to destroy the allied army strung out in a long, vulnerable line of march in New Jersey. Clinton curtly replied that Arnold's proposal was out of the question. He noted how "the bold persevering militia" of New Jersey had shot up the British army when it invaded the state in 1780. Here was a final tribute to the years Washington had spent cultivating a spirit of resistance in the militia. In no other state had the amateurs' readiness to fight beside the Continentals offered better proof of the value of the American Fabius's strategy of victory.

∽

In South Carolina, General Nathanael Greene seemed on his way to presiding over a revived and reunited state. During the hot weeks of August, he had rested his army and acquired some reinforcements. But his force remained pathetically small, about 2,200 men. In Charleston the British were not ready to give up the fight. A new commander, Colonel Alexander Stewart, marched an army about the same size as Greene's to Eutaw Springs, northwest of Charleston. Greene could not ignore the challenge.

Rousing his men at 4:00 A.M. on the morning of September 8, Greene approached the British camp in a formation that was by now almost traditional. In the first line were his militiamen, along with Light Horse Harry Lee's Legion. With the militia were two famous leaders, Francis Marion and Andrew Pickens. Behind them came the Continentals.

The American attack took the British by surprise. But they soon responded with what Greene later called "a tremendous fire." The red-coated regiments were dismayed to discover that the Carolina militia did not run after firing the first round. They blazed away at the British as many as seventeen times—a tribute to the ability of Marion and Pickens to steady their men.

Two British regiments responded with a bayonet charge. Panic un-glued the militia on Greene's right, but he bolstered them with Continentals from North Carolina. Greene later said he could hardly tell which to admire most on both sides of the battle line, the gallantry of the officers or the bravery of the men. As the struggle seesawed, Greene committed his best Continentals, the Maryland and Virginia men, joined by the Delaware regiment. The British left teetered toward collapse. Redcoats and Tory militia started running for safety.

But the battle was far from over. When the pursuing Americans swarmed into the British camp, they could not resist the food and liquor they found in the enemy's tents. Both the militia and some Continental regiments succumbed to temptation. The British, sensing an opportunity, counterattacked. By this time, only a few higher-ranking officers remained to restore order among Greene's rank and file. The

British had learned from American example to pick off the top leaders whenever possible.

Greene's men were also exhausted. The day was unbelievably hot, and they had been fighting for at least four hours. Even more discouraging, the British had seized a big red-stone house on the edge of their camp and turned it into a fortress that resisted all assaults. Greene decided it was time to withdraw. Let the British have the satisfaction of possessing the battlefield.

The Americans reeled back to their camp, seven miles away. Behind them they left a British army staggering under the highest casualties suffered by any force in the entire war: 693 men out of 2,000. Later in the day they limped back to Charleston. It was the last British venture into the South Carolina countryside. Without winning a single battle, Nathanael Greene had rescued the state from the verge of returning to the British Empire.[7]

∽

In Virginia a week later, Washington's and Rochambeau's armies joined forces with Lafayette to trap the dismayed Cornwallis in Yorktown. Almost simultaneously the French fleet arrived from the West Indies to make an escape by water impossible. The British fleet made a desperate attempt to rescue Cornwallis, but the French bested it in an early-September naval battle, forcing it to return to New York for emergency repairs. That decision permitted the French squadron at Newport to bring the army's heavy artillery and tons of supplies safely to the Chesapeake. Soon the allies were digging trenches and bombarding Cornwallis's unfinished defenses in a formal siege, aided by 9,000 militia Washington called up from Maryland and Virginia. Watching from South Carolina, an exultant Nathanael Greene told Washington, "It was no less fortunate for the public than happy for ourselves" that such a good understanding had existed "between Your Excellency the Marquis and myself." Almost playfully, he added, "As you are within the limits of the Southern Department I hope you will communicate your orders [to me] without the least embarrassment; for be assured I shall have no less pleasure in serving under you than I ever had."[8]

⌒

ALMOST ONE hundred heavy guns began pounding the British at point-blank range. The moment was approaching, faster than anyone expected, when the Americans would storm the enemy, his guns silent and his walls breached. On October 15 Cornwallis wrote Sir Henry Clinton a despairing letter: "We shall soon be exposed to an assault in ruined works, in a bad position, and with weakened numbers. The safety of the place is therefore so precarious that I cannot recommend that the fleet and army should run any great risk in endeavoring to save us."

There was no danger of that happening. The second-rate British admiral in command in New York had no appetite for another encounter with the French fleet. He found all sorts of excuses to delay his departure with the 6,000 troops Clinton was ready to put on his ships.

Washington accelerated the British collapse with assaults on two key redoubts on the flank of the British line. One was led by his former aide, Alexander Hamilton; the other was a French affair. Both were stunningly successful, enabling the allies to emplace cannons that could fire into the trenches and dugouts where the British troops were living.

Lord Cornwallis asked his senior officers what he should do. Fight to the last man? Every officer told him that he owed it to his troops to surrender. Silently, Cornwallis nodded his assent. He turned to an aide and dictated a historic letter. "Sir, I propose a cessation of hostilities for 24 hours and that two officers may be appointed on each side . . . to settle terms for the surrender of the posts at York and Gloucester."

During the negotiations, Cornwallis tried to protect loyalists and American deserters in his ranks. Washington agreed to look the other way and permit them to escape punishment. The final terms only made the size of the victory more impressive. Cornwallis surrendered 7,157 soldiers and 840 seamen—far more men than General John Burgoyne had given up. Washington and Rochambeau waited in a nearby captured redoubt and signed the surrender document there. Washington ordered an aide to write above their signatures, "Done in the trenches before Yorktown Virginia, October 19, 1781."

Later that day the British marched out to surrender in a nearby meadow, where they stacked their guns. Their army's regimental bands reportedly played an ironic tune. It was an old English air to which many songs have been written. One set of lyrics was titled "When the King Enjoys His Own Again," but by far the most popular version was "The World Turned Upside Down." This was not a bad summary of the Americans' almost miraculous victory at Yorktown.

An ecstatic Lafayette dashed off a letter to a friend in Paris, announcing, "The play, Sir, is over." When the British prime minister, Lord Frederick North, heard the news several weeks later, his reaction was not dissimilar. "Oh God! It is all over! It is all over!" George III seriously considered abdicating when the House of Commons announced it would issue a vote of no confidence in the North government. But Prime Minister Lord North persuaded the monarch that he would "lose no honor" if he yielded to the decision of the House. The king had "persevered as long as possible in what you thought right." Nevertheless, the House still passed the resolution, forcing North's resignation, and the king had to accept a new prime minister, who promised to begin peace negotiations.[9]

In America, General Washington warned Congress and the American people that the war was not over. Still on the American continent were 25,000 well-armed British regulars—five times the number he could hope to muster if they chose to continue fighting.

When he sent the news of the triumph at Yorktown to Congress, Washington gave one of his most dependable aides, Marylander Tench Tilghman, the honor of delivering the message. Tilghman arrived in Philadelphia exhausted from a full day and night in the saddle—and had to endure several hours of questioning from a congressional committee that wanted a more complete description of the siege and surrender than Washington communicated in his deliberately matter-of-fact letter.

Finally, Tilghman asked if he could retire to a convenient boarding house for some rest. But the messenger of victory had not a cent in his pocket. Like all the other officers in the Continental Army, he had not been paid for years. Uneasy looks flickered around the congressional chamber. There was not a penny in the national treasury. A New Jersey congressman rose to suggest that each member contribute a dollar in hard money from his pocket. Thus the messenger of victory was able to collapse in his bed without fear of arrest for debt. General Washington's strategy of victory had come breathtakingly close to running out of time.

CHAPTER 14

Victory's Unexpected Challenge

Negotiating peace became almost as nerve-racking as winning the war. George Washington had tried to accelerate the process by sending a letter to Ambassador Benjamin Franklin in Paris within a day or two of Cornwallis's surrender, informing him of the amazing news. Washington made a point of enclosing a copy of the surrender document, which made clear that he was the commander in chief at Yorktown, the conductor of the negotiations, and the man in possession of the prisoners and captured weapons. He was ready to acknowledge French assistance but wanted the diplomats to know the American army had played a major role.

To emphasize this point, Washington enclosed a copy of Nathanael Greene's report of the battle of Eutaw Springs. It was a very effective way of informing the diplomats—and the French—that the British were being defeated elsewhere, with no help from France.[1]

⌣

FRANKLIN AND his two colleagues, John Adams and John Jay, had to cope with a galaxy of problems before they could start talking peace with the British. They did not get along with each other. Adams hated Franklin, viewing him with an almost mindless compound of envy and suspicion that he was pro-French. Jay was even more anti-French. Congress had saddled them with a promise to sign nothing without French approval. Meanwhile, France had brought Spain into the war in 1779 by promising it would not sign a peace treaty until Spain acquired the fortress of Gibraltar and the island of Jamaica. Gibraltar would make Spain ruler of the Mediterranean Sea. Jamaica would guarantee her domination of the West Indies. The British were still inclined to resist these threats to their empire with all the violence and cunning in their power.

For most of 1782, while the diplomats talked, war raged in the West Indies and the Mediterranean. Two attempts to take Gibraltar failed. In the West Indies, the fleet that had helped trap Cornwallis suffered defeat in a battle that demolished French and Spanish hopes of dominating the immensely profitable sugar islands. Meanwhile, the diplomats continued to talk. John Jay and John Adams convinced Franklin that they had the right to negotiate without saying a word to the French. Soon they had the makings of a very generous treaty, which extended America's western border to the banks of the Mississippi. Franklin exercised his almost magical powers of persuasion, and the French agreed to go along with it. Bankrupt, they were desperate for peace.[2]

As 1783 began, rumors filtered into Philadelphia from ships recently arrived from Europe. They all reported that Benjamin Franklin and his fellow negotiators in Paris were close to signing a peace treaty with Britain. Now only a treaty between England and France and her European allies, Spain and Holland, was needed to end the war. This glimpse of peace just over the horizon stirred profound excitement and hope in the civilian population. But among the Continental Army's officers, it produced a surge of sullen fury. Congress had not paid them for years. As a reward for their services, it had promised them half pay for life. Now Congress would no longer need them and was reportedly going to welsh on this agreement—and on the years of unpaid back pay. Suddenly a challenge to the strategy of victory came from a new and very dangerous angle.

FLURRIES OF antagonism over pay had flared between Congress and the officers during the Valley Forge winter. In response to Washington's recommendation of a pension for life, Samuel Adams and his fellow New Englanders had done everything but threaten secession from the union to block a vote. Eventually Congress had compromised on half pay for seven years after the war.

In 1780, at Washington's urging, Congress had again extended the pension to half pay for life. Almost immediately, under pressure from New England, the lawmakers got cold feet and rescinded their generosity. Instead they recommended the half pay idea to the individual states, where it got a very mixed reception. When asked to grant Congress the power to tax imports, Connecticut's legislature specified not a single dollar should go to the army's officers for half pay.

⌢

SMALL WONDER a determination was growing on the officers' part to settle matters. They decided to send a three-man delegation to Congress, led by abrasive, outspoken Major General Alexander McDougall of New York. They brought with them a petition from the officers, which General Washington assured Congress was written in "respectful terms." While this was true by and large, some of the language was more than a little threatening. "We have borne all that men can bear," the petition declared. "Our property is expended—our private resources are at an end and our friends are wearied out with our incessant applications" (for loans). "Any further experiments on their [the army's] patience may have fatal effects."

On January 13, 1783, General McDougall and his delegation met with a "grand committee" of one congressman from each state. They had already conferred with Robert Morris, the nation's superintendent of finance, who had said that without new taxes he could not pay them a single dollar. The nation's financial situation was "so alarming," Morris wondered if Congress should create a "confidential committee" to hear the gruesome details without panicking the public. McDougall and the two colonels who accompanied him only reiterated their anger at the on-again, off-again way Congress had dealt with paying them. The approach of peace made them fear they were in danger of being "still more neglected."[3]

⌣

PENSION OPPONENTS soon resorted to slander to block negotiations. They accused Robert Morris of favoring a military dictatorship to collect federal money to balance his budget. One of the most outspoken of these enemies of the army, Arthur Lee of Virginia, accused them of "subverting the revolution." Virtually a certified paranoid, Lee had the good fortune to be the younger brother of the influential Richard Henry Lee, leader of their wealthy powerful clan. McDougall and his committee responded by declaring that the army would not disband until Congress and the states had met their demands. This threat looked more and more like an open door to future calamities.

By this time most readers will have perceived that we are nearing the close of our time-travel journey. Looming ahead was a confrontation that no one had previously imagined. A glimpse of the dimensions of the potential disaster emerged when the committee returned to New Windsor. A group of malcontents was circulating stories that Washington was indifferent to the soldiers' needs. In one letter he called them "the old leven [leaven]"—shorthand for General Horatio Gates and his circle. Gates was still with the army, wearing a mask of "apparent cordiality." In fact, driven by rage and envy, he was working secretly to undermine the commander in chief. His New England congressional friends had protected him from an inquiry into his defeat at Camden, but his military reputation remained in tatters.[4]

Around him Gates had collected a group of hotheaded younger officers, whom he converted into critics of Washington. Soon after McDougall's return, rumors swept through the army that Congress and the states were going to treat the officers shabbily. On March 10, 1783, an anonymous broadside called for a meeting of all the army's field officers (colonels and majors) and company representatives (captains and lieutenants) the following morning (Tuesday) at 11:00 A.M.

The Newburgh address, as it became known, exhorted the officers to abandon "the milk and water style" of their petition to Congress. Failure to act now would condemn them to grow old "in poverty wretchedness and contempt." Peace would benefit everyone but them. It was time to confront the "coldness and severity of the government" and the ingratitude of their fellow citizens, whom the army's courage had made independent. They had only one option left: their swords. They should "suspect the man who would advise them to more moderate and longer forbearance."[5]

This last piece of advice was a shaft aimed directly at General Washington. If peace was at hand and Congress refused them, it was time to give the politicians a taste of steel. If the war continued, "they should all retire to some unsettled country" and laugh when a frightened Congress confronted a revived enemy without the Continental Army's protection.

John Armstrong, a twenty-four-year-old major and Horatio Gates's aide, had written this blast of rage. Rather than challenge this wild emotion, General Washington played the commander in chief. He issued a brisk order banning the Tuesday meeting as "disorderly" and "irregular" and instead called a meeting for noon the following Saturday, at which all the officers and the senior general present at New Windsor—Horatio Gates—would discuss the situation.

The Gates men had no intention of letting Washington outflank them. Armstrong produced another anonymous address, urging everyone to attend the Saturday meeting. Waiting for that conclave could not, Armstrong wrote, "possibly lessen the independence of your sentiments"—another nasty gibe at Washington, implying that he was going to try to preach patience to them.

∽

ON SATURDAY, generals and field officers and one representative from every company stationed in or near New Windsor gathered in a large building the soldiers had constructed in December. Gates had christened it the Temple of Virtue, a name intended to please his New England backers in Congress, who still saw unselfish virtue as the key ingredient in the Revolution. The building's main purpose was to encourage mingling between officers from different states. Balls and theatrical entertainments were held in the main room, which had a stage at the far end.

The officers were soon seated, and General Gates mounted the stage to assume his role as chairman. The faces in the audience displayed a grim satisfaction. They knew Gates was on their side. It was an open secret that his aide, John Armstrong, had authored the anonymous addresses. The main item on the agenda was supposed to be General McDougall's report of his visit to Congress. Before General Gates could say a word, an unexpected visitor stepped onto the stage through a nearby door. General Washington strode to the lectern and asked General Gates if he could say a few words. The flustered Gates could hardly refuse him.

The commander in chief turned to his officers and saw on almost every face a forbidding mixture of surprise and resentment. Many considered his appearance a double cross. He had promised to let them discuss the situation independently. General Washington spread some prepared remarks on the lectern but did not read them. Instead, he swept the room with angry eyes and launched a direct attack on the anonymous addresses. They were "unmilitary and subversive," appealed to "feelings and passions" rather than "reason and good sense," and had "insidious purposes." More to the point they seemed to impugn his readiness to be the army's friend and advocate. He reminded his listeners that he had been among the first to step forward to defend "our common country" in 1775 and since that time "had never left your [the army's] side." After so many years of companionship, how could anyone say he was "indifferent" to their interests?

The faces in the audience remained grim and unconvinced. These men had been disappointed too often to accept Washington as their unchallengeable friend. Wasn't he at least partly responsible for letting them reach this desperate pass?

Washington returned to the attack on the anonymous addresses. He assailed the alternative they proposed—quitting the war and retreating into the wilderness or marching on Congress with drawn swords. "My God!" Washington exclaimed. Can this writer be "a friend to the Army? Can he be a friend to the country? Rather is he not an insidious foe?" He might even be a "secret emissary" from the British in New York. They never stopped trying to sow discord among the Americans.

⌒

SENSING THIS accusation of treason was having the hoped-for effect, Washington assaulted another aspect of the anonymous addresses. He regarded as a personal insult the claim that any man who recommended moderation should be suspected of disloyalty. This was an attempt to suppress freedom of speech so that he and the army could be led away, "dumb and silent . . . Like sheep to the slaughter."

Congress was not the army's enemy, Washington insisted. He knew from speaking to them personally that most delegates had "exalted sentiments" about the army's merits and services. The soldiers needed to remember that "deliberative bodies" always acted slowly. But he vowed to do everything in his power to obtain "complete justice" as a reward for "all your toils and dangers."

Completely passionate now, Washington exhorted the officers "in the name of our common country" and "your own sacred honor" to express their "detestation" of any man who wanted to "overturn the liberties of our country" and "open the floodgates of civil discord." Instead, he begged them to retain their dignity and honor. If they did this he was certain that someday people would praise their "glorious example" and say, "Had this day been wanting the world would never have seen the last stage of perfection to which human nature is capable of attaining."

This surge of emotion stunned most of the listening officers. But it did not change many minds. The men sat silent, their anger still dominant. Washington fumbled in the inner pocket of his coat and took out a copy of a letter he had recently received from Virginia congressman Joseph Jones, describing some of the positive steps Congress was planning to satisfy the officers.

After reading the first few lines, he stopped and peered at the page. Reaching into another pocket, he extracted a set of eyeglasses he had recently received from Philadelphia. No one except a few aides had seen him wearing them. "Gentlemen," he said, "you will permit me to put on my spectacles, for I have not only grown gray but almost blind in the service of my country."

⌒

THESE UNPLANNED words had a huge impact on the audience. A murmur of emotion swept the room. Some men began brushing away tears; a few wept openly. Washington finished reading Jones's letter and departed. General Henry Knox rose to his feet and made a motion to thank Washington for his speech. There were no objections. Colonel Rufus Putnam of Connecticut recommended appointing General Knox and Colonel John Brooks to prepare resolutions for the officers.

Washington had conferred with these men and made sure that these statements were already written. General Knox stepped offstage for a few minutes and then returned to read them. They affirmed the army's unshaken attachment "to the rights and liberties of human nature" and asked Washington to become their spokesman with Congress. Another resolution declared the officers' "disdain" for the "infamous propositions" advanced in the anonymous addresses and also condemned the attempts of "some unknown persons" to collect the officers together for purposes that were "totally subversive of discipline and good order"—a barely concealed swipe at General Gates and his circle.

The officers approved the resolutions overwhelmingly. Only one man rose to object to this endorsement—lean, sour-faced Timothy Pickering of Massachusetts, the army's quartermaster general. He condemned the hypocrisy of denouncing publications that every officer in the army had read with "rapture" during the preceding days. Pickering was obviously trying to reignite the officers' rage. But no one else agreed with him, at least publicly. Each man quietly departed to his quarters. Thus ended the most perilous moment to that point in the brief history of the fledgling United States of America.[6]

⌣

BACK IN Philadelphia, Major John Armstrong was still enraged with Washington and Congress. In a letter to Horatio Gates, who had rushed to Virginia to care for his sick wife, Armstrong reported that unrest was rising among five hundred Continental Army troops stationed in the city. The major included in his letter a copy of Congress's latest attempt to raise money by taxing imports. The delegates said the money would go to commuting the officers' promised half pay for life to a lump sum of five years' full pay. Along with the appeal, Congress added Washington's speech to the officers in Newburgh. The politicians seemed to think that the military men's rejection of the Newburgh addresses would win admiration among civilians everywhere. They would soon learn this presumption was disastrously wrong.

⁓

A WEEK later, on Sunday, March 23, 1783, the *Triomphe*, a French sloop of war, dropped anchor off Philadelphia after a seven-week voyage. Her captain delivered to Elias Boudinot, president of Congress, an electrifying letter from the Marquis de Lafayette. In one hundred joyous words, he reported that all the warring nations had signed treaties of peace; America's eight-year struggle for independence was over. President Boudinot rushed the news to Washington at Newburgh and included some good news of his own. On March 22, in response to a plea from the commander in chief, Congress had formally agreed to commute the officers' promised half pay for life into full pay for five years.

For several days Congress debated about whether to ratify the treaty of peace with Britain. Lafayette's letter convinced most members that this was the best course. In early April the delegates heard from the British commander in New York, General Sir Guy Carleton, that George III had issued a proclamation ending hostilities. On April 11, 1783, Congress ratified the treaty and officially proclaimed the war over. An exuberant President Boudinot wrote to General Washington, "You can only judge from your own feelings on this occasion with what peculiar joy I congratulate your Excellency and the army."

⁓

BOUDINOT AND the rest of Congress were blithely unaware of the army's continuing discontent. By this time Washington had discovered that the officers' unhappiness was infecting the enlisted ranks. The soldiers of the New Jersey brigade informed the commander in chief that when discharged they wanted a clear statement of their exemption from paying taxes as civilians. The sergeants of the Connecticut line sent another petition demanding half pay for life, like the officers were reportedly getting. For a few hours Washington wondered if he should conceal the news of Congress's declaration of peace.

Realizing this deception was impossible, Washington published the proclamation in the next day's orders. He congratulated the men for winning a victory that had rescued "millions from the hand of oppression and laying the foundation of a great empire." He hoped they could now preserve a "perfect . . . consistency of character through the very last act." He was certain that Congress would soon release them with "every mark of distinction and honor."

On April 19, 1783, the eighth anniversary of the first shots fired on Lexington green, officers and men of the regiments on duty marched to the Temple of Virtue. There, a field officer read Congress's proclamation of peace, a chaplain recited a prayer, and the soldiers gave three cheers and sang "Independence," by New England's favorite musician, William Billings.

Washington made this ceremony as low-key as possible in an attempt to keep the army's emotions under control. He was also wrestling with strong feelings of his own. He writhed at the thought that Congress might welsh on its promises to the officers. Immediately after the confrontation in the Temple about the Newburgh addresses, he admonished Congress that if it failed to compensate the officers, "then shall I have learned what ingratitude is, then shall I have realized a tale, which will embitter every moment of my future life."[7]

∽

WASHINGTON URGED Congress to discharge the men who had enlisted for the duration of the war as soon as possible and to let them take their guns and cartridge boxes with them. He predicted these weapons would become family mementos handed down to children and grandchildren. Congress approved this parting gift. But concerned about allowing the army to all but dissolve while a large British army remained in New York, the delegates settled on furloughs. They ordered Washington to send the men home on indefinite leaves that would become permanent with the signing of a final peace treaty.

Washington tried to find money to give the men before they departed. He thought each man—officers and enlisted ranks—should receive three months' back pay, for a total of $750,000. But the bankrupt Congress could not come close to achieving this figure. Washington could only ask the men to accept "Morris notes"—certificates payable in six months, signed by the superintendent of finance. Everyone knew that many of the soldiers would have to sell this pseudo-money to speculators, who were eagerly buying up at discounted prices government promissory notes issued earlier in the war. But the Morris notes were better than nothing.

Morris had to sign each note, which took weeks. On June 2, 1783, an almost frantic Washington rushed a messenger to Philadelphia, begging him to deliver the notes he had already signed. The commander in chief warned that he feared "the worst consequences" if the notes did not arrive soon. He added a lament that Congress could not give the men at least a month's pay in hard money.[8]

On June 5 a committee of officers asked Washington to suspend the furloughs, which they looked on with "a mixture of astonishment and chagrin." The army was being disbanded in front of their eyes without even one of their demands for justice met. They asked Washington to "insist" that no officers be sent home without receiving payment in full, including the commutation of their half pay. They also wanted a gift of $80 for each enlisted man.

Washington could only tell them there was no money to do any of these things. Nor was there any alternative to an immediate departure, for there was also no money to pay the cost of keeping the army together. Almost pathetically he could only ask them to understand that he was merely a servant of the public, required to obey the orders of Congress. He insisted, despite the evidence to the contrary, that the lawmakers still retained "the best disposition toward the army" and would eventually meet their demands. Aware by now of the animosity toward the Continental Army spreading throughout the nation, most soldiers dismissed this attempt at optimism.

No farewell parade or other ceremony marked the departure of the furloughed troops. The regiments of the victorious Continental Army simply marched away. Among the officers, disgust with Congress and with General Washington were almost universal. One friend of General Gates told him with unconcealed glee that the officers had canceled a dinner at which they had planned to make General Washington the guest of honor.

⌒

IN PHILADELPHIA, Major John Armstrong was still hoping for the worst. In another letter to General Gates, he reported that the "little corps at this place"—the five hundred or so Continentals who served as a garrison in the capital—had reacted to the furloughs "very spiritedly." They had sent a message to Congress: "We shall not accept your furloughs and demand a settlement." In Newburgh, Washington was at work on a document that he hoped would keep at a distance "embitterment" with Congress and the nation for their financial failure. His circular letter to the governors of the states urged them to support an "indissoluble union" and to maintain a "sacred regard for public justice." It was another way of exhorting them to pay their debts, to the army above all. He also recommended the creation of a small peacetime "military establishment." Once more he was emphasizing the essential idea of his strategy of victory: a trained regular army, capable of looking an enemy in the face. He sent this sermon to Elias Boudinot, the president of Congress, who mailed it to the governors of the states with a warm letter of approval.

The next day, an agitated Boudinot sent Washington a cry of distress. A menacing ring of Continental Army soldiers had surrounded the Pennsylvania State House and was threatening Congress with fixed bayonets. Some of these troublemakers were part of the city's garrison; others had marched from Lancaster under the command of growling sergeants, who claimed their officers had deserted them. They wanted money, and they wanted it now—and not in Morris notes. Major General Arthur St. Clair, the soldiers' local commander, tried to talk sense to them. They told him to go away. When congressional president Boudinot tried to pass through the cordon of mutineers, they roughed him up and called him unprintable names. The frantic president of

Congress begged Washington to send some dependable troops as soon as possible.[9]

Congress demanded that the state of Pennsylvania call out the militia. Its spokesmen refused, fearing that the amateur soldiers would side with the mutineers. When the mutineers insulted and shoved more congressmen, the theoretical rulers of the thirteen states decided on a drastic solution. They abandoned Philadelphia and moved to the rustic simplicity of Princeton, New Jersey. Delighted, Major Armstrong told General Gates that most Philadelphians deemed the decision of the "Grand Sanhedren of the nation" "not unacceptable." They had long questioned the congressional delegates' wisdom, suspected their virtue, and laughed at their pretensions to dignity.[10]

⌒

FOR THE next seven months, Congress attempted to govern the nation from Princeton. From Philadelphia came sneers in the newspapers that their decision to cut and run "exhibited neither fortitude, dignity nor perseverance." Other newspapers took up this theme with savage alacrity. "The flight of Congress" became sarcastic dinner conversation from Boston to Savannah. European allies were appalled. The Marquis de Lafayette wrote from Paris, wondering if the decision meant "a wane of disposition to the federal union."[11]

Obviously looking to dignify its sojourn in the boondocks, Congress invited General Washington to visit to discuss the chief question on his mind, a peacetime regular army. He was soon on his way with his wife Martha, two aides, and an escort of twelve dragoons—unaware that the idea was already in trouble. A chief opponent of Congress's attempts to raise money to pay the officers, David Howell of Rhode Island, had already attempted to emasculate the invitation. He had forced Congress to vote on a resolution to invite Washington with no mention of the peacetime army.

Congress arranged for Washington to stay in a handsome twenty-room house at nearby Rocky Hill. There he gave a dinner for the twenty-two members of Congress in attendance—another sign of trouble to come. Numerous delegates had gone home in disgust, including Washington's former aide Alexander Hamilton. The commander in chief learned that Congress was debating where to erect a gigantic equestrian statue of him. But he soon saw that its members had little or no interest in his recommendations for a peacetime army. Virginian Arthur Lee joined David Howell and other believers in the power of a virtuous militia to dismiss the idea. It was better for the nation's political health, Lee averred, if Congress remained "a rope of sand rather than a rod of iron." The mindless fear of a standing army seemed impervious to criticism from a theoretical or practical point of view.[12]

Instead of working out plans for a peacetime army, Congress ordered Washington to dismiss the remaining regiments in the service. A handful would remain as token garrisons at Fort Pitt to guard the western frontier and at West Point, where America's artillery and ammunition would be stored. Washington noted with some concern that the British had not yet handed over five northern and western forts as promised in the peace treaty. When Washington sent General Baron Friedrich Wilhelm von Steuben to Canada to discuss this omission with the British and obtain a schedule for the forts' surrender, Steuben got a brusque brush-off. The forts would remain in British hands for another ten years and become strongholds for arming and encouraging Indians to oppose American settlers in the west.

⁓

IN OCTOBER, Washington abandoned his attempt to persuade Congress to create a peacetime army. Instead, he wrote a message that he hoped would resonate with the last regiments that were about to disband and go home. He began his "Farewell Orders to the Armies of the United States" by telling them their victory should inspire "astonishment and gratitude" in every American heart and mind. Better than anyone else, they knew how often they had been reduced to a "feeble condition." But their unparalleled perseverance through "almost every possible suffering and discouragement" had produced a victory that would forever remain "little short of a standing miracle." Men from every state had put aside local prejudices and become "one patriotic band of brothers."

Washington said he was sure they would make the transition from soldiers to citizens by maintaining "the same steady and decent behavior" that had characterized their military careers. He was taking this opportunity not only to praise them but to profess his "inviolable attachment and friendship." He hoped that their country would do "ample justice" to them—and pay them what they deserved. No one else had secured by their courage and devotion "such innumerable blessings for others."

At West Point, where most of the remaining officers had gathered, they decided to write a reply to this farewell. News from the New York state legislature had soured their mood. The lawmakers, under the leadership of Governor George Clinton, had voted to reject the new impost approved by Congress. Under the absurd constitution imposed on the country by the Articles of Confederation, which required every state to agree to any and all forms of federal taxation, this meant there would be no federal money for the commutation of the officers' half pay for life.

Quartermaster General Timothy Pickering volunteered to do the writing. His essay had only minimal praise for General Washington, whom he exonerated from allowing Congress to defraud the officers. "Causes" beyond the general's control were the culprits. But that did not rescue Washington from portrayal as a silent spectator to the massive malfeasance committed by Congress and the states. One historian has described the text as a "snarl of self pity and defiant outrage." Although hand delivery would have been a simple matter, apparently no one was willing to give the order. So they put it in the mail.[13]

Meanwhile, Washington was exchanging polite letters with General Sir Guy Carleton about when he and his troops would evacuate New York. Finally, a date was set: November 25. It turned out to be a clear, cold day with a brisk northwest wind. Washington sent General Knox and some eight hundred Continentals into the city to ensure order. When Knox returned to report all was peaceful, Washington rode beside Governor Clinton to the city line. There numerous civilians joined them. Ahead of them rode a uniformed militia cavalry regiment. Behind Washington and Clinton trudged numerous civilians, many of them New York state officials. Then came Washington's remaining officers. Once more the civilians eagerly played down the Continental Army's role in the victory.

Washington made no attempt to contest this policy. He had more than made his point about the Continentals' contributions in his farewell orders to the army. While the British ships in the harbor, loaded with troops and loyalists, awaited a wind that would enable them to depart, Washington spent the next week attending dinners and receptions at which he was showered with praise. Only someone who understood the power of New England's hostility to a regular army would have been able to understand his acceptance of the situation. Washington, long since determined not to clash with Congress about fundamental issues, made no attempt to combat it.

Finally winds carried the British fleet and army into the open sea for their long voyage home. Washington sent word to his officers that he would welcome a chance to exchange a personal good-bye with them at Sam Fraunces's tavern on the corner of Broad and Pearl Streets. He did not realize that he was about to experience emotions that he and his officers would never forget.

CHAPTER 15

George Washington's Tears

Many people know that General George Washington wept when he said farewell to his officers at Fraunces Tavern on December 4, 1783. Only readers of this book will understand the reason for his tears. Historians have long relied on a memoir written by Major Benjamin Tallmadge decades after the event. By that time memories of the Revolution had become drenched in rose-tinted nostalgia.

Tallmadge made it seem as if Washington were saying good-bye to old and dear friends. In fact, he did not know more than a half dozen people in the room. Most of the veteran officers had long since left on those indefinite furloughs, which were now permanent. The officers of these eight hundred men were almost all newcomers. Moreover, the history of the preceding months makes clear that a sentimental farewell was the least of the reasons for the general's tears.

On the second floor of the brick building, which still stands on the corner of Broad and Pearl Streets, Washington poured himself a glass of wine and raised it to his lips. The officers passed decanters and quickly filled their glasses. Washington gazed at the officers, his lips trembling. He wanted—even needed—to break through the resentment infesting their minds and hearts. He wanted to speak to this small cluster of guarded faces—and somehow reach the whole officers' corps.

He knew all too well about the abuse the Continental Army was taking in the newspapers for the officers' daring to insist on their pensions. Quartermaster Timothy Pickering's angry letter and Washington's admonishment that Congress's failures threatened to leave him perpetually embittered may well have flickered through his mind.

Slowly, Washington raised his glass and said, "With a heart full of love and gratitude, I now take leave of you. I most devoutly wish that your latter days may be as prosperous and happy as your former ones have been glorious and honorable."[1]

Tears began to stream down Washington's cheeks. The officers' anger at this man—if not at Congress—dissolved. They understood that the chief reason for those tears was regret. The general had failed to get them the rewards they needed and deserved—not only the money owed them but the praise and appreciation of a grateful country.

"I cannot come to each of you," Washington said in a choked voice. "But I shall feel obliged if each of you will come and take me by the hand."

A tearful General Henry Knox, standing closest to Washington, extended his meaty hand. Washington embraced him and kissed him on both cheeks. Next came Baron Friedrich Wilhelm von Steuben and, after him, Alexander McDougall, the spokesman of the officers' anger. Washington embraced both men. After them came the other officers, in rough order of rank, to receive a handshake and an occasional embrace. "In the same affectionate manner," Major Benjamin Tallmadge recalled, "every officer in the room parted with his general in chief."

⌒

THREE WEEKS later, in Annapolis, Maryland, General Washington went before Congress and resigned as commander in chief of the American army. Despite his bitter disappointments, he retained his vision of why they had fought the Revolution—to create a nation of free men. He went home to Mount Vernon a private citizen, subject to politicians he neither admired nor respected.

Within two years, he would be sitting on the porch at Mount Vernon, discussing with ex-congressman James Madison how to overhaul the malfunctioning federal government. Washington told Madison he had only one idea to propose. America needed a president with powers coequal to those of Congress. This was his low-key but no less potent solution to Congress's inability to lead the nation. Washington may have suspected that he would become that president. But he did not realize he would find an opportunity to make the essence of the strategy of victory—a trained army to look the enemy in the face—a fundamental part of America's revolutionary heritage.[2]

CHAPTER 16

Major General Anthony Wayne to the Rescue

Not many people had seen President George Washington lose his temper. His self-control was, by this time, legendary. But when he lost it, the unfortunate few witnesses never forgot the explosion. One of the most historic detonations occurred on December 9, 1791, when a messenger from Secretary of War Henry Knox arrived at the president's Philadelphia mansion while Washington was entertaining guests at dinner. His secretary, Tobias Lear, hurried into the dining room and whispered that there was news from the west.

The president excused himself and rushed to a nearby parlor to glance at a dispatch from the commander of the western army, Major General Arthur St. Clair. The previous day, a newspaper had reported a rumor that the army had been mauled in a clash with hostile Indians. Within minutes Washington returned to the table, where he chatted agreeably with his guests until they departed.

Lear followed Washington into the parlor and asked if he was needed for any immediate task. The slight, affable secretary found a man he had never seen before. The president's face was red, his eyes wild. His long arms flailed the air. "IT'S ALL OVER!" he roared. "St. Clair's defeated—ROUTED! The officers nearly all KILLED! I told him when I took leave of him—Beware of SURPRISE! He went off with that as MY LAST SOLEMN WARNING! Yet he let his army be cut to pieces—HACKED—BUTCHERED—TOMAHAWKED —by SURPRISE—the very thing I warned him against! The blood of the slain is upon him—the curse of widows and orphans—THE CURSE OF HEAVEN!"

For another five minutes, Washington damned General St. Clair in language that Lear had never heard before in his genteel young life. He had spent most of the Revolutionary War years at Harvard. The horrified Lear feared the nation's fifty-nine-year-old chief executive would topple to the floor in a fatal fit of apoplexy.

Breathing in rasps, Washington flung himself on a nearby sofa. When he spoke again, his voice was calm and measured. "This must not go beyond this room. General St. Clair shall have justice. I will hear him without prejudice."[1]

Already Washington was thinking beyond General St. Clair, whose military career was over. The president had realized that the disaster could be a blessing in a very unpleasant disguise. Even before Washington became president in 1789, the fledging United States had been fighting an Indian war in the western territory that it had unexpectedly acquired from the British in the treaty of peace that ended the War for Independence.

George III's spokesmen in Canada demonstrated their continuing enmity by refusing to evacuate the forts they had built in the wilderness we now call the Midwest and Congress called the Northwest Territory. His majesty's spokesmen also urged their agents and traders to do their utmost to encourage the Indians to attack the American settlers swarming into the region from the overpopulated states to the east.

The result was a drumbeat of brutal massacres in which Indian war parties slaughtered an estimated 1,500 American men, women, and children. Settlers in Kentucky screamed for vengeance and often retaliated against tribes that were trying to remain at peace with the white man. President Washington sent envoys who attempted to negotiate a peaceful cession of some of the Indians' lands. But the Miamis, Shawnees, and other more warlike tribes evaded or violated these agreements.

To the president's profound frustration, the United States did not have an army to add muscle to his diplomacy. Few Americans know that the Revolutionary War ended in almost mindless antagonism between the regular army and Congress—a dislike that soon took deep roots in the American psyche.[2]

Not even President Washington's enormous prestige—he was elected unanimously—could alter the new Congress's prejudice against a regular army. The politicians refused to recruit more than the single regiment created in 1784. Militia could supply any additional men needed, paid by the day. This reliance on amateurs must have made ex-general Washington wonder if he had been elected president of Never-Never Land. As he had repeatedly told Congress throughout the Revolution, militia specialized in running for the rear the moment they saw British bayonets coming at them. Without a trained army to look the enemy in the face, they would continue to run.

In 1790, America's one-regiment regular army, reinforced by over 1,000 militia, had launched a punitive attack on a cluster of Miami villages from which the whites believed many war parties emanated. About one hundred warriors had ambushed the advance guard. The panicked militia abandoned the regulars in headlong flight. Another surprise attack mauled a second American detachment the following day. The army stumbled back to its base at Fort Washington, near present-day Cincinnati, demoralized and humiliated. The tall, hard-eyed Miami war chief who had commanded the Indians, Me-she-kin-no-quah, known to the white men as Little Turtle, became a hero to the Indians of the Northwest.

A grim president and his secretary of war, Henry Knox, resolved to try again. This time they persuaded Congress to authorize a second regular regiment. They also negotiated permission to raise 2,000 "levies" for six months' service. These soldiers would be considered regulars even though they were closer to militia. To command this second army they chose former major general Arthur St. Clair, one of the first officers who had responded to Washington's insistence on the crucial importance of a trained regular army. St. Clair had, readers will recall, surrendered the bastion of Ticonderoga rather than defend it with a relative handful of Continentals. For this decision, St. Clair had suffered eighteen months of sneers and obloquy from Bunker Hillist New England soldiers and their anti–regular army allies in Congress.

Ideologues in Congress had undermined President Washington's attempt to create a new regular army. Late in 1790 they reduced the regulars' pay and for an entire year did not bother to send them a single penny. As a result, less than 10 percent of the men whose enlistments expired that year signed up again. When General St. Clair reached Fort Washington, he found the First Regiment had dwindled to 299 men. Recruiting for the new second regiment faltered disastrously, leaving the regulars 50 percent below their authorized strength. St. Clair's six-month levies were barely trained, forcing him to call out 1,160 militia.

Meanwhile, the Indians gathered a 1,500-warrior army under the leadership of Little Turtle. At dawn on November 4, 1791, the war chief attacked. The militia and the six-month levies fled, and the American campground became a scene of indescribable slaughter. An appalling sixty-four officers and 807 enlisted men were killed or wounded, with even more horrendous casualties among the packhorse drivers and other civilians. General St. Clair had joined the fugitives on one of the few surviving horses.

∽

PRESIDENT WASHINGTON informed Congress and the newspapers that the country was now embroiled in a full-scale war, with the future of the United States at stake. Were we going to let the British and their Indian allies confine America to a strip of states along the Atlantic seaboard? The chastened politicians suspended their paranoia and gave the president the soldiers he wanted. There would be four regular regiments, with men enlisted for three years' service, plus a squadron of cavalry. As a sop to a still vocal minority of regular army haters in Congress, Secretary of War Knox decided the new force would be called the Legion of the United States rather than the United States Army.

Washington and Knox studied a list of revolutionary commanders and chose Anthony Wayne of Pennsylvania to command this new entity. The president still remembered with pride and pleasure Wayne's 1779 midnight assault on the British Hudson River fort, Stony Point. Wayne had also demonstrated other leadership skills. In 1782, with only a few hundred regulars, he had wrested control of Georgia from a much larger British army.

Wayne instantly accepted the president's offer. He was floundering in a morass of debt and impending bankruptcy due to an ill-fated attempt to prosper as a rice grower on a plantation the grateful Georgians had given him for his 1782 liberation of their state. Wasting no time, Wayne headed for Pittsburgh. Told that his army would await him there, he discovered on arriving a grand total of forty morose recruits. It took another ten months for the Legion of the United States to reach 1,200 men. Low pay and the prospect of confronting the tomahawk wielders who had slaughtered St. Clair's army did not attract the best and brightest. Like the Continentals before them, Wayne's recruits were almost all poor, landless, and frequently illiterate.[3]

⌒

WAYNE WENT to work on turning this collection of fugitive farm boys and urban drifters into serious soldiers. Back in Philadelphia Knox and Washington had found it necessary to mollify another vocal minority of congressmen who still thought diplomacy could persuade the Indians to cede land to importunate settlers. The president forbade Wayne to launch any offensive operations while envoys conferred with various tribes and tried to convene a "grand council" at which the two sides would resolve their irreconcilable differences. The British did their utmost to stall and otherwise derail this meeting.[4]

⌒

MEANWHILE, MAJOR General Wayne was making clear to his recruits that his "Mad Anthony" nickname was a misnomer. He was a professional soldier with very high standards of military performance. His men soon learned this meant unremitting discipline. Within five weeks in the fall of 1792, he executed seven deserters. Anyone found sleeping on duty or revealing "an intention to desert" got one hundred lashes.

Anyone on parade in a soiled uniform got twenty lashes. He cashiered drunk and disorderly officers with equal ruthlessness.

The new general moved the army some twenty-two miles into the wilderness to escape the taverns and swarming prostitutes of Pittsburgh, at this time a raw frontier town. He christened their camp Legionville and resumed his training routine with new intensity. The men spent dozens of hours firing at targets "waist band high," using a cartridge that contained one ball and three heavy buckshot instead of the standard single ball—a combination Wayne thought would be far more effective in fighting Indians in the forest. He also redesigned their muskets, enabling the men to load and fire more rapidly.

To nerve his tyro soldiers for the shock and terror of combat, Wayne sent part of the army into the woods with orders to imitate Indians. They stripped off their shirts and painted their bodies and faces. The remainder of the army launched an attack. The pseudo-Indians whooped and howled and fired blank cartridges, producing a very realistic version of the tumult of battle. The attackers blasted back at them, roaring defiance.

In the spring of 1793, Secretary of War Knox ordered Wayne to bring his men into the disputed Northwest Territory by boat. At Cincinnati, a cheering crowd of over 1,000 lined the bank of the Ohio River, greeting them as saviors. The Indians, especially the warlike Miamis, were not pleased with the proximity of Wayne's soldiers. They accused the United States of speaking "with a double tongue."[5]

While diplomacy continued, Wayne asked the governor of Kentucky to call out 1,500 mounted militia. The Kentuckians replied that their militia insisted on the right to act independently of Wayne's command. Kentucky had recently become the fourteenth state, and as followers of Thomas Jefferson and his new Democratic-Republican Party, they had no great affection for federal power.

An infuriated Wayne pointed out that Kentucky's militia were in the pay of the United States and would obey his orders or else. In an eloquent letter, he warned them that he was fighting not a few Indian tribes but "a hydra"—a widespread confederation that hoped to build a chain "around the frontiers of America." The Kentuckians grudgingly agreed to obey the general.

Meanwhile the army's contractors failed to deliver more than a third of the promised provisions. Wayne accused them of trying to sabotage the legion in league with antiregular ideologues in Congress. In the spring of 1793, news from Europe added another complication: war had broken out between Great Britain and Revolutionary France. British officials in Canada became even more determined to retain the loyalty of the Indians, in case the Americans attacked the "fourteenth colony" on behalf of their former ally.

The Indians responded to British backstairs encouragement by announcing that they would tolerate no Americans north of the Ohio River. The American negotiators told them this demand was unacceptable. Thousands of Americans already lived on these lands, sold by the US government in good faith based on previous treaties with individual tribes. For a while it looked as if a climactic battle would erupt at any moment.

Wayne marched his army forty miles north from Cincinnati to the American outpost at Fort Jefferson. Six miles farther along, the road ended in an impassable wilderness. Here Wayne decided to build a winter camp and stand his ground, despite being in the heart of the territory the Indians claimed would remain forever theirs. His soldiers built a fort that enclosed fifty acres, with huts for the men and roomy quarters for the officers. Wayne called it Fort Greeneville, in honor of his best friend in the Continental Army, General Nathanael Greene, who had died after a brief illness in 1786.

⌒

DURING THE winter, Wayne discovered he had another problem. His army's second in command, Brigadier General James Wilkinson, had been in charge at Fort Jefferson and several other outposts in the Northwest Territory. A born liar and intriguer, Wilkinson wanted Wayne's job. We now know he was on the payroll of the Spanish government as "Agent 13" and hoped to make a fortune by persuading

Kentucky to declare its independence, backed by the gold that poured into Spanish coffers from the mines of Mexico.

For the moment, getting rid of Wayne was Wilkinson's immediate goal. Suddenly newspapers in the east blossomed with stories portraying Wayne as corrupt, cruel, incompetent, and stupid. Antiregular congressmen gleefully fanned the flames. But President Washington kept his temper under tight control and soon had pro-administration papers printing no-holds-barred rebuttals.

Wayne remained strangely reluctant to see Wilkinson and a group of officers around the brigadier as the source of these smears. Further belying his "Mad Anthony" nickname, he decided the best answer to his enemies was victory. By this time the Indians were artfully playing the diplomacy game directly with him. Envoys from various tribes claimed they wanted peace. If Wayne brushed the negotiators aside and attacked, they would use his intransigence to turn out every warrior in sight.

Instead, while insisting to the Indians that he was willing to parley, Wayne marched eight companies twenty miles north to the battlefield where General St. Clair's army had been slaughtered in 1792. The area was littered with the bones of the unburied dead. After interring the remains in a mass grave with suitable military honors, Wayne ordered his men to build another bastion, which he named Fort Recovery. With the help of a few men captured in the battle who had later escaped, he found the cannons St. Clair had abandoned and the Indians had buried, hoping to use them another day. Wayne installed the big guns on the walls of Fort Recovery—an added touch of defiance that he made sure the Indians heard about.

THE INDIANS listened to Canadian governor Guy Carleton, Lord Dorchester, the former general who had deftly defended the colony against the Americans' 1775 invasion—and presided over the final British withdrawal from New York at the close of the Revolution. Dorchester told the Indians that he expected war between Britain and America to begin within a year. If they remained loyal to their benevolent "father," George III, they would regain all the land they had lost since 1783. The British would scour the Americans from every foot of ground west of the mountains. To prove his sincerity, Dorchester ordered another Revolutionary War veteran, Lieutenant Governor John Graves Simcoe, former colonel of the Queen's Rangers, to build a fort on the Maumee River, well within American territory, and call it Fort Miami, in honor of the tribe led by Little Turtle.[6]

THE EMBOLDENED Indians decided to strike at Fort Recovery. On June 30, 1794, Little Turtle led an estimated 1,700 warriors through the forest. One British officer called it the most formidable Indian army in history. They launched the assault with a classic ambush. They caught a 360-horse pack train leaving the fort after bringing badly needed supplies and annihilated it, killing a third of the soldiers in its one-hundred-man escort.

Whirling bloody scalps, the screaming warriors charged the two-story fort. It was the first test of General Wayne's eighteen months of training and discipline. His troops greeted the Indians with musket blasts of buck and ball fired through loopholes. Cannons flung grape shot into their ranks. The stunned warriors took cover behind tree stumps and fired back for several hours. Recognizing that the fort was impregnable, they abandoned their siege the following day.[7]

The impact on the fragile Indian confederacy was devastating. More than six hundred warriors had come from the Great Lakes tribes, lured by British agents. They blamed the Miamis and Shawnees for the mismanaged attack and went home. Meanwhile, an exultant General Wayne hailed the victory. He informed Secretary of War Knox that his army would advance on the main Miami villages as soon as the 1,500 mounted volunteers from Kentucky joined his ranks.

On July 29, 1794, in blazing summer heat, the army began its advance. Ignoring pleas from his aides to be careful, Wayne frequently rode with the advance guard. Each day they camped well before sundown and built fortifications against a surprise attack. On August 2, after an advance of about forty miles, Wayne paused to build another fort where he could store supplies. The men felled huge trees and sawed them into logs.

At around 3:00 P.M. on August 3, Wayne retired to his tent to escape the burning sun. As he rested, a gigantic beech tree crashed into the tent, smashing an empty cot next to Wayne and badly bruising the general. His aides immediately suspected the friends of General Wilkinson were at work. Some historians, including this one, are inclined to agree with them. But Wayne dismissed the attempted assassination as an unfortunate accident.

❧

BACK IN Pittsburgh, the legion faced a new threat to its existence. To finance the army and other federal expenses, Secretary of the Treasury Alexander Hamilton had persuaded Congress to pass a tax on whiskey. This "excise" had infuriated not a few people in western Pennsylvania and elsewhere along the frontier. Making whiskey was a main source of revenue for many small farmers. On July 15, 1794, a huge riot erupted. A mob burned the house and barn of John Neville, the federal tax collector for the district, and fought a pitched battle with a squad of soldiers ordered to defend the premises.

The rioters talked wildly of seceding from the United States. Several proposed asking for help from the British in Canada. At a huge meeting outside Pittsburgh, a man wearing the uniform of a major general gave a rousing speech, predicting they were about to form a new independent nation in the West. President Washington issued a proclamation condemning the rebellion and called out 13,000 militia to suppress it.[8]

There was no longer much doubt that the future of the United States depended on the success of General Wayne's army. Resuming its march, the legion crunched forward, building a good road as it progressed. On August 8 the men reached one of their objectives, the Miami settlement of Grand Glaize, which had hundreds of cabins in fertile fields full of growing corn, beans, and other crops.

To Wayne's surprise, the Indians had abandoned this prize without a fight. They fled so swiftly that one chief left $859 in a trunk for a lucky soldier to find. Wayne called the Glaize "the grand emporium of the hostile Indians of the West" and began building another fortification, which he called Fort Defiance. Meanwhile his soldiers filled their knapsacks and wagons with fresh produce and trampled the rest underfoot. The cabins they burned, leaving a virtual wasteland.

The Indians' retreat signaled a growing disarray in their ranks. In late July Little Turtle had gone to Detroit and tried to extract an explicit pledge of military support from the British. He wanted infantry and cannons. Instead he got only vague promises. After the news of Wayne's destruction of Grand Glaize, the British rushed two companies of regulars to Fort Miami, plus additional cannons and one hundred barrels of food for the swarming refugees from Grand Glaize, who were close to starvation.

The Indians convened a grand council at which Little Turtle amazed everyone by urging peace negotiations. The war chiefs of the Shawnees, Ottawas, and other tribes dismissed him scornfully. Little Turtle resigned command of the army to Blue Jacket, a six-foot-two Shawnee leader known for his fancy clothes and hatred of white men. He had 1,300 warriors ready to follow him, plus a 70-man company of Canadian militia who would paint their faces and fight as Indians.

⌒

On August 20, a day of rain showers and oppressive heat, Wayne's army moved up the Maumee River valley toward Fort Miami, laboring across deep ravines and through thick woods. They marched in two columns, with a heavily armed battalion of picked troops as an advance guard and cavalry on both flanks. Wayne was still determined that they would not be taken by surprise. The general was in agony from an attack of gout, but he thrust the pain aside and rode at the front of the left column.

Ahead, muskets barked, followed by a volley. Messengers came racing back to report they were facing the Indian army. The warriors had chosen to fight in a part of the forest that had been struck by a tornado, leaving hundreds of felled trees in a gigantic tangle. The site already had a name, Fallen Timbers. To the Indians it seemed heaven-sent as a place that cavalry could not charge and that infantry would find difficult to penetrate in a compact mass, wielding the weapon the Indians feared, the bayonet.

The opening volley killed the two leaders of the advance guard, and the rest of the Americans began falling back, firing as they retreated, not a few turning to run. It had all the appearances of another triumphant ambush, and Ottawas and Potawatomis in the center of the Indian line charged from their tangled timber defense line, expecting a harvest of scalps. They collided with the main body of Wayne's army and found themselves fighting in tall grass and open forest, where American marksmanship took a stunning toll.

"Charge the damned rascals with the bayonet!" Wayne roared, and his men obeyed with alacrity. On the right, where General Wilkinson was in command, the Indians took one look at the oncoming "long knives" and ran. On the left, the Canadian militia met the charge with "a most heavy fire" until a company of mounted Kentucky militia hit them from the flank. The entire enemy line, whites and Indians, broke in disorder. Some fled across open ground, and Wayne's Kentucky horsemen ruthlessly rode them down.

An Ottawa war chief mounted a rock and began exhorting his men to make a stand. In midsentence, he toppled to the ground. One of Wayne's riflemen had put a bullet through his heart. Other war chiefs also fell, trying to rally their men. Little Turtle was carried from the field, streaming blood, and flung across the back of a horse that would take him to Fort Miami.

The British bastion now became the Indians' last hope. They would find refuge there with their English brothers and perhaps fight the long knives another day. To their dismay, when they reached the fort, they found the gates shut and British soldiers on the ramparts waving them away.

At that moment the central illusion that had fueled the Indians' defiance came crashing to the ground. They could only keep fleeing north as a routed rabble. Within an hour, the battle of Fallen Timbers was over. American casualties were thirty-three dead and about one hundred wounded. The Indian losses were thought to be about forty, but the humiliation of the rout and the collapse of the British-Indian alliance transcended numbers.

⌒

Two MONTHS later, President Washington's militia army marched into western Pennsylvania to stamp out what has become known as the Whiskey Rebellion. A defeat of Anthony Wayne's army at Fallen Timbers might well have encouraged the British to ship these rebels guns and ammunition. Instead, the king's men glumly watched from Canada while the cowed leaders surrendered to the federal government's display of overwhelming force.

At Fort Greeneville the following July, General Wayne negotiated a treaty with the Indians that opened the Northwest Territory—the future states of Indiana, Ohio, Illinois, Michigan, and Minnesota—to massive American settlement. Not so coincidentally, in London negotiations with President Washington's special representative, John Jay, the British government agreed to evacuate all its forts on American territory. It became more and more apparent that Anthony Wayne's victory at Fallen Timbers was a crucial turning point in American history. In the context of this book it was also the last battle of the Continental Army (disguised as the Legion of the United States) in the War for Independence. In the person of Major General Anthony Wayne, the principles of a strategy for victory in revolutionary warfare conceived by General George Washington were applied one last time— with victorious results.

The victories of Fallen Timbers and the militia army that disarmed the Whiskey Rebellion impressed some members of Congress. They proposed a resolution to send their thanks to Major General Wayne. But many other congressmen clung to their antiregular antagonism, declaring it would be inappropriate for the virtuous Congress of the United States to thank a major general of the regular American army. President Washington, not in the least surprised by this reaction, calmly informed the legislators that he, the president of the United States, would thank General Wayne. This worked an almost magical change on the naysayers. They realized the totality of Wayne's victory would make them look foolish. Soon the resolution passed unanimously.[9]

Meanwhile, the war that raged in Europe between Napoleonic France and Great Britain and her allies convinced even the most hostile antiregular politicians that some kind of trained force was necessary for the nation's security and peace of mind. While the opposition party now grouped around Jefferson still vocally opposed a standing army in Congress, some of its leaders were already saying the opposite privately. Henry Dearborn, who would become President Jefferson's secretary of war, admitted, "This country should abandon any idea of depending on militia to prosecute a war."

In 1796, with steady pressure from President Washington, who firmly reiterated the need for a small peacetime army, Congress abolished the Legion of the United States and passed an "Act to Ascertain and Fix the Military Establishment." Soon Washington's secretary of war, James McHenry, changed the four legions into regiments and reassigned officers to their new units. The force acquired a name that would become familiar to generations of Americans: the United States Army. This change pleased no one more than America's Fabius, the creator of the strategy of victory, George Washington.[10]

Afterword

s we reach the end of our journey, perhaps we should ask ourselves the meaning of the history we have traversed between 1775 and 1796. We have seen the emergence of George Washington as a thinking general and president. We have watched him deal with an egocentric ally—France—with its own agenda in the war. Above all we have acquired a new understanding of how and why average Americans fought—or failed to fight—in the long struggle. Year in, year out, they confirmed the profound truth of Washington's conclusion: that self-interest far more than patriotism was the prime factor in persuading men to remain loyal as the years of war accumulated. This insight was crucial to understanding and recruiting a strong officer corps—the soul of every army. Ultimately this book describes the difficult, troubled birth of the US Army.

Nothing is more important than understanding this surprising truth. So many people, in and outside Congress, denigrated and suspected the regular army. The New England idea that virtue and its self-satisfactions comprised a far superior motive held a profound appeal for thousands of people. It justified the dark suspicions and irrational contempt of a regular army that pervaded Congress during Washington's two terms as president.

Perhaps even more surprisingly, these emotions, expressed in different terms and for seemingly different reasons, have survived over the ensuing two centuries. One of the most memorable moments of my life was a conversation I had in 1965 with a new superintendent of West

Point, Lieutenant General Donald V. Bennett. He invited me to his office to discuss the impact of the unpopularity of the war in Vietnam on the cadets. "I've decided to order the history department to help these kids—and not a few of our faculty—deal with the vituperation and insults that are flung at them every day," he said. "Cadets can't wear their uniforms on leave without getting insults flung in their faces. Officers and their wives get midnight phone calls calling them vile names. I'm ordering our historians to start telling our cadets that the regular army has never been popular. The praise the army received during World War II was an aberration."

Those words and the reality they describe deepen the achievement of the men who founded the US Military Academy at West Point and gave it a philosophy that enabled their fragile creation to flourish and become an essential part of America's history. Their motto, "Duty, Honor, Country," played a huge role in this achievement. Those words put the US Army above politics and enabled its members to endure and even accept the eruptions of hostility that would have demoralized many men.

As I end our journey, my mind is rich with images of memorable soldiers, starting, of course, with George Washington and Nathanael Greene. After them comes a galaxy of men who have preserved the United States of America in both war and peace: Winfield Scott, Ulysses S. Grant, William Tecumseh Sherman, John J. Pershing, Dwight Eisenhower, Matthew Ridgway. They march in ghostly but still meaningful procession through my mind and heart and (I hope) through the minds and hearts of my readers. They all owe their fame to George Washington's search for a strategy of victory that would realize his vision of a nation of free men and women, shielded by an army prepared to look the enemy in the face.

Around these famous soldiers are the armies they created and led. I have a share in one of those regiments and battalions. My father fought in World War I, in the 312th Regiment of the 78th Division. He was in all the major battles. In the Argonne he was promoted from sergeant to lieutenant when all the officers in his company were killed or wounded. He never won a medal, but he once told me that some of the bravest men went undecorated. Many of them died trying to help a wounded buddy. On the wall of his bedroom, he had a framed copy of the poem "My Buddy." It is a heartbreaking—and ennobling—commentary on the "band of brothers" that George Washington constantly urged his Continentals to become.

Who was it met me with a smile
And stayed beside me all the while
And helped me o'er each weary mile?
My buddy

Thus the men (and now women) of the US Army have continued their voyage through the centuries.

Notes

Introduction

1. Henry Mintzberg and James Brian Quinn, *The Strategy Process: Concepts, Contexts, Cases* (New York: Prentice Hall, 1996); Max McKeown, *The Strategy Book* (New York: Prentice Hall, 2011); Andrew Wilson, *Masters of War: History's Greatest Strategic Thinkers* (Chantilly, VA: Teaching Company, 2012).

Chapter 1: The First Stroke

1. Arthur Bernon Tourtellot, *William Diamond's Drum* (New York: Doubleday, 1959), 19–23.

2. Allen French, *The Day of Concord and Lexington: The Nineteenth of April, 1775* (Boston, MA: Little, Brown, 1925), 140.

3. Allen French, *General Gage's Informers: New Material upon Lexington and Concord* (Ann Arbor: University of Michigan Press, 1932), 53.

4. Tourtellot, *William Diamond's Drum*, 138–139.

5. Tourtellot, *William Diamond's Drum*, 203.

6. Tourtellot, *William Diamond's Drum*, 203.

Chapter 2: Propaganda Meets Reality in 1776

1. Philip C. Davidson, *Propaganda and the American Revolution, 1763–83* (Chapel Hill: University of North Carolina Press, 1941), 165.

2. Thomas Fleming, *1776: Year of Illusions* (New York: W. W. Norton, 1975), 38 (Adams's quote).

3. Merrill Jensen, ed., *Tracts of the American Revolution, 1763–1776* (Indianapolis: Bobbs-Merrill, 1967), 436–439. Looking back on *Common Sense* decades later, John Adams

called it "a crapulous mass." David Freeman Hawke, *Paine* (New York: Harper & Row, 1974), 43–49.

4. Edmund C. Burnett, ed., *Letters of Members of the Continental Congress*, vol. 1: *August 29, 1774 to July 4, 1776* (Washington, DC: Carnegie Institution, 1921), 256, 279.

5. Ron Chernow, *Washington: A Life* (New York: Penguin, 2010), 195.

6. Letter to John Augustine Washington, March 31, 1776, in George Washington, *Writings*, ed. John Rhodehamel (New York: Library of America, 1997), 220.

7. Edward G. Lengel, *General George Washington: A Military Life* (New York: Random House, 2005), 131.

8. Douglas Southall Freeman, *George Washington: A Biography*, 7 vols. (New York: Charles Scribner's Sons, 1951), 4:166.

9. Joseph Plumb Martin, *A Narrative of a Revolutionary Soldier* (New York: Signet Classics, 2001), 4.

10. Freeman, *George Washington*, 4:180.

11. Edmund C. Burnett, ed., *Letters of Members of the Continental Congress*, vol. 2: *July 6, 1776 to December 31, 1777* (Washington, DC: Carnegie Institution, 1923), 83.

12. Freeman, *George Washington*, 4:180.

13. Fleming, *1776*, 478.

14. Freeman, *George Washington*, 4:317.

15. Martin, *Narrative of a Revolutionary Soldier*, 30–31.

16. Terry Golway, *Washington's General: Nathanael Greene and the Triumph of the American Revolution* (New York: Henry Holt and Co., 2005), 96.

17. Chernow, *Washington*, 261–262.

18. Leonard Lundin, *Cockpit of the Revolution: The War for Independence in New Jersey* (Princeton, NJ: Princeton University Press, 1940), 159.

19. Thomas Fleming, *New Jersey: A History* (New York: W. W. Norton, 1984), 66.

20. Jared Sparks, ed., *The Writings of George Washington* (Boston: New York Public Library, 1834), 228.

21. Burnett, *Letters of Members of the Continental Congress*, 232.

22. "Henry Knox to Lucy Knox, 7 January 1777," Gilder Lehman Collection, #GLC02437.00514.

Chapter 3: The Year of the Hangman

1. James Kirby Martin and Mark Edward Lender, *"A Respectable Army": The Military Origins of the Republic, 1763–389* (Hoboken, NJ: Wiley, 2013), 90–94; also see Douglas Southall Freeman, *George Washington: A Biography* (New York: Charles Scribner's Sons, 1951), 4:387–89.

2. "Alexander Hamilton to Robert R. Livingston, 28 June 1777," Founders Online, https://founders.archives.gov/documents/Hamilton/01-01-02-0201.

3. E. Capps et al., eds., *Plutarch's Lives* (New York: Loeb Classical Library, 1916), 3:119–295.

4. "Alexander Hamilton to Robert R. Livingston, 28 June 1777."

5. Terry Golway, *Washington's General: Nathanael Greene and the Triumph of the American Revolution* (New York: Henry Holt and Co., 2005), 126.

6. Washington to George Clinton, *The Writings of George Washington from the Original Manuscript Sources, 1745–1799*, vol. 9: *August 1, 1777–November 3, 1777*, ed. John C. Fitzpatrick (Washington, DC: US Government Printing Office, 1933), 77.

7. Thomas Anburey, *With Burgoyne from Quebec* (Toronto: Macmillan of Canada, 1963), 268–271.

8. Entry for July 14, 1777, in James Thacher, MD, *A Military Journal During the American Revolution* (Boston: Cottons & Barnard, 1827).

9. David B. Mattern, *Benjamin Lincoln and the American Revolution* (Columbia: University of South Carolina Press, 1998), 41.

10. "To George Washington from Major General Philip Schuyler, 14 July 1777," Founders Online, http://founders.archives.gov/documents/Washington/03-10-02-0273.

11. Paul David Nelson, *Anthony Wayne: Soldier of the Early Republic* (Bloomington: Indiana University Press, 1985), 55–57.

12. Mattern, *Benjamin Lincoln*, 47.

Chapter 4: The Perils of Fabius

1. Richard Henry Lee to Samuel Adams, November 23, 1777, in *Letters of Delegates to Congress: 1774–1789*, vol. 8: *September 19, 1777–January 31, 1778*, ed. Paul H. Smith et al. (Washington, DC: Library of Congress, 1976), 311–314.

2. Smith et al., *Letters of Delegates*, 314n.–315n.

3. "Letter from John Adams to Abigail Adams, 25 October 1777," Adams Family Papers: An Electronic Archive, Mass Historical Society, https://www.masshist.org/digitaladams/archive/doc?id=L17771025aa.

4. James Lovell to Horatio Gates, November 27, 1777, in Smith et al., *Letters of Delegates*, 329.

5. Lovell to Gates in Smith et al., *Letters of Delegates*.

6. Thomas Nelson Winter, "The Strategy That Gave Independence to the US," *The Classical*, Bulletin 53, November 1976, Files, 1A.

7. Jonathan Dickinson Sergeant to James Lovell, November 20, 1777, in Smith et al., *Letters of Delegates*, 296.

8. Smith et al., *Letters of Delegates*, 315n.

9. Ron Chernow, *Alexander Hamilton* (New York: Penguin, 2004), 116.

10. Terry Golway, *Washington's General: Nathanael Greene and the Triumph of the American Revolution* (New York: H. Holt, 2005), 153.

11. Cornelius Harnett to William Wilkinson, December 8, 1777, in Smith et al., *Letters of Delegates*, 390–391.

12. "To George Washington from Major General Horatio Gates, 19 February 1778," Founders Online, http://founders.archives.gov/documents/Washington/03-13-02-0502. Original source: Edward G. Lengel, ed., *The Papers of George Washington*, vol. 13: *December 1777–February 1778*. Revolutionary War Series (Charlottesville: University of Virginia Press, 2003), 26.

13. William Cresson, *Francis Dana: A Puritan Diplomat at the Court of Catherine the Great* (New York: Lincoln Mac Veagh, Dial Press, 1930), 46.

14. Friedrich Kapp, *Life of Fredrich William von Steuben: Major General in the Revolutionary Army* (Gansevoort, NY: Mason Bros., 1859), 115–116.

15. Edmund Cody Burnett, *The Continental Congress: A Definitive History from Its Inception in 1774 to March, 1789* (New York: Macmillan, 1941), 332.

16. James Thomas Flexner, *George Washington*, vol. 2: *In the American Revolution: 1775–1783* (Boston: Little, Brown and Co., 1967), 290–291.

Chapter 5: General Double Trouble

1. Letter to Dr. Rush, June 4, 1778, in Edward Langworthy and Charles Lee, *Life and Memoirs of the Late General Charles Lee* (New York: Richard Scott, 1813), 342.

2. From George Washington to Major General Horatio Gates, May 26, 1778, in *The Papers of George Washington*, vol. 15: *May–June 1778*, ed. Edward G. Lengel. Revolutionary War Series (Charlottesville: University of Virginia Press, 2006).

3. Johann von Ewald, *Diary of the American War: A Hessian Journal* (New Haven, CT: Yale University Press, 1979), 139.

4. "Council of War, 24 June 1778," Founders Online, http://founders.archives.gov /documents/Washington/03-15-02-0543.

5. Terry Golway, *Washington's General: Nathanael Greene and the Triumph of the American Revolution* (New York: H. Holt, 2005), 175–176.

6. Ron Chernow, *Washington: A Life* (New York: Penguin, 2010), 342.

7. "From George Washington to John Augustine Washington, 4 July 1778," Founders Online, https://founders.archives.gov/documents/Washington/03-16-02-0026. Original source: David R. Hoth, ed., *The Papers of George Washington*, vol. 16: *July–September 1778*. Revolutionary War Series (Charlottesville: University of Virginia Press, 2006), 25–26.

8. "From Alexander Hamilton to Elias Boudinot, [5 July 1778]," Founders Online, https:// founders.archives.gov/documents/Hamilton/01-26-02-0002-0012. Original source: Harold Coffin Syrett, ed., *The Papers of Alexander Hamilton* (New York: Columbia University Press, 1961), 510–514.

9. Phillip Papas, *Renegade Revolutionary: The Life of General Charles Lee* (New York: New York University Press, 2014), 259.

Chapter 6: A Surplus of Disappointments

1. James Thomas Flexner, *George Washington*, vol. 2: *In the American Revolution: 1775–1783* (Boston: Little, Brown and Co., 1967), 319.

2. Ron Chernow, *Washington: A Life* (New York: Penguin, 2010), 347.

3. Flexner, *George Washington*, 324.

4. Sydney George Fisher, *The Struggle for American Independence* (Philadelphia: J. B. Lippincot, 1908), 2:211.

5. Christian M. McBurney, *The Rhode Island Campaign* (Yardley, PA: Westholme, 2011).

6. Washington to Gouverneur Morris, October 4, 1778, in *The Writings of George Washington from the Original Manuscript Sources, 1745–1799*, vol. 13: *October 1, 1778–January 11, 1779*, ed. John C. Fitzpatrick (Washington, DC: US Government Printing Office, 1933), 325–327.

7. Todd W. Braisted, *Grand Forage 1778: The Battleground Around New York City* (Yardley, PA: Westholme, 2016), 59–60.

8. Braisted, *Grand Forage 1778*, 138–141.

9. Braisted, *Grand Forage 1778*, 138–141.

10. David B. Mattern, *Benjamin Lincoln and the American Revolution* (Columbia: University of South Carolina Press, 1998), 55–57.

11. Allen D. Gaff, *Bayonets in the Wilderness: Anthony Wayne's Legion in the Old Northwest* (Norman: University of Oklahoma Press, 2004), 26.

12. Paul David Nelson, *Anthony Wayne: Soldier of the Early Republic* (Bloomington: Indiana University Press, 1985), 94–100.

13. Douglas Southall Freeman, *George Washington: A Biography* (New York: Charles Scribner's Sons, 1951), 5:121.

14. Freeman, *George Washington*, 5:127.

15. Mattern, *Benjamin Lincoln*, 82. General Lincoln angrily protested the admiral's statement when they met.

16. Mattern, *Benjamin Lincoln*, 83–87.

17. William B. Wilcox, *Portrait of a General: Sir Henry Clinton in the War of Independence* (New York: Knopf, 1964), 293.

18. Freeman, *George Washington*, 5:123.

19. Robert D. Bass, *The Green Dragoon: The Lives of Banastre Tarleton and Mary Robinson* (New York: Henry Holt and Co., 1957), 72–77.

20. Mattern, *Benjamin Lincoln*, 107–108.

Chapter 7: Lexington Repeated—
with an Army to Look the Enemy in the Face

1. "The Line of March," Von Jungkenn Papers, William L. Clements Library, Ann Arbor, Michigan, Document 174.

2. The Ernest L. Meyer map of Elizabethtown in 1780 shows an orchard a few hundred yards inland from De Hart's Point and pasture running parallel to the shore. The map is from the Archives of the New Jersey Historical Society.

3. "The Line of March," Von Jungkenn Papers. The two German regiments were the Landgrave, the household regiment of the Landgrave of Hesse-Cassel, and the Regiment de Corps, often called Leib after its colonel. Also see Ernest Kipping, *The Hessian View of America, 1776–1783* (Monmouth Beach, NJ: P. Freneau Press, 1971), 40.

4. For additional material on William Franklin's relationship with his father and his arrest in 1776, see Thomas J. Fleming, *The Man Who Dared the Lightning: A New Look at Benjamin Franklin* (New York: William Morrow and Co., 1971), 291–343. For even more details, see William H. Mariboe, *The Life of William Franklin* (PhD diss., University of Pennsylvania, 1962).

5. W. H. W. Sabine, ed., *Historical Memoirs of William Smith, 1778–1783* (New York, 1971), 317.

6. *Orderly Book of Adjutant General Alexander Scammell* (Newark: New Jersey Historical Society, 1780), 120–121.

7. W. D. Ford, ed., *Correspondence of and Journals of S. B. Webb* (New York: Wickersham Press, 1894), 1:232–245.

8. Letter of June 4, 1780, to Moore Furman, Deputy Quartermaster General of New Jersey, in Nathanael Greene, *Papers of Nathanael Greene*, William L. Clements Library, Ann Arbor, Michigan.

9. *Orderly Book of Adjutant General Alexander Scammell.*

10. "From George Washington to Elias Dayton, 21 May 1780," Founders Online, http://founders.archives.gov/documents/Washington/99-01-02-01938.

11. Sabine, *Historical Memoirs*, 271; Edwin F. Hatfield, DD, *History of Elizabeth, New Jersey* (New York: Carlton & Lanahan, 1868), 488.

12. Papers of George Washington, Library of Congress, 137 LC, f 16, Series 4: Reel 67. Hereafter referred to as Papers of GW.

13. Colonel Aaron Ogden, *Autobiography* (Paterson, NJ: Press Print. & Pub. Co., 1893), 12–13.

14. Ogden, *Autobiography*, 13; for Ogden's wound, see Lucius Q. C. Elmer, *The Constitution and Government of the Province and State of New Jersey: With Biographical Sketches of the Governors from 1776 to 1845 and Reminiscences of the Bench and Bar, During More Than Half a Century* (Newark: M. R. Dennis, 1872).

15. *Historical Magazine*, 2nd ser., 8 (July 1870): 55–56; see also Theodore Sedgwick Jr., *A Memoir of the Life of William Livingston* (New York: Harper, 1833), 349–350.

16. Previous historians have described this signal as a "lofty pole with a tar barrel on top" (e.g., James Connolly, *Proceedings of the NJHS* 14, 411). In *The Pictorial Field-Book of the Revolution: Or, Illustrations, by Pen and Pencil, of the History, Biography, Scenery, Relics, and Traditions of the War for Independence* (New York: Harper & Bros., 1850), Benson John Lossing included a drawing of a pole with a tar barrel on its apex, but it happens to be a picture of such a signal device on Beacon Hill, Boston. This Boston beacon was first erected in 1635 and never replaced after 1789, so Lossing could never have seen it. Contemporary New Jersey sources support the description of the beacon I have used. See also the *New Jersey Gazette* of January 18, 1778; John C. Fitzpatrick, ed., *The Writings of George Washington from the Original Manuscript Sources, 1745–1799*, vol. 14: *January 12, 1779–May 5, 1779* (Washington, DC: US Government Printing Office, 1936), 284; William Henry Smith, ed., *The St. Clair Papers: The Life and Public Services of Arthur St. Clair, Soldier of the Revolutionary War; President of the Continental Congress; and Governor of the Northwest Territory; with His Correspondence and Other Papers* (Cincinnati, OH: Robert Clarke & Co., 1881), 1:469; Minutes of the Council of Safety of New Jersey, November 17, 1777; Ambrose Ely Vanderpoel, *History of Chatham, New Jersey* (Chatham, NJ: Chatham Historical Society, 1959).

17. Unpublished correspondence of William Livingston and John Jay, edited by Frank Monaghan, *Proceedings of the New Jersey Historical Society*, July 1934, 144.

18. David Bernstein, *New Jersey and the American Revolution: The Establishment of a Government Amid Civil and Military Disorders, 1770–1781* (PhD diss., Rutgers University, 1969), 329.

19. *Weekly State of the Continental Army Under the Immediate Command of His Excellency General Washington*, General Services Administration, National Archives, Miscellaneous, June 3, 1780.

20. "The Line of March," Von Jungkenn Papers.

21. Extract from a letter to the Landgrave of Hesse by Lieutenant General Knyphausen, July 2, 1780, translated by Gerhard Mueller and published in the Milburn and Short Hills *Item*, January 31, 1963. Mr. Mueller discovered this letter in the Hessian State Archives in Marburg, Germany.

22. Major Carl L. Baurmeister, *Revolution in America: Confidential Letters and Journals, 1776–1784, of Adjutant General Baurmeister of the Hessian Forces*, ed. and trans. B. A. Uhlendorf (New Brunswick, NJ: Rutgers University Press, 1957), 348; Sabine, *Historical Memoirs*, 271. In his memoir, *The American Rebellion: Sir Henry Clinton's Narrative of His Campaigns, 1775–1782*, ed. William B. Willcox (New Haven, CT: Yale University Press, 1954), 192, Clinton says that his aide-de-camp, presumably Crosbie, did not arrive in time to stop Knyphausen because the frigate on which he sailed, "happening to fall in with some of our cruisers off the port of New York and mistaking them for an enemy, was through a mutual ignorance of signals repeatedly driven off the coast, and thereby retarded in her arrival at least a fortnight longer than necessary." But both Baurmeister and William Smith note Crosbie's arrival on the sixth of June. In fact, Baurmeister, on 352, says that Knyphausen "had just embarked" when Crosbie arrived.

23. Clinton, *The American Rebellion*, 191.

24. Baurmeister, *Revolution in America*, 353, tries to excuse Knyphausen by writing, "All the troops had already embarked when Major Crosbie arrived. No decision had been reached as to whether or not this expedition should be carried out. I am constrained to believe the whole affair was a scheme of Generals Robertson and Skinner."

25. Sabine, *Historical Memoirs*, 278, 281.

26. *New Jersey Journal*, July 12, 1780.

27. Marquis de Chastellux, *Travels in North America in the Years 1780, 1781, 1782*, rev. trans. Howard C. Rice Jr. (Chapel Hill: University of North Carolina Press, 1963), 125. Even though the marquis traveled through New Jersey in the late fall, he still found that "the beauty of the country . . . everywhere corresponds to the reputation of the Jerseys, called the garden of America." In the Condict Transcripts, *Jemima Condict: Her Book* (South Orange: New Jersey Daughters of the American Revolution, 1930), militiaman David Ammerman recalled that when Connecticut Farms was burnt, "flax and oats were eight inches high."

28. Hatfield, *History of Elizabeth, New Jersey*, 488–489; for the visibility of von Wurmb's troops from the Short Hills, see Joseph H. Jones, ed., *Life of Ashbel Green, V.D.M.* (New York: Robert Carter and Bros., 1849), 96: "On a clear day, with a good telescope, the city of New York may be seen from these heights."

29. John C. Fitzpatrick, ed., *The Writings of George Washington from the Original Manuscript Sources, 1745–1799*, vol. 19: *June 12, 1780–September 5, 1780* (Washington, DC: US Government Printing Office, 1936), 134–136.

30. John C. Fitzpatrick, ed., *The Writings of George Washington from the Original Manuscript Sources, 1745–1799*, vol. 18: *February 10, 1780–June 11, 1780* (Washington, DC: US Government Printing Office, 1937), 488.

31. Entry for June 7, 1780, in Diary of Sylvanus Seeley, ms., Morristown National Historical Park Library.

32. Charles B. Bullard, "Some New Jersey Sidelights on Revolutionary Days," *Proceedings of the New Jersey Historical Society* 8 (1923): 191–192.

33. For the Newark volunteers, see Joseph Atkinson, *The History of Newark* (Newark, NJ: W. B. Guild, 1878), 116–117; for Jonathan Crane, see Ellen Crane, *Geneaology of the Crane Family*, Elizabeth Public Library, 473.

34. Richard H. Ammerman, "Treatment of American Prisoners During the Revolution," *Proceedings of the New Jersey Historical Society* 78 (1960): 299; also see *New Jersey Journal*, August 9, 1780; Henry G. Steinmeyer, *Staten Island Under British Rule* (New York: Staten Island Historical Society, 1949), 17; Charles W. Lang and William T. Davis, *Staten Island and Its People: A History, 1609–1929* (New York: Lewis Historical Pub. Co., 1930–1933), 1:190. FitzRandolph began the game by kidnapping Colonel Christopher Billopp, commander of the loyalist militia on Staten Island.

35. Letter of William Maxwell to Governor Livingston, June 14, 1780, in *The Historical Magazine and Notes and Queries Concerning the Antiquities, History and Biography of America* (New York: Charles B. Richardson, 1859), 3:211.

36. Elizabeth Ellet, *Domestic History of the American Revolution* (Philadelphia: J. B. Lippincott, 1876), 239–241; see also Charles A. Philhower, *Brief History of Chatham, Morris County, New Jersey* (New York: Lewis Historical Pub. Co., 1914).

37. Philhower, *Brief History of Chatham*, 20.

38. Colonel John Womack Wright, *Some Notes on the Continental Army* (Vails Gate, NY: National Temple Hill Association, 1963), 70. A British infantry soldier carried sixty-three pounds.

39. *Diary of the "Excellent" Geide Jaeger Corps*, Morristown National Historical Park Library, Morristown, NJ.

40. Sabine, *Historical Memoirs*, 271.

41. Letter of William Maxwell to Governor Livingston, June 14, 1780.

42. *Diary of the "Excellent" Geide Jaeger Corps.*

43. Record of Jacob Sisco, *Proceedings of the New Jersey Historical Society* 7 (January 1922): 29.

44. All the details are contained in the depositions of Catherine Benward, Abigail Lennington, and Mrs. Patience Wade and published under the title "Certain Facts Relating to the Tragic Death of Hannah Caldwell, Wife of Reverend James Caldwell," *New Jersey Journal* 81 (September 6, 1780). Caldwell concluded from this testimony that his wife was murdered. But he was in no position to be an objective judge of this tragedy.

45. Entry for June 7, 1780, in Diary of Sylvanus Seeley.

46. Entry for June 7, 1780, in *Diary of the "Excellent" Geide Jaeger Corps.*

47. Letter of William Maxwell to Governor Livingston, June 14, 1780.

48. *Proceedings of the New Jersey Historical Society.*

49. Carlos E. Godfrey, *The Commander in Chief's Guard: Revolutionary War* (Washington, DC: Stevenson-Smith Co., 1904), 68.

50. See *Historical Magazine*, 2nd ser., 3 (1868): 24–25, for correspondence between Nathanael Greene and historian William Gordon. Original source: Nathanael Greene

to Mr. Gordon, undated, 1785, L. W. Smith Collection, Morristown National Historical Park.

51. Sabine, *Historical Memoirs*, 281.

52. Sedgwick, *A Memoir of the Life of William Livingston*.

53. Lieutenant John Charles Philip von Krafft, *Journal of Lieutenant John Charles Philip von Krafft*, Collections of the New York Historical Society for the Year 1881, 112.

54. Entry for June 8 in *Diary of the "Excellent" Geide Jaeger Corps*.

55. Von Krafft, Collections of the New York Historical Society for the Year 1881, 112.

56. John Barber and Henry Howe, *Historical Collections of the State of New Jersey* (New York: S. Tuttle, 1845), 198.

Chapter 8: Enter the Outraged Conqueror of Charleston

1. Entry for June 9 in *Journal of Lieutenant John Charles Philip von Krafft*, Collections of the New York Historical Society for the Year 1881, 113.

2. John C. Fitzpatrick, ed., *The Writings of George Washington from the Original Manuscript Sources, 1745–1799*, vol. 18: *February 10, 1780–June 11, 1780* (Washington, DC: US Government Printing Office, 1937), 500–501.

3. Fitzpatrick, *The Writings of George Washington*, 18:505–507, 509–511.

4. Major Carl L. Baurmeister, *Revolution in America: Confidential Letters and Journals, 1776–1784, of Adjutant General Baurmeister of the Hessian Forces*, ed. and trans. B. A. Uhlendorf (New Brunswick, NJ: Rutgers University Press, 1957), 354–355.

5. "Mathew's Narrative," *Historical Magazine*, April 1857, 105.

6. Fitzpatrick, *The Writings of George Washington from the Original Manuscript Sources, 1745–1799*, 18:504. See also vol. 19: *June 12, 1780–September 5, 1780*, 1.

7. Fitzpatrick, *The Writings of George Washington*, 19:14–15.

8. James Thacher, MD, *A Military Journal During the American Revolution* (Boston: Cottons & Barnard, 1827), 239.

9. "Lieutenant Colonel Joseph Barton," *Proceedings of the New Jersey Historical Society* 69 (1951): 190–191.

10. Tallmadge to George Washington, Papers of GW, vol. 6:13–80, ed. Dorothy Twohig (Charlottesville: University of Virginia Press, 1983).

11. Fitzpatrick, *The Writings of George Washington*, 18:508–509; also see entry for June 15 in Thacher, *A Military Journal*, 235–242.

12. Fitzpatrick, *The Writings of George Washington*, 19:32–33; also see letters of Quartermaster Joseph Lewis (typewritten copies at Morristown Historical Park).

13. Papers of GW, 138 LC, Series 4, Microfilm Reel 67, Forman to GW, June 18, 1780.

14. Fitzpatrick, *The Writings of George Washington*, 19:26–28.

15. Sir Henry Clinton, Clinton Papers, William L. Clements Library, Ann Arbor, MI, 192.

16. Sir Henry Clinton, Clinton Papers, 192.

17. Sir Henry Clinton, Clinton Papers, 193.

18. Papers of GW, 139 LC, f 139–6.

19. Papers of GW, 139 LC, f 139–23.

20. Von Krafft, Collections of the New York Historical Society for the Year 1881, 114; Lieutenant Colonel John Graves Simcoe, *Simcoe's Military Journal* (New York: Bartlett & Welford, 1844), 96.

21. Fitzpatrick, *The Writings of George Washington*, 19:51–52.

22. Simcoe, *Simcoe's Military Journal*, 96; entry for June 22 in *Diary of the "Excellent" Geide Jaeger Corps*, Morristown National Historical Park Library, Morristown, NJ.

23. Evidence that the Americans were aware of their strategic problems appears in a letter from Major Henry Lee to former Washington aide Governor Joseph Reed of Pennsylvania, written at the "advance post" on June 20, 1780. Published in Henry Lee, *Memoirs of the War in the Southern Department of the United States* (New York: University Publishing Company, 1870), 25.

24. William Gordon, *History of the Rise, Progress, and Establishment, of the Independence of the United States* (London: Printed for the author and sold by Charles Dilly, 1788), 3:368–374.

25. Greene to Washington, June 24, 1780, in *New Jersey Archives*, 2nd ser., 4, 480–484.

26. Christopher Ward, *The War of the Revolution* (New York: Macmillan, 1952), 373 ff.

27. *Weekly State of the Continental Army Under the Immediate Command of His Excellency General Washington*, General Services Administration, National Archives, Miscellaneous, Jacket 16-5.

28. Fitzpatrick, *The Writings of George Washington*, 19:57–59. Washington also rushed a letter to the Continental Congress Committee of Cooperation, which was still at Morristown, begging them to find wagons to remove the army's stores. His doubts about Greene's ability to hold off Knyphausen are also visible in the postscript to this letter: "Morristown is become an ineligible place for the Committee. As I wish to have their support and aid, I beg leave to recommend their removal" (57–58). The Meade letter is in Papers of GW, 39 LC, f 70; also see *Orderly Book of Adjutant General Alexander Scammell*, 179–180.

29. John Barber and Henry Howe, *Historical Collections of the State of New Jersey* (New York: S. Tuttle, 1845), 190.

30. Springfield Historical Society, Bulletin No. 6, March 1961, 7.

31. Springfield Historical Society, Bulletin No. 6, March 1961, 6–10.

32. Thacher, *A Military Journal*, 235–242.

33. *Proceedings of the New Jersey Historical Society* 8 (1923): 191.

34. *Proceedings of the New Jersey Historical Society* 9 (January 1924): 51, 53 (from Condict Transcripts).

35. *New Jersey Journal*, July 14, 1780, New York Historical Society.

36. Nicholas Murray, *Notes on Elizabethtown* (rpt.; New York: Columbia University Press, 1941), 97.

37. Simcoe, *Simcoe's Military Journal*, 96–97.

38. Simcoe, *Simcoe's Military Journal*, 96–97.

39. Simcoe, *Simcoe's Military Journal*; Andrew Sherman, *Historic Morristown, New Jersey: The Story of Its First Century* (Morristown, NJ: Howard Pub. Co., 1905), 368–370.

40. Simcoe, *Simcoe's Military Journal*, 96–97.

41. Joseph H. Jones, ed., *Life of Ashbel Green, V.D.M.* (New York: Robert Carter and Bros., 1849), 117.

42. Mrs. Williams, *Biography of Revolutionary Heroes; Containing the Life of Brigadier General William Barton and Also of Captain Stephen Olney* (New York: Wiley & Putnam, 1839); original Olney letter in L. W. Smith Collection, Morristown National Park Library.

43. Washington Irving, *Life of George Washington* (New York: G. P. Putnam, 1857), 4:61–72. This is the earliest reference I have been able to find for this story, which has a strong oral tradition. Irving spent a good deal of time in New Jersey, and his biography of Washington was a serious historical effort. In 1857, there were still many men alive in New Jersey whose fathers had fought at Springfield. This convinces me that the story is substantially true.

44. Williams, *Biography of Revolutionary Heroes*.

45. Papers of GW, 139 LC, f 61, Microfilm Series 4, Reel 67.

46. Greene to Washington, June 24, 1780. This letter is also in Jared Sparks, ed., *The Writings of George Washington* (Boston: Little, Brown and Co., 1835), 7:506–509.

47. Simcoe, *Simcoe's Military Journal*, 97.

48. The Trial of Honorable Colonel Cosmo Gordon of the 3rd Regiment of the Foot Guards for Neglect of Duty Before the Enemy on the 23rd of June, 1780, near Springfield in the Jerseys (London, 1783), 102. Testimony of Lieutenant Colonel Joseph Barton. The loyalist urged Gordon to take the flowers out of his hat; they were attracting bullets and cannon balls.

49. The Trial of Lt. Colonel Thomas of the 1st Regiment of Foot Guards on a Charge Exhibited by Lt. Colonel Cosmo Gordon for Aspersing His Character (London, 1781), 93.

50. Simcoe, *Simcoe's Military Journal*, 98; also see *New Jersey Archives*, 2nd ser., 4, 474–477.

51. John Peebles, *Notebook of Captain John Peebles During the War of Independence*, 13 volumes in manuscript, original in Scottish Record Office, microfilm copy in Library of Congress.

52. Jones, *Life of Ashbel Green*, 117–118.

53. Stephan Popp, *The Hessian Soldier in the American Revolution*, privately printed, 1953. No other account of the battle mentions this, and other details of Popp's narrative on June 23 are confused. The comment about the pigsty is, however, widely corroborated.

54. Thacher, *A Military Journal*, confirms this body count; also see *Diary of the "Excellent" Geide Jaeger Corps*.

55. Simcoe, *Simcoe's Military Journal*.

56. Jones, *Life of Ashbel Green*, 119.

57. See entry for June 23 in *Diary of the "Excellent" Geide Jaeger Corps*; Von Jungkenn Papers, William L. Clements Library, Ann Arbor, MI; von Wurmb letter of July 1, 1780.

58. Simcoe, *Simcoe's Military Journal*, 99–100.

59. "Return of the Killed, Wounded & Missing of the Troops Under the Command of His Excellency Lieutenant General Knyphausen in Jersey the 7th and 8th of June, 1780," Sir Henry Clinton, Clinton Papers, William L. Clements Library, Ann Arbor, MI, June 23, 1780, in Sparks, *The Writings of George Washington*.

60. Leonard Lundin, *Cockpit of the Revolution: The War for Independence in New Jersey* (Princeton, NJ: Princeton University Press, 1940), 433.

61. Jones, *Life of Ashbel Green*, 121.

62. *The Journals of Major Samuel Shaw* (Boston: Wm. Crosby and H. P. Nichols, 1847), 74; Thomas Balch, ed., *Papers Relating Chiefly to the Maryland Line During the Revolution* (Philadelphia: 1857), 110–111.

63. Harold Coffin Syrett, ed., *The Papers of Alexander Hamilton* (New York: Columbia University Press, 1961), 2:347–348.

64. Fitzpatrick, *The Writings of George Washington*, 19:63–65.

65. Charles K. Bolton, *The Private Soldier Under Washington* (New York: Scribner, 1902), 126.

66. Entry for July 12, 1780, in Diary of Sylvanus Seeley, ms., Morristown National Historical Park Library.

Chapter 9: How Much Longer Can Fabius Last?

1. "From George Washington to Mesech Weare, 30 June 1780," Founders Online, http://founders.archives.gov/Washington/99-01-02-02323. Weare was president of New Hampshire.

2. "From George Washington to Fielding Lewis, 6 July 1780," Founders Online, http://founders.archives.gov/documents/Washington-99-01-02-01653.

3. Terry Golway, *Washington's General: Nathanael Greene and the Triumph of the American Revolution* (New York: H. Holt, 2005), 227.

4. Lieutenant Colonel Banastre Tarleton, *A History of the Campaigns of 1780 and 1781 in the Southern Provinces of North America* (London: T. Cadell, 1787), 18–19.

5. Robert D. Bass, *The Green Dragoon: The Lives of Banastre Tarleton and Mary Robinson* (New York: Henry Holt and Co., 1957), 79–82.

6. Patrick K. O'Donnell, *Washington's Immortals* (New York: Atlantic Monthly Press, 2016), 245–246.

7. Bass, *The Green Dragoon*, 99–100.

8. Thomas Fleming, *Liberty! The American Revolution* (New York: Viking, 1997), 310.

9. James Thomas Flexner, *George Washington*, vol. 2: *In the American Revolution: 1775–1783* (Boston: Little, Brown and Co., 1967), 386.

10. George Washington to John Mathews, October 23, 1780, in Golway, *Washington's General*, 230.

11. "To George Washington from Nathanael Greene, 19 November 1780," Founders Online, https://founders.archives.gov/documents/Washington/99-01-02-03982.

Chapter 10: A Plan So Daring Even
Daniel Morgan Feared the Worst

1. George Washington Greene, *Life of Major General Nathanael Greene* (New York: Hurd and Houghton, 1871), 70.

2. "To George Washington from Nathanael Greene, 28 December 1780," Founders Online, http://founders.archives.gov/documents/Washington/99-01-02-02251.

3. Don Higginbotham, *Daniel Morgan: Revolutionary Rifleman* (Chapel Hill: University of North Carolina Press, 1961), 96–116.

4. Greene, *Life of Major General Nathanael Greene*, 129.

5. "From George Washington to Nathanael Greene, 2 February 1781," Founders Online, https://founders.archives.gov/documents/Washington/99-01-02-04731.

6. Bass, *The Green Dragoon*, 114; for Cornwallis quote, see 102.

7. Bass, *The Green Dragoon*, 113, 117 (Marion quote).

8. Bass, *The Green Dragoon*, 176–178; also see Edward McCrady, *A History of South Carolina in the Revolution* (New York: Macmillan, 1902), 820–823.

9. Bass, *The Green Dragoon*, 121–125; also see H. Butterfield, *George III, Lord North and the People, 1779–80* (London: G. Bell and Sons, 1949). The book describes the so-called Yorkshire Movement, an attempt to mobilize massive popular resistance to the established government.

10. Clyde R. Ferguson, *General Andrew Pickens* (Ann Arbor, MI: University Microfilms, 1973), 108–109.

11. Bass, *The Green Dragoon*, 142–143.

12. Bass, *The Green Dragoon*, 148–149.

13. Robert D. Bass, *Ninety Six: The Struggle for the South Carolina Back Country* (Lexington, SC: Sandlapper Store, 1978), 142–143.

14. Bass, *Ninety Six*, 292.

15. Bass, *Ninety Six*, 295–297.

16. Bass, *Ninety Six*, 305.

17. Bass, *Ninety Six*, 307. Bass says Pickens had ninety-five men; other accounts say sixty.

18. McCrady, *A History of South Carolina in the Revolution*, 61–67.

19. Chalmers Davidson, *Piedmont Partisan: The Life and Times of General William Lee Davidson* (Davidson, NC: Davidson College, 1951), 49.

20. James Graham, *The Life of General Daniel Morgan of the Virginia Line of the Army of the United States* (Cincinnati, OH: H. W. Derby & Co., 1856), 268.

21. Graham, *The Life of General Daniel Morgan*, 268.

22. Graham, *The Life of General Daniel Morgan*, 274–275.

23. Nathanael Greene Papers, William Clements Library, Microfilm in the author's possession.

24. Graham, *The Life of General Daniel Morgan*, 285–286.

25. North Callahan, *Daniel Morgan: Ranger of the Revolution* (New York: Henry Holt and Co., 1961), 197.

26. Graham, *The Life of General Daniel Morgan*, 285–286.

27. Graham, *The Life of General Daniel Morgan*, 261.

28. Bass, *Ninety Six*, 321, gives Pickens most of the credit for deciding to fight at Cowpens.

29. Jones, *Life of Ashbel Green*, 545.

30. Lieutenant Thomas Anderson, *Journal of Lieutenant Thomas Anderson of the Delaware Regiment, 1780–1782* (Morrisania, NY: Henry B. Dawson, 1867), 209.

31. "General Richard Winn's Notes—1780," *The South Carolina Historical and Genealogical Magazine*, ed. Samuel C. Williams (January 1942).

Chapter 11: Downright Fighting

1. Lieutenant Colonel Banastre Tarleton, *A History of the Campaigns of 1780 and 1781 in the Southern Provinces of North America* (London: T. Cadell, 1787), 213–212.

2. Tarleton, *A History of the Campaigns*, 250.

3. Bass, *Ninety Six*, 298.

4. Adrian B. Caruna, *Grasshoppers and Butterflies: The Light Three Pounders of Pattison and Townshend* (Bloomfield, Ontario: Museum Restoration Service, 1979), 16–32.

5. Higginbotham, *Daniel Morgan*, 77.

6. *Magazine of History* (October 1881): 277–279.

7. Higginbotham, *Daniel Morgan*, 134.

8. Joseph Johnson, MD, *Traditions and Reminiscences Chiefly of the American Revolution in the South* (Charleston, SC: Walker & James, 1851), 446.

9. James Collins, "Autobiography of a Revolutionary Soldier," in Mrs. S. G. Miller, *Sixty Years in the Nueces Valley, 1870 to 1930* (San Antonio, TX: Naylor Print. Co., 1930), 51–55.

10. Bass, *Ninety Six*, 322.

11. Graham, *The Life of General Daniel Morgan*, 297.

12. Quoted in Johnson, *Traditions and Reminiscences*, 453.

13. William Seymour, *Journal of the Southern Expedition, 1780–1783* (Wilmington: The Historical Society of Delaware, 1896), 13.

14. "John Eager Howard: Patriot and Public Servant," *Maryland Historical Magazine* 62 (1967).

15. Tarleton, *A History of the Campaigns*, 217.

16. Bass, *The Green Dragoon*, 158.

17. Johnson, *Traditions and Renaissances*, 451–452.

18. Rev. J. D. Bailey, *History of Grindal Shoals* (Gaffney, SC: Ledger Print, n.d.), 39.

19. Tarleton, *A History of the Campaigns*, 252.

20. Graham, *The Life of General Daniel Morgan*, 334.

Chapter 12: Fight, Get Beat, Rise and Fight Again

1. "To George Washington from Nathanael Greene, 24 January 1781," Founders Online, http://founders.archives.gov/documents/Washington/99-01-02-04635.

2. "To George Washington from Nathanael Greene, 24 January 1781."

3. Terry Golway, *Washington's General: Nathanael Greene and the Triumph of the American Revolution* (New York: Henry Holt and Co., 2005), 249.

4. Golway, *Washington's General*, 249.

5. James Graham, *The Life of General Daniel Morgan of the Virginia Line of the Army of the United States* (Cincinnati, OH: H. W. Derby & Co., 1856), 318; for quote, see Edmund C. Burnett, ed., *Letters of Members of the Continental Congress*, vol. 5: *January 1, 1780 to February 28, 1781* (Washington, DC: Carnegie Institution, 1921), 568.

6. Golway, *Washington's General*, 247–248.

7. Golway, *Washington's General*, 248.

8. "To Thomas Jefferson from Daniel Morgan, 1 February 1781," Founders Online, http://founders.archives.gov/documents/Jefferson/01-04-02-0608.

9. John Buchanan, *The Road to Guilford Courthouse* (Hoboken, NJ: Wiley, 1997), 340–341.

10. "To George Washington from Nathanael Greene, 5 February 1781," Founders Online, http://founders.archives.gov/documents/Washington/99-01-02-04859.

11. Buchanan, *Road to Guilford Courthouse*, 363–364.

12. Golway, *Washington's General*, 255.

13. Buchanan, *Road to Guilford Courthouse*, 274–275.

14. Patrick K. O'Donnell, *Washington's Immortals* (New York: Atlantic Monthly Press, 2016), 320–321.

15. "From George Washington to Nathanael Greene, 18 April 1781," Founders Online, http://founders.archives.gov/documents/Washington/99-01-02-05444.

16. "To George Washington from Nathanael Greene, 18 March 1781," Founders Online, http://founders.archives.gov/documents/Washington/99-01-02-05132.

17. "To George Washington from Nathanael Greene, 29 March 1781," Founders Online, http://founders.archives.gov/documents/Washington/99-01-02-05238.

18. "From George Washington to Major Nathanael Greene, 22 April 1781," Founders Online, http://founders.archives.gov/documents/Washington/99-02-02-1159.

Chapter 13: From Mutiny and Despair to Improbable Victory

1. Paul David Nelson, *Anthony Wayne: Soldier of the Early Republic* (Bloomington: Indiana University Press, 1985), 118–125.

2. "[Diary entry: 1 May 1781]," Founders Online, http://founders.archives.gov/documents/Washington/01-03-02-0007-0001-0001. Original source: Donald Jackson, ed., *The Diaries of George Washington*, vol. 3: *1 January 1771–5 November 1781* (Charlottesville: University of Virginia Press, 1978), 356–357.

3. "To George Washington from Marquis de Lafayette, 24 May 1781," Founders Online, http://founders.archive.gov/documents/Washington/99-01-02-05856.

4. "Comte de Rochambeau to Admiral de Grasse, June 11, 1781," in Henri Doniol, *Histoire de la participation de la France à l'établissement des États-Unis d'Amérique: Correspondence diplomatique et documents* (Paris: Imprimerie national, 1890), 4:647.

5. Terry Golway, *Washington's General: Nathanael Greene and the Triumph of the American Revolution* (New York: Henry Holt and Co., 2005), 271.

6. William B. Wilcox, *Portrait of a General: Sir Henry Clinton in the War of Independence* (New York: Knopf, 1964), 404–408.

7. Golway, *Washington's General*, 280–284.

8. "To George Washington from Nathanael Greene, 17 September 1781," https://founders.archives.gov/documents/Washington/99-01-02-06976.

9. Don Higginbotham, *The War of American Independence: Military Attitudes, Policies, and Practice, 1763–1789* (New York: Macmillan, 1971), 383.

Chapter 14: Victory's Unexpected Challenge

1. "To Benjamin Franklin from George Washington, 22 October 1781," in *The Papers of Benjamin Franklin, May 1 thru October 31, 1781*, ed. Barbara Oberg (New Haven, CT: Yale

University Press, 1999), 637–638. Letter cites source for Greene's report on the battle of Eutaw Springs.

2. Thomas Fleming, *The Man Who Dared the Lightning: A New Look at Benjamin Franklin* (New York: W. Morrow and Co., 1971), 415–462.

3. Entry for January 20, 1783, in Robert Morris, *The Papers of Robert Morris, 1781–1784*, vol. 7: *November 1, 1782–May 4, 1783*, ed. John Catanzariti (Pittsburgh, PA: University of Pittsburgh Press, 1988), 329.

4. "To Alexander Hamilton from George Washington, 4 March 1783," Founders Online, http://founders.archives.gov/documents/Hamilton/01-03-02-0171. Original source: Harold Coffin Syrett, ed., *The Papers of Alexander Hamilton* (New York: Columbia University Press, 1962), 3:277–279.

5. *Journals of the Continental Congress* (Washington, DC: Government Printing Office, 1906), 4:207.

6. Douglas Southall Freeman, *George Washington: A Biography* (New York: Charles Scribner's Sons, 1951), 5:431–437; also see James Thomas Flexner, *George Washington*, vol. 2: *In the American Revolution: 1775–1783* (Boston: Little, Brown and Co., 1967), 505–508.

7. "From George Washington to Elias Boudinot, 18 March 1783," Founders Online, http://founders.archives.gov/documents/99-01-02-10856.

8. "From George Washington to Robert Morris, 3 June 1783," Founders Online, http://founders.archives.gov/documents/Washington/99-01-02-11365.

9. "To George Washington from Elias Boudinot, 12 April 1783," Founders Online, http://founders.archives.gov/documents/Washington/99-01-02-11042.

10. John Armstrong to Horatio Gates, June 26, 1783, Gates Papers. Cited in Mary A. Y. Gallagher, "Reinterpreting the 'Very Trifling Mutiny' at Philadelphia in June 1783," *Pennsylvania Magazine of History and Biography* 119, no. 1/2 (January–April 1995): 25.

11. Varnum Lansing Collins, *The Continental Congress at Princeton* (Princeton, NJ: Princeton University Press, 1908), 30–39.

12. Arthur Lee, "Congress—Notes on Debates, Feb. 21, 1783," in *The Papers of James Madison*, ed. William T. Hutchinson et al. (Chicago: University of Chicago Press, 1969), 5:231–234. Also see Louis W. Potts, *Arthur Lee: A Virtuous Revolutionary* (Baton Rouge: Louisiana State University Press, 1981).

13. Gerald H. Clarfield, *Timothy Pickering and the American Republic* (Pittsburgh, PA: University of Pittsburgh Press, 1980), 84.

Chapter 15: George Washington's Tears

1. Benjamin Tallmadge, *Memoir of Col. Benjamin Tallmadge*, ed. Henry Phelps Johnston (New York, 1904), p.97.

2. Stuart Leibiger, *Founding Friendship: George Washington, James Madison and the Creation of the American Republic* (Charlottesville: University of Virginia Press, 1999), 50–54, 70–73.

Chapter 16: Major General Anthony Wayne to the Rescue

1. Douglas Southall Freeman, *George Washington: A Biography* (New York: Charles Scribner's Sons, 1951), 6:336–337.

2. Charles Royster, *A Revolutionary People at War: The Continental Army and American Character, 1775–1783* (Chapel Hill: University of North Carolina Press, 1996), 358.

3. Paul David Nelson, *Anthony Wayne: Soldier of the Early Republic* (Bloomington: Indiana University Press, 1985), 228–229.

4. James Thomas Flexner, *George Washington*, vol. 3: *George Washington and the New Nation, 1783–1793* (Boston: Little, Brown and Co., 1970), 304–307. The Miamis fired on negotiators carrying flags of truce. Some were killed. Yet Washington persisted until he had demonstrated that "conciliation had been proved utterly hopeless." John C. Fitzpatrick, *The Writings of George Washington from the Original Manuscript Sources, 1745–1799*, vol. 31: *January 22, 1790–March 9, 1792* (Washington, DC: US Government Printing Office, 1939), 81; also, vol. 32: *March 10, 1792–June 30, 1793* (Washington, DC: US Government Printing Office, 1939), 205–206.

5. Nelson, *Anthony Wayne*, 243.

6. Richard Norton Smith, *Patriarch: George Washington and the New American Nation* (Boston: Houghton Mifflin, 1993), 198.

7. Nelson, *Anthony Wayne*, 259. As the Indians retreated, the garrison of Fort Recovery emerged to taunt them.

8. Thomas P. Slaughter, *The Whiskey Rebellion* (New York: Oxford University Press, 1986), 183–187, 212–221.

9. Nelson, *Anthony Wayne*, 272. Secretary of War Knox informed General Wayne, "It is with great satisfaction, the President of the United States directs the communication of the Unanimous Thanks of the House of Representatives to you, your army and the Kentucky Volunteers."

10. Edward L. Coffman, *The Old Army: A Portrait of the American Army in Peacetime, 1784–1898* (New York: Oxford University Press, 1986), 5–7; also see Richard H. Kohn, *Eagle and Sword: The Federalists and the Creation of the Military Establishment in America, 1783–1802* (New York: Free Press, 1975), 184–187; Letter of James McHenry to Congress, March 14, 1796, "Ought the Military Force of the United States to Be Diminished?," in *American State Papers, Class V: Military Affairs*, ed. Walter Lowrie (Washington, DC: Gales and Seaton, 1832–1861), 1:114.

INDEX